W9-BNS-199

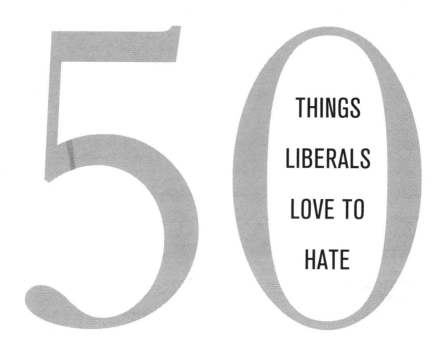

50

THINGS
LIBERALS
LOVE TO
HATE

MIKE GALLAGHER

THRESHOLD EDITIONS

NEW YORK   LONDON   TORONTO   SYDNEY   NEW DELHI

Threshold Editions
A Division of Simon & Schuster, Inc.
1230 Avenue of the Americas
New York, NY 10020

This Threshold Editions paperback edition June 2013

THRESHOLD EDITIONS and colophon are trademarks of Simon & Schuster, Inc.

For information about special discounts for bulk purchases, please contact
Simon & Schuster Special Sales at 1-866-506-1949
or business@simonandschuster.com.

The Simon & Schuster Speakers Bureau can bring authors to your live event.
For more information or to book an event, contact the
Simon & Schuster Speakers Bureau at 1-866-248-3049
or visit our website at www.simonspeakers.com.

Designed by Ruth Lee-Mui

Manufactured in the United States of America

1 3 5 7 9 10 8 6 4 2

Library of Congress Cataloging-in-Publication Data is available.

ISBN 978-1-4516-7926-7
ISBN 978-1-4516-7927-4 (ebook)

To my Denise,
whose love of life and hearty laugh made the world a better place.
You are always in my heart.

This book is for everyone on the right, left, and middle who is willing to laugh a little and realize that we truly don't have to "hate" each other just because we disagree.

Contents

CONTENTS

Introduction

This book is about liberals. Not Democrats, who are not that much different from Republicans in many respects. No. This book is dedicated to that peculiar brand of American who self-identifies as a liberal, lives life as a liberal, and wishes more of us in America were liberal. Think Michael Moore. Think Nancy Pelosi. Think your local college professor. Think the checkout help with the Masters in Gender Studies wearing the Che Guevara headband at your local Whole Foods. You get the picture.

It doesn't take much heavy lifting to understand the surface characteristics of liberals. Most of them are exceedingly well educated, and rarely miss an opportunity to tell you so. Most of them are exceedingly upper middle class, which I know because it takes real money to support a twice-a-day double-decaf habit at Starbucks, not to mention yoga sessions for the wife and pets.

They tend to gather in clusters, huddling up in tight quarters like San Francisco, Boston, Washington, D.C., and New York City, all places where sushi is readily available.

And they dominate professions that leave a large cultural footprint on this country. Professions like journalism, the arts, academia, the music industry, and America's fastest-rising group of entertainers—Cirque du Soleil acrobats.

But that large footprint has little to do with the size of the liberal population in America. A recent Gallup/*USA Today* Poll revealed that 42 percent of Americans called themselves conservative, 35 percent moderate, while 20 percent used the "L" word to describe themselves.

Who are these people who call themselves liberals? And how does such a small group have such a big impact on our culture? What motivates them?

I am in an excellent position to answer those deeper questions because I've been watching liberals closely for over thirty years. I've studied liberals like Jane Goodall studies her chimps. In their natural habitats, and without judgment. In silence mostly, because we barely speak the same language.

I have been tireless in my research. I lived with liberals, and broke bread with them. I've humored them, teased them, prodded them, imitated them, and yes, even loved them. Some of my best friends are liberals. Some are even members of my own family.

My commitment to understanding liberals sometimes worried my conservative friends. Some even questioned my mental health. But my passion to understand this misunderstood minority knew no boundaries. For as many years as I can remember, I read the *New York Times* from cover to cover each day. And yes, that included Paul Krugman's column. And even . . . gasp . . . Frank Rich's.

I read *New Yorker* magazine. I went to see *The Vagina Monologues,* and listened to NPR whenever I got the chance. And I even watched my carbon footprint. As much as a guy can who loves V-8s and has owned a well-cooled 3,750-square-foot home in the Dallas suburbs. Boy, I watched it, all right.

I also made sacrifices for the cause. I went without meat for a week, put off NASCAR races for two, went without church, skipped Dallas Cowboys home games, and some years ago, took the deepest dive of all and rented an apartment in the Ground Zero of liberalism—New York City. All in order to get inside the liberal mind.

What did I learn from my three decades of research? I learned that liberals don't love many things about this world. They are endlessly trying to correct, fix, mend, and adjust every aspect of other people's daily lives.

I learned that they spend a whole lot of time thinking about America's faults, and how to correct them. About America's ills, and how to cure them. Liberals love to hate things most Americans love, and spend the rest of their lives endlessly trying to take those things away from us. And they are convinced they do it all because they love us.

Thus was born this book, *50 Things Liberals Love to Hate.*

This list is not dispositive, but suggestive. Indeed, I urge those of you who know a liberal, work with a liberal, have a liberal friend or a liberal lover, to add to this list.

For all of you who call yourselves liberals, know that this book was written with the deepest care, and yes, with love. You may not like what you read in the chapters to come, but you will recognize yourself. And you will stumble upon some truths that only someone who cares deeply about you would tell you.

So think of me as your ideological psychotherapist. No. That's too 1970s Woody Allen. It's too *Annie Hall.* Think of me as your ideological life coach.

Consider this the cheapest self-help book you'll ever buy. And the best.

50 McDonald's

"Who stole my happy meal?!"

If you could build a time machine and go back in time—not far, say fifty years or so—and you told the first American you saw that in the future, man would walk on the moon, that we'd all carry video telephones the size of a deck of cards, and that poor Americans would be fat, I guarantee you the response would be: "Wow! Really? Poor people are *fat*?"

Because, of course, poor people are supposed to be skinny. They're *poor*.

But the astonishing rise in standards of living since the 1950s, coupled with advances in food preservation—not to mention the brilliant invention of the triple cheeseburger—have meant that the

5

once-universal indicator of wealth, the big fat belly, is now an indicator of the working class.

Rich people in America today look like old photographs of poor people during the Great Depression. Poor people today look like the corpulent, trouser-bursting cartoon sketches of the Robber Barons of the 1890s.

Hollywood liberals go on juice fasts and colon cleanses—don't ask; it's as appetizing as it sounds—and eat organically raised tofu. Normal Americans cruise though the drive-in and stop off for a slice of pizza.

Now obviously, it's not good that so many Americans are fat. The skyrocketing levels of obesity and Type 2 diabetes that affect so many of us—especially children—are something to worry about and something to address.

But here's how liberals want to address it: They want to pass laws.

Laws against sugar and junk food, as liberals in San Francisco are trying to get enacted. Laws against buying certain kinds of food with food stamps, as liberals in Florida are trying to pass. Laws about portion size, about the location of fast-food restaurants, about what parents can pack into school lunchboxes—all of which have been suggested by liberals all across the country.

Conservatives see a fat person and think: "Lay off the bread. Take the stairs. Would it kill you to have a salad once in a while?"

Liberals see a fat person and think: "We should immediately pass laws forbidding this kind of obesity, establish new federal programs and guidelines to correct this behavior, and create ways to federally subsidize weight-loss programs."

Here's the problem with the liberal approach: We tried it. It doesn't work.

In 1992, the United States Department of Agriculture—which is supposed to be focused on *growing* food, not *eating* food—published the first American food pyramid.

The official federal government guidelines—what the feds *wanted* you to eat, in other words—is now recognized by pretty much every nutritional expert as a horrible mistake.

Eat bread, is what they said. Lots of it. And pasta, too. Go easy on animal proteins and fat. Load up on the carbs.

Let me repeat: This is what the federal government *recommended* to Americans.

That was good news for people like me, who see an entire bread basket in a restaurant and think: "Come to Papa," but bad news for the over 25 million Americans with Type 2 diabetes, which is a disease you get from, essentially, bread and sugar. The diabetes epidemic in America is so huge, it's impossible to target a specific cost.

It's somewhere between $83 billion and $185 billion a year, but it doesn't really matter what the exact cost is—because we all know it's going up. Way up. There are about 2 million new cases each year.

Any enterprising businessman could have looked at the food pyramid and made a fortune investing in Size XXXXL T-shirts.

The federal government seems to be hell-bent on making us all fat and sick.

But who do they blame?

McDonald's.

Why? Because they sell delicious—and fattening—burgers and fries, along with salads and McNuggets and a whole lot of other things. Even the beloved Happy Meal is under assault by politicians around the country, and by some who call themselves scientists. One group with a very officious-sounding name—The Center for Science in the Public Interest—threatened to sue McDonald's if the burger giant didn't stop selling Happy Meals. In typical nanny-statist hyperbole, they equated what the burger giant did to kids with child abuse, and worse, child molestation.

"McDonald's is the stranger in the playground handing out candy to children," CSPI's litigation director, Stephen Gardner, said in a prepared statement. "It's a creepy and predatory practice that warrants an injunction. . . ."

It was Gardner's statement that sounded creepy to even the most ordinary liberal who occasionally treats the kids to lunch at McDonald's.

"Multi-billion-dollar corporations make parents' job nearly impossible by giving away toys and bombarding kids with slick advertising," CSPI's director Michael Jacobson added.

I'd love to see the parties over at CSPI's offices. They must be a real riot. Can you spell BUZZ KILLERS?

One could make the same argument about chocolate in the candy aisles, and ice cream at gas stations and cookies after dinner. The fact is, it's a whole lot easier to be a parent than one might imagine. We are a lot bigger than our kids. It may come as a surprise to the folks at CSPI's offices, but parents can actually say "no" to their kids. It happens every day in this great country.

The fact is, liberals hate McDonald's—and its competitors—because they symbolize everything about America they despise: our entrepreneurial zeal, our ability to deliver high quality in a uniform way, our love of convenience and speed, and especially our ability to inspire and support businesses that can be franchised across the globe and that provide millions of jobs.

They really hate that last part. *McJobs* is what they call them. Because, to a liberal, a job isn't something that's intrinsically useful. To a liberal, the fact that fully 25 percent of all working Americans—and that percentage is much larger for Americans under thirty—have worked at McDonald's, or one of its competitors, is truly alarming. It's not clear why, exactly. Working for a large company is a great way to learn useful job skills, like time management and customer service.

For liberals, that's a red flag.

The hate of McDonald's knows no limits. In his really gross 2004 documentary *Super Size Me,* writer/actor/activist Morgan Spurlock (yes, that's really his name) hated McDonald's so much that he decided to eat McDonald's food, and only McDonald's food, for thirty straight days—three times a day—and film what happened.

And surprise of surprises, he gained twenty-four pounds, he had a 13 percent body mass increase and a cholesterol level of 230, and he experienced mood swings and sexual dysfunction.

I suspect that would have happened if Spurlock had decided to eat at IHOP three times a day for a month. Or Taco Bell. Or Mortons. And especially if he chose to eat only their very worst meals to make his tedious point.

The fact is, Spurlock wasn't interested in anything but vilifying McDonald's, and helping to bring attention to the work of some food tort lawyers, who were at the time thinking of ways to shake down the burger and shake giant for some kind of cash settlement for selling a product that people like, and that, if eaten to excess, can harm you.

Why didn't Spurlock, I wondered, choose to instead eat Breyers ice cream by the half-gallon every day and do a documentary about that? Or Gouda cheese? Or canned ham? Or popcorn? Or pounds of cherries, and only cherries, for thirty days?

Because that would just be a really, really gross idea, sans the villain. There'd be no one to vilify but Spurlock himself for making stupid daily food choices.

Oddly enough, Spurlock never disclosed his actual daily McDonald's intake. Moreover, if he had chosen to, Spurlock could have picked the many good and hearty salads McDonald's offers its customers. Rather than stuff himself with double cheeseburgers, Big Macs, and extra-large milkshakes, with an extra-large Coke chaser, he could have gone with the single burger. Or the grilled chicken wrap.

But that would not have made Spurlock famous. That would not have made Spurlock the Michael Moore of his generation. Actually,

Spurlock should have followed Michael Moore around and filmed what *he* eats every day. That would have been a fun movie!!

The truth is, *Super Size Me* was less a documentary than a filmed stunt, and what it really did was Super Size Spurlock's bank account. And as a capitalist, I am all for that! Even if he is not.

Fitness expert Chazz Weaver came out with a documentary to rebut Spurlock's, but got very little media buzz. He ate at McDonald's for thirty days, too, but with a very different meal selection, and with exercise. The result? He lost eight pounds and improved his blood pressure, cholesterol, and triglycerides.

The food fascists love to hate on McDonald's, but many other possible targets are somehow spared. Starbucks, which sells sugared carbohydrates by the crate, and high-calorie "coffee" drinks—which are essentially fancy milkshakes—is somehow curiously exempt from the fast-food hate you hear from the liberals.

Starbucks, of course, is a very left-leaning company, so despite the fact that there are plenty of Starbucks drive-throughs, and that Starbucks has a tight top-down corporate culture that's almost McDonaldian in its discipline and structure, they get a free pass from the Fat Police.

In other words: if you get fat on Double Quarter Pounders with Cheese, liberals want to start passing laws. If you get fat on Venti Mocha Lattes with a Caramel Shot and a Currant Scone, liberals are perfectly delighted to look the other way.

But what they both represent is American ingenuity and entrepreneurial risk. What Ray Kroc, the founder of McDonald's, and Howard Schultz, the founder of Starbucks, have in common is that both of them took something that all Americans loved and figured out a way to serve it faster and better than anyone else.

Faster and better? Liberals dislike that!

Job skills training? On an *actual* job? Liberals *hate* that!

Serving up food that's delicious and fattening, which requires individuals to exercise self-control and personal responsibility? Liberals *really* hate that!

All that hate wrapped up in a cardboard box, tucked into a sesame-seed bun. With melted cheese, a little ketchup, special sauce, a pickle, maybe some fries on the side?

If you're a liberal and you're feeling a little bit hungry right now, I've got some bad news for you.

You just might be a conservative.

49 Flag Pins

"That pin!"

Let me make a confession: Sometimes, when I find myself in a really liberal part of town—you know the parts of town I'm talking about, right? Yoga studios, lots of electric cars around with "Vegan On Board" bumper stickers, that sort of thing—I make sure that I'm wearing my American flag lapel pin somewhere really conspicuous.

It's kind of a silly game I play with myself. I'm baiting them, I know. But for some reason, I can't help myself. Liberals really hate those pins.

I'm not sure why liberals hate the American flag lapel pin. They hate it more than the actual American flag, it seems to me. In those same neighborhoods, you see the American flag flying high in some places. Maybe a holdover fourth-generation Ford dealer. Probably the local VFW hall, if there is one. Possibly the local school and town hall, but only because to *not* have a flag up would be aggressively unpatriotic.

And if there's one thing liberals hate, it is aggression.

No, better to stick with their passive-aggressiveness when it comes to being unpatriotic.

Maybe it's because the lapel pin is smaller, and at eye level. It's in your face. And it's personal. It's in a place it's not usually found, rather than at the top of a flagstaff or next to a judge. You can't ignore it. It just pops into eye's view.

I'll be at the counter with my purchases, or I'll ask someone a question, and I'll see their eyes flicker from my face to my lapel, and I'll see that look—you know the look I'm talking about—the look of confusion *(Hey, what's that?)* followed by alarm *(What's wrong with this guy?)* and winding up with a shudder of disgust *(Probably some kind of America freak; I'll bet one of those right-wing nuts, too)*.

It's as if I had a swastika on my lapel.

But surely that's not why they hate it, is it? I mean, when I wear my American flag pin, I'm not making a big political statement. I'm not talking about who to vote for in the next election. I'm not saying anything about taxes or foreign policy or the deficit or any of the issues that fill the airwaves and editorial pages.

The American flag lapel pin that I wear—and that millions of Americans wear every day—just means this: I'm grateful to live in a country that honors and protects freedom, that offers boundless opportunities to its citizens, and that does its best to nurture the noblest parts of the human spirit.

When I wear my pin I'm just saying, when you get right down to it, I love my country.

Now that I think about it, that's probably why they hate it so much.

You see, many liberals don't really love America. Oh, sure, they have the vocabulary down. They know how to frame the sentence so that it sounds like a declaration of patriotic feeling. "I love America," they'll say. And then they'll add, "I mean, I love the *idea* of America . . ." and then comes that inevitable "but."

And the parade of horribles soon follows.

They'll start listing all of the things that America has done to let them down, all of the injustices and failings of the country from the moment the Pilgrims landed on Plymouth Rock to the most recent midterm election. They love America, but it's with qualifications and quibbles, like one of those asterisks next to a baseball player's stats on the back of his baseball card. *He was an okay player. But we've got reservations.*

I wonder if liberals do this with their wives. I love you . . . "but."

"I love you, darling, but that extra few pounds on your hips weren't there when we met, and it would be great if you lost 'em."

"The way you kiss me, it's nice, but a little too rough. I knew a girl who had a soft, gentle way of kissing, and she really made me forget about all of my troubles when her lips touched mine."

That's the kind of guy women love. The kind whose love is filled with qualifiers and quibbles, and who can't wait to remind you about them each and every day.

Liberals have reservations about everything American. When they see an American flag, they automatically put an asterisk next to it. *Yes, but . . .* they want to say. Yes but we're too rich and drive too much and eat too much and we're too American. Yes, we saved Europe and are a beacon of liberty for the world, but we don't recycle enough and we're too religious to be a really sophisticated country.

During his run-up to the election, then-senator Barack Obama got into a few flag flaps. There was the scene at an event with all of the Democratic candidates standing on a stage in Iowa, listening to our national anthem while facing the American flag. All but one had a hand firmly over the heart. Guess who? Hint: his initials are B.H.O.

No big deal, you say?

Then there was that AP story in October 2007. The one where he went out of his way to stop wearing an American flag lapel pin. He explained his position at a campaign stop in Independence, Iowa: "My attitude is that I'm less concerned about what you're wearing on your lapel than what's in your heart. You show your patriotism by how you treat your fellow Americans, especially those who serve. You show your patriotism by being true to our values and ideals. That's what we have to lead with is our values and our ideals."

No big deal, you say?

Try that with your wife. "I love you, honey, but I am not buying you those sweet diamond earrings because I'm less concerned with what you wear on your ears than what's inside our hearts."

Give that a shot. See where it gets you.

President Obama was asked again about the pin in an interview with KCRG-TV in Cedar Rapids. "The truth is that right after 9/11 I had a pin," he said. "Shortly after 9/11, particularly because as we're talking about the Iraq War, that became a substitute for I think true patriotism, which is speaking out on issues that are of importance to our national security."

It just kept getting worse. The pin he said he didn't like, he actually used to like, until everyone in America started liking it. And so he stopped liking it.

In that interview, he actually referred to the American lapel flag pin as "that pin." The same way that Bill Clinton referred to Monica Lewinsky. "That woman."

Obama came around. "That pin" he stopped wearing because it didn't show what was in his heart, he is wearing near his heart now. It's one of those cheesy, jingoistic things you just have to do as president.

When he returns to civilian life, the thing I suspect he'll like the most is ditching that silly pin once and for all. Maybe he'll replace it with a United Nations flag pin.

That simple little American flag pin—honestly, the thing is no bigger than a nickel—makes liberals terribly uncomfortable. It forces them to go into all of those reservations and critiques in their minds. It makes their subconscious go into overdrive, whirring and clicking away like one of those old adding machines, totaling up the many, many ways in which they cannot bring themselves to actually love this country.

And it confuses them, too, because here's a guy in their store or coffee shop—me—who seems nice enough, who's smiling and being polite. I mean, I don't foam at the mouth or shout or make a spectacle of myself. I'm just standing there, with a tiny American flag on my lapel, minding my own business, announcing in the quietest, most reserved way possible that I'm grateful to live in America.

That's all. Just gratitude.

Gratitude for the sacrifices of my forebears. Gratitude for the opportunities this country affords. Gratitude for the men and women who serve the flag in the military. Gratitude for being a part of this amazing, ennobling experiment in representative democracy.

Boy, liberals hate that. Because for them, to be grateful for being an American means, for some reason, whitewashing all of the not-so-great things about this country and her past. America isn't perfect. We've made mistakes in the past, with our callous disregard for the rights of all people, irrespective of race. And we're making mistakes right now, with our callous disregard for the rights of the unborn. But we always try to be better. We're always moving toward the good, toward what Lincoln called the "better angels of our nature."

Liberals don't see it that way.

Because if they saw it that way—if they saw the America that I see—they'd be forced to admit something awful, something painful, something that would shake the foundation of their beliefs.

They'd be forced to admit that America is a pretty great place. And that Americans are a pretty great people. And that it's okay to show your gratitude by wearing a small symbol on your lapel. And they can't admit that, so they see my pin and have only one choice: They have to hate it.

It's kind of cruel, I'll admit, to bring such mental anguish to people. And I'm not proud of it, but it always gives me a kind of kick to watch their eyes flicker from the pin to me, back to the pin, back to me, as they enter the sad echo chamber that is the liberal attitude toward this country.

America, to them, is just okay. Not good. Not great. Certainly not exceptional.

Just . . . okay.

About as okay as Sweden. Not quite as okay as France.

When I walk out of the store or the coffee shop, I have to admit that I chuckle a little to myself, because I can hear them behind me still trying to figure it all out.

48 NASCAR

If you Google the phrase "Liberals who love NASCAR," you get exactly three hits.

That's not a typo: *three* hits.

And that's surprising, because NASCAR is one of the fastest-growing and most popular sports in America.

On the other hand, it's *not* so surprising when you remember that each NASCAR event begins with an invocation, a presentation of the colors, and the national anthem. And all of that happens *before* a lot of gas-guzzling cars roar to life and zip around a track a couple of hundred times.

There's a lot of stuff in there that makes liberals completely freak out: patriotism, religion, turning fossil fuels into noise. Liberals hate all of that stuff. But it's the fact that people are all gathered together, in one arena, that sends their hate-ometers skyward.

A NASCAR event is a celebration of American excess, sure—there are RVs in the parking lot, burgers on the grill, plenty of cold beer, noise—and it's also got a distinctly southern cast. In the parking lots and on the ballcaps, you occasionally catch glimpses of the old Stars and Bars, and a NASCAR event without a country music star singing the national anthem is almost impossible to imagine.

That immediately eliminates NASCAR from contention as a favorite anything for liberals. Liberals hate the American South. (* See #37.)

But they especially hate the *unapologetic* American South.

And that's really the root of their NASCAR animosity. It isn't the noise and the crowds—ever been to Madison Square Garden?—and it's certainly not the threat of physical injury. (Two professional hockey players going at it on the ice can probably do more damage to each other than one NASCAR driver, one car, and one guardrail.) What upsets liberals about NASCAR is that everyone there is having a good time, everyone there is drinking and eating and cheering away, there's fatty food and country music, and no one there seems troubled in the least that *liberals disapprove.*

Stop being so tacky! The liberals want to shout at the guys in their T-shirts and the ladies in their bedazzled denim.

Stop having such a good time! They want to scold the guys with their Styrofoam beer Koozies and bald eagle caps.

Don't you know that you people are horribly, horribly working class? Ah, yes. There it is.

Don't you know you should be doing better things with your day off? Like shopping at Whole Foods, or watching some PBS documentary, or catching up on this week's issue of the *New Yorker?*

Liberals love to swan around as champions of the lower orders, and love to extol themselves as the friend of the working man, but they really hate it when the working man doesn't go along with the edicts and offerings of their wannabe masters. When the working man chooses to do what he wants with his free time.

Like watching grown men speed in high-performance cars around an oval racetrack at breakneck speed, inches apart, taking endless left turns, with an occasional brush with death.

Liberals love to talk endlessly about how much they *care* about the working class, but they don't want to *know* any of them.

On February 18, 2001, NASCAR legend Dale Earnhardt was locked in a battle for third place when his Chevrolet grazed another car and hit a concrete wall while buzzing around a banked turn at the Daytona 500. His car was cruising at between 157 and 161 mph, and he was killed instantly. He was cut from his battered car and pronounced dead of head injuries at a hospital. Earnhardt's teammate Michael Waltrip won the race, and his son, Dale Jr., was second.

The nation was stunned. Racing fans had lost a legend. A tough man, and a self-made man, he was known as the "Intimidator" for his aggressive driving style, but was adored by fans for his straight talk and for his monumental racing success. He won seventy-six races and earned more than $41 million in a NASCAR career that spanned more than twenty-five years.

But what the people loved most about him was his reputation as being a regular guy. In fact, Earnhardt was so loved that some math teachers in the South taught kids their 1s, 2s, and 3s this way: 1, 2, Earnhardt, 4. It has a ring to it! NASCAR itself has unofficially retired the number 3, and no driver has had the temerity to adopt the number 3 as his own.

Somehow, the *New York Times* didn't quite understand the nature of the connection between Earnhardt and the public, and the paper with the line "All the News That's Fit to Print" on its masthead didn't waste much type—or ink—on his death. At least not on the first or second day.

It took a few days for their news team to understand the profound connection Earnhardt had with millions of Americans.

Now if Cher had died, the *Times* would have been all over it. Or Billie Jean King. But a guy from North Carolina who made his living taking left turns in front of race fans with a two-pack-a-day habit and six-pack mentality? Please!

All of this cultural condescension makes sense when you remember the roots of NASCAR. Its origins go back to the days of Prohibition—another grand experiment in government overreach, when "progressives" decided that Americans needed to be protected from themselves—and the black-market business of making and transporting moonshine.

Deep in the "hollers" of Appalachia, families that had been distilling their own eye-watering, throat-burning liquor for hundreds of years suddenly discovered that, thanks to Prohibition, they had a thirsty market for their product. So they ramped up production and soon the valleys of Appalachia were filled with backyard distilleries bubbling away.

All they needed were drivers. Fast drivers. Drivers that could outrun the federal agents charged with enforcing the Volstead Act. On days off, the best drivers would race each other for fun. And when the Volstead Act was finally repealed, it didn't take much for a new national sport—with its roots in hell-raising, law-skirting, and southern culture—to be born.

So from the very start, NASCAR drivers and their fans were happy to stick a thumb in the eye of polite and uptight society. From its first days, NASCAR and its followers didn't much care for the approval of the "right" kind of people. They were only interested in a few very American things: have some fun, make some noise, put some money in your pocket.

Okay, so, let's be fair: These aren't the most *elevated* American traits. The guy in the stands at the track in Bristol, Tennessee, with the beer-can hat and the slightly profane T-shirt isn't going to end up on the ten-dollar bill as one of America's leading intellectual and moral lights. But there is something truly American—and heroic, in a way—in those principles.

They were the ones who moved out West to build a new nation. They were the ones who didn't wait for permission. They were the ones who didn't follow the rules. With every spin around the track, NASCAR and its fans are celebrating the American renegade.

NASCAR fans also know how to laugh at themselves, and that's another character trait liberals don't like. Here are just a few of the better NASCAR Redneck Jokes: You Might Be a NASCAR Redneck If . . . You think the last four words of the national anthem are "Gentlemen, start your engines!" . . . You've ever written Richard Petty's name on a presidential ballot . . . You're not actually able to read *The Richard Petty Story*, but you sure do like to look at the pictures . . . The only book you own is *The Richard Petty Story* . . . You spell out NASCAR in Christmas lights . . . You've spent more time on the top of a Winnebago than in one . . . You know the "back way" to Talladega . . . You can change a tire faster than you can change a diaper.

But in the end, what underlies the hatred that liberals have for NASCAR and its fans is the sense that they simply don't care what anyone thinks of them.

If you walked up to that guy in Bristol and told him that some liberals in New York City or Los Angeles or any of the places where liberals gather to scoff and disapprove didn't much like his choice of sport, or headgear, he'd probably smile and shrug and then say something unprintable about what, exactly, those liberals can do to themselves.

And then he'd probably offer you a beer and a few of his nachos.

Because NASCAR fans are almost always friendly. Even when they're cursing, they're smiling. The only problem is, they just don't know their place.

Which is why the liberals really hate them.

47 Steakhouses

Beef, cigars, and booze

One of the things they always ask you, when you sit down at a fancy steakhouse, is, "Have you been here before?"

I invariably say "no," because I enjoy what happens next.

The waiter or waitress will go through a wonderful description of everything on the menu—at some steakhouses, they even wheel up a cart piled high with steaks and vegetables and a live lobster or two. It's an amazing—and mouth-watering—way to see all of that great food, and all of those choices, in one place.

But great steakhouses don't have to be fancy.

One of the best and most quintessential places to dive into a juicy steak is Cattlemen's Steakhouse in the heartland of steak country,

Oklahoma City. At Cattlemen's, the prices are reasonable, the portions are huge, and the waiter or waitress always says the same thing when your steak arrives at the table.

They ask you to cut into it to make sure it's cooked the way you like it.

That's the thing about steak: Everybody likes it cooked exactly the way they like it cooked.

If you go to a steakhouse with friends, pretty much everyone at the table has a particular way to describe what they like—medium, rare, medium rare, medium well, well, not-quite-rare, medium *medium* rare, we've all got our own personal choice. I have a friend who likes it charred on the outside and almost raw in the inside. He ordered it that way once, he told me, at a local steak joint, and the waitress didn't even blink an eye.

"You want it *black and blue*?" she asked.

"Is that what they call it?" he said.

She nodded.

And when she brought him his steak, it was just the way he liked it: *black and blue*.

That's what I love about steakhouses—they offer delicious only-in-America food, gigantic portions, and best of all, they want to make sure it's *exactly* the way you want it.

Liberals hate that.

I love that Americans have so many types of steak to love; there's the T-bone, the porterhouse, the strip steak, and the sirloin. There's the rib eye, the ranch steak, the round steak, and the hanger steak. There's the filet mignon, the chuck steak, and the flap steak. And believe me, I've tried them all.

All of those choices of *anything* drive liberals crazy.

And that many options for eating red meat will drive all but the most caffeinated liberals into a state of depression.

Liberals spend sleepless nights tortured by the idea that some

American, in some steakhouse, is having a good meal. Actually, liberals hate *everything* about the great American steakhouse. It's a celebration, after all, of the bounty of America's pasture land. It's a place for American appetites and American tastes.

I even saw, one night at Cattlemen's in Oklahoma City, a table of six adults who had just been served bow their heads in prayer.

When was the last time you saw that at the local vegetarian spot?

You can't get a sushi roll at a steakhouse, and you can't get a vegan appetizer, either. Most steakhouses make some accommodation for the fish eaters among us—there's almost always some kind of tuna or salmon to be had, somewhere—but that's about as far as it goes. When you walk into a steakhouse, there's no question that you've walked into a temple of American culture—an unabashed, unapologetic celebration of American-ness and red meat.

Put it this way: You can find a terrific French restaurant in Chicago. And you can find a delicious Japanese restaurant in Tucson. Nothing wrong with that.

But you can't find a great steakhouse anywhere but in this country. You can't dive into a juicy T-bone anywhere but here. Steak—and steakhouses—are American through and through.

Liberals hate this.

But here's what else they hate about steakhouses. It's the atmosphere. There are the great, long wooden bars, with the old-fashioned bartenders who'll laugh if you ask for one of those wishy-washy liberal drinks—a cantaloupe vodka with a spray of Sprite, for instance.

And then there are the cigarettes. And the cigars.

Drag a lib, if you can, into the local steak palace and watch his nose crinkle and his lips curl. Everything about the typical steakhouse décor—the cowboys on the wall, the waiters and waitresses in sharp-looking uniforms, the rolling cart laden with red meat on display, and the smoke—it's as if it was all designed to drive liberals crazy, it is so perfectly, delightfully politically and gastronomically incorrect.

Liberals, in fact, are the only people who can get a heart attack from just *thinking* about all of that steak.

They hate the piles of red meat, the smell of caramelizing fat, the noise of a knife and fork cutting into a juicy porterhouse. But they *especially* hate the choice! How do you want your steak cooked? For liberals, the answer to that question—and to every question—is "Who cares? You'll eat it the way we want you to eat it!"

Of course, liberals don't want you to be eating steak in the first place. If they had their way, the answer to the question "How do you want your steak cooked?" would be, "Never, thanks. I'll have the steamed tofu instead."

We're not supposed to be eating these steaks, according to the lefties. We're supposed to be nibbling on lettuce shards and sipping miso broth. Our vegetables are supposed to be drab and spotted—*organic,* you see, is code for *brown*—and everything else is required, by liberals, to be *artisanal.*

Have a seat in a liberal restaurant, and you're assaulted with all sorts of rules and information. No substitutions. Everything organic. They'll tell you the name of the farm the lettuce comes from, the variety of tomato in the salad, and probably even the name of the hard-working chicken who donated the eggs.

But they won't ask you how you want your steak. They won't ask you anything, actually. At liberal restaurants, they *tell* you what you're going to have.

And what you're going to have isn't going to satisfy you nearly as much as a slab of juicy steak, some potatoes, a wedge of lettuce slathered in blue cheese dressing, and something sweet for dessert.

You see, for liberals, that might put some color into your cheeks. That might make you *happy,* and they can't have that.

The folks who eat and work in liberal, organic, vegan places always have the same pale complexion. The same yellowish pallor. They always look worn out and tired, wrinkly and sad. I mean, ask yourself: Have you ever seen a bubbly, happy vegan? Have you ever had a meal with a cheerful vegetarian?

Please.

What on earth do they have to be happy about, with every day filled with sad little tofu wraps and piles of beans and odd-looking grains? Liberal food is even hard to spell—is it "quinoa"? "Quenoa"? And what *is* quinoa, anyway?—and even when you can spell it, it doesn't sound very appetizing. Bulghur, quinoa, spelt—these sound like the noises your stomach makes after a big vegan meal.

Maybe that's why they all look so miserable. It's not an emotional problem. It's *gastric distress*!

Look, I love liberals—I try to love all of God's creatures—but I'd prefer not to take a long car ride with one after they've had a big vegan meal. If you get my drift.

So even though liberals hate steakhouses, do what you can to get one to cross the threshold. Promise them anything—just get them to the table and get some red meat into them.

They'll resist, of course, but try to get them to the table. They'll freak out at the selection, at the size of the portions, and especially at the whole notion that the customer has a *choice*. But keep saying soothing words, encourage them to relax, and before you know it, they'll be sitting back in their chairs and savoring the environment.

And when the steak arrives at the table, you will have won the day.

My guess is that for a lot of liberals, that's all it's going to take. One big bite of a red and dripping strip, maybe an onion ring or two, and for some of them it's going to be the beginning of a long journey from tofurkey socialism to steakhouse free-market capitalism.

So do your civic duty.

Buy a liberal a steak.

46 The Pilgrims

Here's what we all agree about the Pilgrims: They were deeply religious, wore funny black hats and buckles on their shoes, their clergyman shouted at them every Sunday, and they celebrated the first Thanksgiving with the local Indians.

Here's what the *liberals* agree about the Pilgrims: They were religious fanatics, wore funny hats and buckles on their shoes, burned witches at the stake, and celebrated the first Thanksgiving with the local indigenous Native American peoples. And then decided to kill them.

Here's what's *true* about the Pilgrims: pretty much everything in the two paragraphs above—though I might phrase it differently—but liberals and conservatives often forget this one interesting fact:

29

The Pilgrims were communists.

Well, okay, maybe not *communists,* but they were about as socialist as you could be in the seventeenth century. Put it this way: they were a lot more socialist than the French.

And, of course, that's why they almost starved to death.

Liberals hate the Pilgrims, and it's never made any sense to me why they do. It seems like a match made in heaven—a rigid, dogmatic group of people in weird clothes trying to survive in a communelike setting.

Isn't that a liberal's idea of paradise?

In fact, except for their unwavering religious faith and strict code of self-discipline—which I admit are two pretty big things—it's hard to tell the difference between the early Pilgrim settlements and one of those hippie communes where everyone walks around naked and they sit in a circle and drum.

I may be exaggerating here, but only a little.

It's the religious stuff—the belief in God and the Bible and a Plan that rules us all—that keeps liberals from embracing the Pilgrims as the long-lost cousins that they are.

Liberals hate religion. Well, not all religions. When God or Jesus enters the conversation, they just freeze up. But mention Hinduism, Kabbalah, Islam, radical Wicca—those are okay; start getting into Jesus, though, and the alarm bells go off.

If liberals could just get past the religion obstacle, they'd find they have a lot in common with the Pilgrims.

For instance, in the early years of the Pilgrim experiment, the community didn't believe in private property. They farmed and harvested as a collective farm might. No one owned the livestock. No one owned the land they tilled.

Doesn't that sound like it would appeal to liberals? Doesn't that sound *exactly* like what a political science professor at the local college would describe as his dream set-up?

The problem with all of that was, when no one owns anything, nothing gets done.

The crop yield on the Plymouth Plantation became perilously—dangerously—low. As was the whole animal husbandry operation. Most people today erroneously think that the Pilgrims suffered from harsh weather and hard-to-cultivate land, but what was threatening their existence was really bad public policy.

Because of "community ownership" (known today as progressivism, or "spreading the wealth around"), the industrious Pilgrims were forced to subsidize the lazy Pilgrims. And the lazy Pilgrims—the very first Occupy protesters—had no incentive to put in an honest day's work. So long as they knew they could profit from the industriousness of Other Pilgrims' Work, why bother?

Americans learned early on about what economists call the "free rider" problem, and its regrettable effects. And they learned early on the effects of bad liberal policy.

Who loved the idea of reaping the fruits of OPW (Other Pilgrims' Work)? The lazy Pilgrims, that's who!

As you can imagine, this didn't sit well with the industrious Pilgrims. Why bother to work, only to have the fruits of your labor passed along to those who don't? Collectivism, it turns out, pitted Pilgrim against Pilgrim. Sound familiar?

Here is how William Bradford's history of the colony recorded the early discord. His comments make it clear that common ownership demoralized the community and gave rise to conflicts that were much more serious than any others they confronted.

The strong, as Bradford put it, "had no more in division of victuals and clothes" than the weak. The older men felt it disrespectful to be "equalized in labours" with the younger men.

Unlike modern liberals, the leaders at Plymouth took swift action. They didn't appoint a blue-ribbon panel to study the behavior of the slackers, or a commission to understand the greed of the industrious Pilgrims. Who had the time?

They didn't accommodate the free riders with more food and more goodies. They didn't empower the lazy Pilgrims by asking—or forcing—the hard-working Pilgrims to give more.

The Pilgrim leaders had a better idea. What if we just all work for ourselves? What if we *own* the land we work? And that, as they say in the comic books, was a "lightbulb" moment.

And so it was decided.

Here is how William Bradford described the policy change: "At length, after much debate of things, the Governor (with the advice of the chiefest amongst them) gave way that they should set corn every man for his own particular, and in that regard trust to themselves; in all other things to go in the general way as before. And so assigned to every family a parcel of land, according to the proportion of their number."

And thus was born private property in Plymouth.

When the Pilgrims started to be responsible for their own little piece of the Plymouth Plantation pie, when they got a piece of Plymouth Rock, suddenly things got more efficient. The crop yields went up. Livestock increased. And the slackers were exposed. Free riding no longer yielded any benefits. And so the free riders started working.

The whole place started to hum with the kind of flinty industriousness we've come to expect from tough, winter-beaten New Englanders. In a few years, they had enough prosperity and leisure time to take up cultural pursuits, like burning witches and whipping adulterers. You can't do that kind of thing when you're gaunt and weak from hunger.

In that same history recorded by Bradford, he described the results of this paradigm shift from "community ownership" to private property this way: "It was a very good success."

You think?

All over the world—and at every moment in modern

history—people have learned this simple lesson. Private property and personal responsibility are the best, most effective ways to get a turkey on the dining room table. And if you want pumpkin pie, you're going to have to make a deal with the guy who owns the pumpkin patch, so you better have something to trade.

Liberals refuse to learn that lesson. To them, it's always 1620. They always think that this time it'll be different.

Poor liberals. If it weren't for the rest of us, they'd starve to death.

Liberals hate the Pilgrims for their religious faith and devotion, but they *should* hate the Pilgrims because the Pilgrims learned the hard way that liberalism just doesn't put food on the table. Collective farming is a recipe for collective starvation. No sense of ownership means no sense of personal responsibility.

The Pilgrims learned it in 1620. The French learned it in 1789. (Although they could stand to learn it again.) The Soviets learned it in 1989. The Chinese are learning it right now. And when everyone is hoping that someone else will put food on their table, it creates not only starvation—it creates discord.

Worst of all, it confers a heck of a lot of power on the leaders of the collective, because it will be they who decide who gets food. And who doesn't.

Actually, that's why despots *love* collectivism.

Because it pits the people against each other, and gives the despots the ultimate control. It's the leaders themselves who will choose who eats what. And when.

And what liberal doesn't love that kind of power?

45 John Wayne

What's so great about the Duke?

"If you've got them by the balls
their hearts and minds will follow."
—JOHN WAYNE

No one would confuse that John Wayne quotation with anything Alan Alda ever said on *M*A*S*H*—or anything else Alda ever said, for that matter. Liberals of course tend to like Alda (who is himself an inveterate liberal) and they cannot stand Wayne.

Or, at a minimum, they cannot stand what Wayne stands for.

Interestingly, Alda is from the Bronx—he studied in Paris and acted in Rome and Amsterdam before becoming an actor in the States. Kind of heavy on the euro-influence, wouldn't you say?

Wayne—from the Midwest—played football at Southern Cal until he started hanging around movie studios for bit parts. Most of the parts were cowboy parts. Kind of light on the European influence.

'Nuff said.

In fact, liberals hate John Wayne so much that they thought it would be an insult to call George W. Bush a cowboy.

Uh, memo to liberals: Most Americans love cowboys.

In fact, the whole world loves American cowboys.

Well, except the French, who like Jerry Lewis.

Yes, I know that some George W. Bush insiders bought into this cowboy hatred and convinced him not to be the cowboy, which is why Bush limped off the world stage with 26 percent approval ratings—but that's another story. Bush was loved while he was the cowboy. History will judge this good and decent man well.

Without a doubt, John Wayne was the quintessential American cowboy for many decades, and not just because most of his big-time movie roles were westerns. Wayne simply represented and gave face to everything that folks around the world love about America in general, and American cowboys specifically. There was an air about Wayne that was unmistakably American. It oozed out of every pore.

That's why liberals hate John Wayne.

Take a test: Fly in to a place like New York City or Los Angeles and attend any of the dozens of so-called film festivals or film seminars or film discussions that pass themselves off as entertainment.

You know the kind. The kind where everyone watches some old important film nobody ever watched, and then—afterward—some experts come on to the stage to tell everyone why the film they just slept through was so important to the history of film.

Liberals love that kind of thing.

Liberals love films.

Americans love movies.

I think what they actually hate most about John Wayne is that some of his movies actually reached the realm of art. Without his ever trying.

They are so deep, so brooding, so profound, and his performance so towering, that they approach American classics.

The kind of movies—like *The Godfather*—that the masses love. And that are actually so good they deserve to be studied.

John Ford's *The Searchers* is just that movie. And it could not have been the classic it was without John Wayne.

No Marlon Brando, no *The Godfather*.

No John Wayne, no *The Searchers*.

Period.

Here's the plot of that 1956 classic, which won no Oscars but was named the Greatest American Western of all time by the American Film Institute in 2008.

In 1868, Ethan Edwards (played by Wayne) returns from the Civil War to the home of his brother Aaron in the wilderness of West Texas, having just fought for the Confederacy.

Liberals already hate it.

We know that Ethan is no Boy Scout; wrongdoing in his past is suggested by his three-year absence, a large quantity of gold coins in his possession, a Mexican revolutionary war medal that he gives to his young niece Debbie, and his refusal to take an oath of allegiance to the Texas Rangers.

This is a flawed man, brimming with anger. And sin.

Shortly after Ethan's arrival, cattle belonging to his neighbor are stolen, and when Captain Samuel Clayton leads Ethan and a group of Rangers to follow the trail, they discover that the theft was a ploy played out by Comanche Indians to draw the men away from their families. When they return home, they find the Edwards home in flames; Aaron, his wife, and their son are dead. Debbie and her older sister Lucy are abducted.

The movie tracks this flawed man's relentless—and often brutal—search to get them back.

Of course, there are countless critics of John Ford's classic, and the charges of racism and bigotry soon follow, because John Wayne killed Indians in this movie. And John Wayne hated Indians in this movie.

But of course John Wayne didn't hate Indians; the character in the movie did. And he didn't hate the Indians only because they were Indians. Indeed, his character spoke the language of the Comanches he so relentlessly hunts down in the movie.

It was revenge he was seeking.

And he also knew that it was revenge Comanches were seeking for the many deaths perpetrated against their people by white men.

It's like in the movie *Gran Torino*. Clint Eastwood played a racist old widowed white guy who ends up loving the neighbors he thought he hated. He ends up loving his Hmong friends more than members of his own white family.

Both movies are about racism. And so much more.

But not the politically correct kind liberals approve of.

Whether John Wayne was on a horse or on a beach in the Pacific theater of World War II, he was a cowboy and an American patriot. He was also a winner and destined to win. And winning for Wayne generally meant he was going to kill some Indians or Japanese soldiers.

Liberals really hate that.

Americans—in the movies—often killed Indians. Soldiers—in the movies and in real life—often killed the Japanese or Germans. This, too, is what real life Americans did. If we had not done so, there wouldn't be a single Starbucks or spinning class in the entire country.

Besides, John Wayne was always convinced that he was on the side of right. He was American, which made his side right, period.

Here are just a few of the famous quotations from John Wayne that irritate the heck out of liberals:

"Courage is being scared to death but saddling up anyway."

"Life is tough, but it's tougher when you're stupid."

"If everything isn't black and white, I say, 'Why the hell not?' "

"Talk low, talk slow, and don't say too much."

"I stick to simple themes. Love. Hate. No nuances. I stay away from psychoanalyst's couch scenes. Couches are good for one thing."

And John Wayne once said, "Sure I wave the American flag. Do you know a better flag to wave? Sure I love my country with all her faults. I'm not ashamed of that, never have been and never will be."

All of those quotations irritate liberals.

Keep that in mind when considering something less serious, like the way liberals bend over backward to pronounce certain foreign names. The American pronunciation is always wrong in the liberal mind. Remember how upset they were when George H. W. Bush would pronounce Saddam more like sadam—as in madam? Meanwhile, liberals go to great pains to appear worldly, even if they sound absolutely ridiculous, if not pompous, trying to do it.

Recently we've been treated to Barack Obama talking about "Pockey-stonn" (Pakistan). I bet the people laughing the hardest actually live in Pockey-stonn!

And who among us can ever forget pompous John Kerry and "Jenjis Con" (Genghis Khan)? I mean, I tried, but I can't forget.

Well, John Wayne would have none of that Pockey-stonn or Jenjis Con stuff. Nope, not even in a movie.

In fact, when forced to share a film with a French character named Paul Regret, Wayne went out of his way to call Monsieur Paul Regret (MISS-yur paul reGRAY) MON-sewer paul reGRET. He really did!

And he repeatedly referred to "the mon-sewer" throughout the film. I'm not sure exactly what a "mon-sewer" is, but I figure it sure ain't from Pockey-stonn and has nothing to do with Jenjis Con.

And that was one of the great things about Wayne.

We're not sure he was ever really acting. He was just being, well, John Wayne.

And by being John Wayne, he was simply not going to betray certain principles of real life even as a character in a movie. He had principles and morals and there were certain lines that he would not cross even as a fictional character.

Principles and morals are threatening to liberals, especially if you believe them.

And whatever Wayne said, we knew he meant it. The character he was playing meant it but so did the real John Wayne. In Wayne's last film, *The Shootist,* he plays a rather unpleasant sort—well, a jerk, frankly—a hired gun who has a few scores to settle before he succumbs to a terminal disease.

The script called for Wayne's character, John Bernard Books, to kill a man by shooting him in the back. Nope. Not happening. Wayne insisted that the scene be changed because in 250 films he had never shot a man in the back and his interpretation of his character, Books—regardless of how unpleasant Books was—would not allow it.

This was John Wayne being John Wayne.

Even John Bernard Books had to live by John Wayne's standards.

Which is why liberals cannot abide John Wayne. No one can be that principled and that certain that he is right. It just can't happen. But it did, every day with John Wayne, and in every appearance.

It's why most Americans love John Wayne.

Because John Wayne loved America.

It's why folks from all over the globe who love America love John Wayne, too.

To quote Wayne as Books: "I won't be wronged. I won't be insulted. I won't be laid a hand on. I don't do these things to other people, and I require the same from them."

That's what Wayne believed. It's why Americans believed in him.

44

George Bailey

Doesn't anyone believe in 20 percent down anymore?

We've all been there, at some point or another.

Standing at a cash register, having just handed over the VISA card to pay for the pile of purchases or groceries or whatever, and we've all, at some point in our lives, said the same silent prayer:

Please let the card go through.

Or maybe we're at a restaurant, and we open the little plastic folder that holds the restaurant bill, we slip our card into the slot, flip the booklet closed with a snap, hand it back to the waiter, and as he takes it away we half-close our eyes and pray:

Please let the card go through.

It's our national mantra. It doesn't really matter if we know, for certain, that the card is fully operational and loaded with untapped credit; it doesn't matter if we're the clean-living pay-it-off-each-month type; it doesn't matter if it's an American Express Platinum or Centurion card. The lady takes it, swipes it through the machine, and we stare, in tense silence, as the display on the thingy goes from "Connecting" to "Transacting" to "Approved."

The waiter makes his way back to our table through the crowded restaurant and we scan his facial expression for clues: Does he look like he's about to have an awkward conversation with us? Does he look suspicious or disapproving or ready to call the police department?

But when the display shows "Approved" or the waiter plops down the check, ready for signature, it's like a little victory. A narrow escape.

It has nothing to do with creditworthiness or ability to pay—when you eat a meal or buy something and pay for it not with cash but with a promise, you're a borrower, a mooch, what they call in Yiddish a *schnorrer*. You're Wimpy from Popeye: I will gladly pay you at the end of this month's billing cycle a defined minimum payment for a pile of stuff from Target today.

And it's a pretty good system. Credit cards are called *unsecured* debt because the bank-issuer can't come after your assets if you end up welching on the deal. But in a practical sense, their potential losses are covered by the rest of us who pay the fees and the interest and the minimum payment each month, those of us who wouldn't *dream* of walking away from our obligations, and who hand over our cards with almost-confidence, though we can be heard to murmur, despite our good credit and 401(k)s and bank statements:

Please let the card go through.

The hard rock foundation of the American financial system—not the big Wall Street banks but the smaller, local banks—was that normal Americans just wanted a place to save some money, borrow to buy a house, and build a secure financial future.

This was the guiding principle behind the savings and loan industry—exactly the kind of small-town banking that the character George

Bailey practiced in Frank Capra's immortal movie *It's a Wonderful Life*. George Bailey—played by the pitch-perfect Jimmy Stewart—was a small-town proprietor of a savings and loan bank.

He lent money to his neighbors based on their character, background, and ability to make their monthly payments.

For all of his homespun neighborly generosity, George Bailey understood that the most important thing to remember about the mortgage business is that the borrower has to be able to pay it back.

Make a lot of home loans to people who can't—or won't—pay, and you just end up hurting everyone. Good borrowers end up footing the bill, in fees and higher interest rates, for all of the bad borrowers. If that happens often enough, it starts to rattle the confidence of lenders, depositors, small regional banks, big national banks, and maybe even the entire worldwide financial system.

Seems to me we've seen this movie recently.

George Bailey was a nice guy—hey, the whole town loved him—but he wasn't a sucker, and he wasn't an irresponsible lender.

And that's why liberals hate George Bailey—not the movie character exactly, but what he represents, which is sound lending based on a borrower's ability to keep up with his monthly obligations.

That's how George Bailey stayed in business.

That's how he had money to lend in the first place—because his borrowers kept current with their mortgage payments.

To liberals, this is a terrible way to run a financial system. To liberals, it's *unfair* to decide to whom you're going to lend money based on something so silly and trivial as their ability to pay it back. To liberals, if someone can't make the monthly payments, if someone has a spotty credit history or intermittent bouts of unemployment, the *government* should step in to help.

Liberals hate George Bailey and the prudent lending he represents. So they fired him and hired Fannie Mae and Freddie Mac instead.

Fannie Mae and Freddie Mac didn't care if a borrower had a job, or could afford the monthly mortgage. Why trouble yourself with those pesky details, when you know that each and every subprime loan, each and every bad credit risk, each and every defaulting mortgage is going to be backstopped by the limitless pockets of the American taxpayer?

Why worry about anything, really, when you've got the system so perfectly rigged? The liberals in government offered the perfect deal: Every dollar Fannie and Freddie made, it got to keep. Including rich bonuses and stock options for the rotating cast of liberal Democratic politicians and former politicians who ran the place.

But every dollar it lost was *covered* by that hapless mark, that sap, that chump—the American taxpayer. Liberals have never much cared what happens to him. He's just the guy at the end of the line, left to pay the bills and clean up the mess.

Until the entire system exploded in 2008, Fannie Mae and Freddie Mac were the best scams that liberals ever came up with. It was like having a credit card that you never, ever had to worry about. It was never having to say, for any reason,

Please let the card go through . . .

. . . because of *course* it was going to go through.

Fannie and Freddie lent money with abandon. They distorted the mortgage markets and made loans to folks who could never meet their obligations, all in the name of *fairness* and *equality*. But the more money they lent, the higher real estate prices soared, so by 2006 or so, they were making bad loans to bad risks at severely inflated prices.

Which is something George Bailey never would have done.

And that's why the liberals hate him.

Because he knew the importance of making the right loans to the right people. Because he knew that even when you know the card is good, it's not a necessarily a bad thing to wonder, every now and then, if it'll go through.

It keeps you on your toes.

Don't have the 20 percent down to buy that dream house?

George Bailey would sit you down and explain why renting was what you needed to keep doing until you had 20 percent down, and six months of savings in the bank for all the things that can go wrong with that new or used house. And six months more in case the breadwinner in the family loses his job.

That kind of common sense and decency did not prevail with Fannie and Freddie at the helm, and all of America suffered.

But since when did words like responsibility, decency, and common sense apply to federal bureaucrats and politicians?

On February 19, 2009, Rick Santelli was on the floor of the Commodities Exchange doing his daily report for CNBC, when he was asked about plans by our government to offer "loan modifications" to people who were underwater on their mortgages.

"Loan modifications" was Washington-speak for getting the people who worked hard and put down 20 percent on their mortgages to cut a check (our tax dollars) to the people who were playing "Flip My House" with their homes, putting no money down, and as prices rose, using their home equity to island-hop in the Bahamas.

These people were playing "Wheel of Fortune" with their houses, and it's my problem? Really?

So let's go back to that classic Santelli speech that ignited the Tea Party Movement.

> **SANTELLI:** In terms of modifications—I'll tell you what, I have an idea. How about this, president and new administration? Why don't you put up a website to have people vote on the internet as a referendum to see if we really want to subsidize the losers' mortgages; or would we like to at least buy cars and buy houses in foreclosure and give them to people that might have a chance to actually prosper down the road, and reward people that could carry the water instead of drink the water?
>
> **JOE KERNEN:** (coanchor): Hey, Rick, did—(*the traders roar*) They're like putty—they're like putty in your hands.

SANTELLI: No they're not, Joe. They're not like putty in our hands. This is America. How many of you people want to pay for your neighbor's mortgage that has an extra bathroom and can't pay their bills? Raise their hand. *(The audience roars "NO!")* President Obama, are you listening?

JOE KERNEN: This is like mob rule here. I'm getting scared.

SANTELLI: We're thinking of having a Chicago tea party in July. All you capitalists that want to show up to Lake Michigan, I'm gonna start organizing.

I wondered as I heard all of that talk about loan modifications what George Bailey would have said to that couple who got a zero percent loan down the block, purchased a house they couldn't afford, and when the prices shot up, took a home equity loan and partied like it was 2009—that is until the 2008 crash happened.

Add to the root cause of all of the bad banking decisions the implicit government guarantees that Fannie and Freddie engendered.

What would George Bailey think of those bailouts for the big banks? And the Dodd-Frank bill, which has made it more difficult for smaller banks like Bailey's to compete with the big boys on Wall Street? Big banks that can afford all of those big government regulations and compliance costs?

In Kingwood, Texas, we found an answer. It turns out that Thomas Depping, chairman of Main Street Bank, announced he was surrendering his charter and selling the four branches that had been around the region for twenty-seven years.

"The regulatory environment makes it difficult to do what we do," he told the *Wall Street Journal*.

Depping isn't Bailey.

But liberals sure hate him.

They hate everything about small bankers like him and George Bailey. No "Wonderful Life" for them.

43 Walmart

What's wrong with "Everyday Low Prices"?

Malcolm McLean had a problem. Along with his brother, he built one of the largest trucking companies in America. By the early 1950s, McLean—who never graduated from high school—owned and operated the largest trucking company in the South, but when his trucks headed to the ports of Charleston or Savannah, they were held up for days.

Back then, cargo had to be loaded and unloaded by hand. Stevedores, as the men who did the loading were called, were part of a powerful labor union that resisted all attempts to modernize and simplify the process.

Sound familiar?

For McLean and his drivers, this was a pocketbook issue. Time spent waiting at port was time they weren't moving loads, earning money.

For manufacturers and factory workers, this was a bottom-line issue. It took a long time to get the product from your factory to the customer, and time is money.

For consumers, it was a price issue. Manufacturers and shippers pass the cost of everything on to the buyer, who passes those costs on to the end user. All of those extra days just meant products were more expensive.

But McLean was a visionary. He figured out that if he could somehow ship everything in uniform containers—if, in other words, a rail car and a truck trailer were the same thing, and could be removed and stacked up like cordwood in the belly of a cargo ship—then he could cut the waiting time down from days to hours. Shipping would be faster, prices would go down, everyone—from his investors to his drivers, from factory owners to the end-of-the-chain consumers—would be happy.

Everybody, that is, except for the stevedores and their powerful union bosses, who fought him all the way. There were bloody strikes at almost every large American port, with clashes and confrontations happening all the way up until the moment that McLean's simple, elegant solution—how had no one thought of it before?—took root.

Containerized shipping was born. Transportation costs plummeted.

All because a smart, visionary entrepreneur—a self-made man, a high school dropout—knew that there must be a better way.

Which leads me to Walmart, every liberal's favorite company to hate.

Barely ten years later, Sam Walton, a shop owner in Bentonville, Arkansas, had a big idea. If he could somehow keep his costs dependably low, he could undersell his competition. With that competitive advantage, he could expand—and by expanding, he could get goods even more cheaply, and sell them at a deeper discount.

You know how this American success story ends.

Walmart, barely fifty years after Sam Walton opened his first store, is one of the world's largest and most successful companies. It operates all over the globe, employs over two *million* people, and delivers low-cost goods to consumers in a reliable and consistent way.

It does this by building on what Malcolm McLean started: It applies efficiencies in purchasing and shipping, squeezing (sometimes ruthlessly) costs out of the supply chain in order to turn those savings into lower prices for the consumer.

That means lower prices for 100 *million* Americans per week. That's about one-third of the country. A Global Insight study in 2005 revealed that Walmart saves the average American family nearly twenty-five hundred dollars a year.

That barely covers the annual sushi budget for your average city hipster. But it's a really nice vacation for your average American family. Or an old but utterly reliable used car for your seventeen-year-old son.

How do they manage to keep costs down, and keep the customers coming?

Former Walmart CEO Lee Scott was on *Charlie Rose* a few years back, and was asked what it was like to work for Sam Walton. Scott had a great story about Walton:

SCOTT: When you didn't perform, Sam would have a direct conversation with you.

ROSE (laughing): What's a direct conversation?

SCOTT: Well, you go around the room on a Friday morning meeting and there's twenty people in that room in the spring of 1980, the year after I joined, and I'm sitting in that meeting with all of the officers in the company—at that time twenty—and Sam would have a P&L—a profit and loss statement—that wasn't particularly good, and he got to me. Now when he was mad at me, he'd point his finger at me, and he said "Scott, your driver uniform costs were up 30 percent this month. What's going on?" And you better know what it was. The interesting thing was that the whole cost of drivers' uniforms was fifteen hundred dollars.

ROSE: But that amount of money meant something to Sam.

SCOTT: You're darn right it did. And it taught me that it meant a lot.

Tell that story to your average liberal, talk to that person about Sam Walton's commitment to pass along savings to his customers, and it changes nothing. Talk about Walmart's state-of-the-art distribution and delivery system, and you'll get a yawn.

Because liberals hate Walmart for their own reasons.

Look, let's face some facts: Walmart is a giant and relentless corporation that delivers prices so low and a selection so broad that it's hard for smaller, local retailers to compete. A lot of them end up closing.

The same could be said for what Walgreens and CVS did to local pharmacists. And what Home Depot did to lots of local hardware stores and lumber yards. But the Walmart haters give the others a pass.

There's Walmart's unceasing focus on driving costs down, which means that it's tough on hourly wages and tight with benefits. But not that much tighter than the rest of its industry.

The fact is that Walmart pays only slightly less per hour than the average American retailer—$11.75. But that is an average, and many of Walmart's workers are part-timers.

At a time when jobs are in short supply, and any job is better than no job, and where any job can actually lead to a better job, even a management position, liberals should be thanking Walmart. The company employs a staggering 1.4 million Americans. That's a remarkable 1 percent of the United States' total workforce of 140 million.

But liberals—and their allies in the big labor unions—instead tap out a steady drumbeat of criticism of Walmart for its labor practices.

Liberals hate Walmart for its success and its influence, and big labor unions hate Walmart for the same reason they hated Malcolm McLean all those years ago. Businesses can only grow and expand if they innovate, and innovation often means that some jobs disappear.

But many other jobs appear.

Through cost-cutting and supply-chain management, Walmart has raised the standard of living for every American, without question. And employed all kinds of Americans.

Liberals hate this. They don't value efficiency and progress. And they certainly don't appreciate bringing low-cost consumer goods to the heartland of America.

Liberals would be a lot happier if Malcolm McLean had failed in his attempt to revolutionize transportation. They'd prefer the trucks to be unloaded by hand—liberals love it when something is handmade, by artisans, don't they?—and for the local shops to be tiny and quaint.

Liberals don't care if the store has that discounted flat-screen television you want. Liberals don't think you should want it in the first place.

You see, it's not really Walmart that liberals hate. What they really hate about Walmart is what it represents.

The future. Progress. Innovation.

Walmart represents the full energy of a free-market, capitalist enterprise trying to deliver what every economist knows is the engine of economic growth: low cost, lots of choice, good service, and tight management.

Think about those words for a moment: low cost, choice, service, management.

The only enterprise that's larger than Walmart is the federal government.

Does *it* offer any of those things?

Does *any* big government program, beloved by the liberals, offer a fraction of the efficiency and service that *every* Walmart offers, every day?

Ask yourself: Who would you rather have delivering your health care? The federal government? Or Walmart?

Who would you rather have running the local school system? The local teachers' union? Or Walmart?

Who would you rather have delivering the *mail,* for heaven's sake?

Liberals don't hate Walmart for its antiunion stance. Or for its low prices. They hate Walmart because Walmart works.

And liberalism doesn't.

42 Football

War with cleats and pads

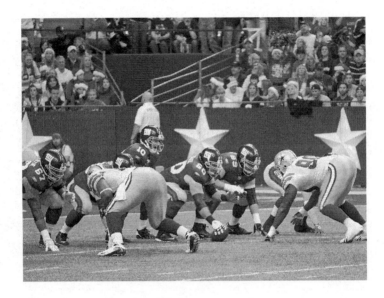

There are a lot of reasons liberals hate football, but chief among them may be that American football is not *futbol*—er, soccer. Soccer, of course, is the preferred liberal sport, and American football is the antithesis of soccer. Thus, the hatred.

You may be thinking that it's ridiculous to say liberals hate football because most Americans love football. There's something to that point, yet the essence of football flies in the face of almost every liberal foundational sacred cow.

Football is aggressive, violent, and brimming with all kinds of risk-reward, free enterprise–type calculations.

With the violence and emphasis on competition, and the

winner-take-all mentality that prevails on the gridiron, football is like two institutions liberals hate: the U.S. military and our free-market economy.

Make no mistake about it, the hatred liberals have for our military and free markets manifests itself in very dangerous and damaging legislation, not to mention insufferable political talking points on MSNBC and CNN.

Think about it. Our soldiers go off to war to win. Not to survive, not to tie, and certainly not to lose. In Vietnam, liberals rooted for us to lose.

Former *New York Times* reporter and journalist Chris Hedges was at Rockford College to deliver a commencement speech in 2005. The students were hoping for the usual graduation uplift, and instead got treated to a twenty-minute critique of the U.S. military, and our foreign policy.

> Following our defeat in Vietnam we became a better nation. We were humbled, even humiliated. We asked questions about ourselves we had not asked before. We were forced to see ourselves as others saw us and the sight was not always a pretty one. We were forced to confront our own capacity for an atrocity—for evil—and in this we understood not only war but more about ourselves.

Liberals actually think losing is good for us! In Iraq, those same liberals rooted for us to lose. And in Afghanistan, they are hoping we'll lose.

When confronted, they'll invariably reply: "We're for our soldiers, but against the war." That's like sitting in Giants Stadium and saying: "I'm for the players, but against the team."

Or: "I love Eli Manning, it's the coaches and owners I hate. It's the NFL I hate."

Whatever.

What also irritates liberals about football is the way scores can mount up quickly, ensuring that the losers in a one-sided contest will escape without a shred of phony self-esteem. You know, a rout in football is 35–0! That's going to invariably leave a mark on someone's self esteem. In soccer, 2–nothing is a rout. Come to think of it, saying "nothing" instead of "zero" is another way to hurt someone's feelings.

But 2–0? Meh. No big deal. Must have been a very close game. Can we all have our participation trophies now?

Think about it. Is it any different from Barack Obama saying he is "not comfortable with the notion of victory" in Iraq? Can't you smell that same liberal odor wafting through all of our rules of engagement?

Then there is the actual language of football, which is itself violent. As the late comedian George Carlin opined, football is full of strategies like "the bomb," "the blitz," and other military-sounding terms. Soccer has "the offside trap" which sounds like an IRS audit.

No wonder liberals love soccer.

The most aggressive-sounding position in soccer is "striker"— which appeals to the union mind-set. Union thugs are the only folks liberals want to be overtly aggressive and successful.

But the essential difference between the two sports is the way risk-reward is handled. Without getting buried in minutiae, the offside rule in soccer is more or less like making the bomb illegal in football or the fast break illegal in basketball. In this way, the rule-makers of soccer are like government bureaucrats. Their job is to make sure no one has too much fun, or gets too far ahead of the other team.

Can you imagine football without the possibility of the bomb or basketball without the notion of the fast break?

Ever heard of a Hail Mary pass?

And what about a great punt return or kickoff return?

It doesn't seem fair to a liberal that one play like that could make up for points yielded in a long, time-consuming, perfectly executed drive. But that's football. The rules may not always seem fair, and may generate unfair results, but who cares?

You can beat your opponents up and down the field all day, pound them on the line of scrimmage, and in total yards and total time of possession, but in the end, only one thing matters: who scored more points.

And no one really cares how.

Life is like that, too. At least in America. At least up until now.

I mean, David Hasselhoff made millions doing some really bad acting on *Baywatch,* while thousands of more talented actors in Los Angeles waited tables, donated blood at the local Red Cross, and posed naked for cash at the local art students league.

The guy who invented the Flowbee is rich beyond belief, and for what? Creating a hair vacuum? All of that money coming into that silly business, while thousands of other hardworking businesses go bust?

It's not fair, a liberal would say.

"Get a helmet. Who said life's fair," is what we say.

But back to the soccer comparison. With Europe's brand of football, it's not fair that you might take a chance to weaken your defense in order to spring a man deep downfield behind the other team's players with a clear shot at the goal. That would be unfair!

No, you must allow the defense to stay between you and your goal. You cannot simply use talent and daring to beat them downfield until you have the ball.

So ingrained is this in the soccer psyche that many of the world's best defenses in this sport employ the aforementioned "offside trap." Here, a defenseman gets beaten downfield *on purpose* to get a call against his opponent.

This is like your average liberal employee who gets fired on purpose so he can sue the employer for wrongful termination.

Contrast this with football, where getting beat downfield leads to six quick points for the other team, a humiliating end zone dance accompanied by a spiked football—and all magnified by endless replays on network TV and the ol' jumbotron.

Then there are all the risk calculations. Should we blitz and leave our secondary exposed? Will we be vulnerable to a screen pass, too? If we go with the dime package, will they run it down our throats?

If we call the bomb, will we risk our QB getting hit? If we run the ball on first down, do we risk having a second and long? And so on.

Every decision has a competitive calculation, which makes football much like running a business in a free-market economy. Or fighting a war.

Should we hire more employees? Should we expand the fleet? If we don't open that market, will we lose share forever to our competitor? And so it goes. This of course is anathema to the liberal mind-set, where there is no tolerance for risk-taking, and an obsession with ensuring equal outcomes for everybody.

Now okay, you're saying football is so popular that there's no way liberals can hate it. Well, you're right. But you're wrong, too. Liberals are always enjoying the fruits of the very pursuits that they're totally opposed to.

They hate free enterprise, but they love to absorb tax revenues from it. They love to exploit it for the right industries (like moviemaking and software development), while hating the wrong industries (well, just about everything else).

Living with contradictions is easy for liberals. They do it every single day.

Football flies in the face of yet another liberal fantasy, which is that men and women are the same, save some minor plumbing differences. Football is one profession in which men and women will NEVER do the same job; men will wear helmets and pads, women will wear the Daisy Dukes, the little tops, and the white cowboy boots.

I'm fine with that. So are millions of football fans.

And no liberal sport would be complete without a generous dose of self-importance and snobbery. Liberals love telling real football fans that their fake football is the world's most popular sport. I guess they are technically right. But they're also wrong.

You see, American football is the world's most popular sport, if by popular you mean what is chosen by people who actually have a choice.

Soccer is the world's most common sport.

There is a difference. To say soccer is more popular than football is like saying dirt is more popular than gold simply because there is more of it.

Liberals hate choices more than anything, which is why they love soccer.

Last time I checked, soccer seems to be popular where starvation and badminton are the main alternatives. Given that, I'd take soccer, too. Where soccer has to compete with football, basketball, baseball, UFC, the X Games, and even high school cheerleading contests . . . well . . . it doesn't fare as well.

Here's to all those wonderful Sunday afternoons plopped in front of the TV set with a big bag of chips watching two NFL teams squaring off in living color. That's the American way.

41 Conservative Women

Mouthy girls

If eye-rolling was an Olympic sport, liberals would win the gold medal every time. To see some truly elaborate eye-rolling, just drop the following words into your next conversation with a liberal:

"I was thinking about something Sarah Palin said the other day . . ."

Stand back. Let the huffing and puffing and sighing begin.

It doesn't matter how you finish the sentence. You could say, "Sarah Palin likes chocolate ice cream," or, "Sarah Palin thinks coffee is good as a breakfast beverage," or, "Sarah Palin thinks panda bears are cuddly," the result is going to be a kind of deranged, automatic rejection of anything Sarah Palin says or thinks.

Try it with *Ann Coulter.*

Same reaction.

Actually, try it with any well-known female who is unapologetically nonliberal, and you'll get the identical eye-rolling incredulity.

Liberals hate mouthy conservative women.

They hate this new generation of independent, conservative, brash-talking female that rejects the 1970s-era feminist dogma. It's insulting to liberals that for all of the wonderful things they've done for women, some of them just refuse to show any gratitude.

Liberals have worked so hard to break down the barriers of sexism that when Sarah Palin burst onto the scene with her unique brand of cheerful conservatism, they had no choice but to attack her for . . . her looks. For her hair. For her outfits. For her accent. For her education. For her children. For her makeup.

For a group of folks that have tried so hard to eliminate sexism from the national discourse, liberals sure know how to use it when they need to.

It's the same with Ann Coulter. She's attacked for her looks, her hair, her weight.

Governor Palin takes it all in stride. So does Ann. These are big girls, and they can—and do—give as good as they get. But it's interesting, since we're talking about looks, to note the remarkable, um, *improvement* over the years in the physical charms of women in the political realm. Google Betty Friedan, one of the first feminists to emerge in the early 1960s. Now Google S. E. Cupp.

There's something to be said for the progression of liberal feminist to conservative commentator.

What sends liberals around the bend, though, is the refusal of the women in the conservative aisle to toe the line on big issues like abortion and welfare.

You're not a "real" woman, the liberals insist, if you're not in favor of abortion on demand. You're not a "real" woman if you claim to have a conscience about an unborn child, because a "real" woman isn't allowed to deviate from the strict liberal line.

Liberals find it incredible that women—who carry life in their bodies, who nurture and protect life from the moment of conception—have strong feelings about it, feelings that come from a conscience and a faith, and not from the majority opinion of a Supreme Court decision.

"Real" women, according to liberals, believe in a larger welfare state, government-sponsored day care, and free abortion.

Do Sarah Palin, Ann Coulter, and nearly every other conservative woman in the national political conversation think a woman should be paid as much as a man for the same job? Of course they do. Basic fairness requires that all citizens be treated equally.

But liberals can't stop at basic fairness. It's not enough that women are paid the same for the same job. Women, liberals think, should be paid based on something called "comparable worth," which means that all jobs—hotel maid, eye surgeon, makeup counter saleswoman, say—need to be ranked and compared according to their "worth" and their "value," and the salaries need to be adjusted accordingly.

Why should the guy at the AT&T store get paid more than an office receptionist? Why should the guy working IT at a company get paid more than the woman who cleans the bathrooms?

What we need, liberals think, is to sort out who's worth what.

Who does the sorting? Do I really have to say?

Liberals! That's who!

They're eager to convene a Federal Commission on Occupational Worth and Compensation, complete with Diversity Regulations, Compensation Penalties, and, probably, some kind of federal jail somewhere for companies that pay their vice presidents more than their secretaries.

But more than that, they're eager to silence the conservative women who just won't stay on the reservation, who insist on talking, out loud, about things like unborn babies, motherhood, families, taxes, and what *real* women care about.

And, worse, they insist on doing it while looking really amazing.

Maybe that's why liberals hate the women on the conservative side. They make conservative values seem so . . . well, *hot.*

There was nothing that matched the media elite's reaction to the sudden ascension of Sarah Palin; sudden, of course, unless you consider the fact that she was the enormously popular sitting governor of the largest state in America.

The sudden ascension of Barack Obama from utter obscurity, of course, bothered no one in the mainstream media. The man had a resume so reed-thin that—even double-spaced and with extra-large fonts—it could barely take up one page.

Community organizer: Mid-1980s. No exact dates.

Attorney: "Practice" specialty—Civil rights law. No precise dates.

Writer: Wrote two memoirs (one wasn't enough). While "practicing" law.

Illinois State Senate: Voted "Not Present" a lot.

U.S. Senator from Illinois. Barely served.

And yet the mainstream media fell in love with this "highly qualified" applicant. And fell in love with him because they liked the trifecta of the first black, male, liberal president more than the first white, female, conservative vice president trifecta.

And it didn't hurt that he went to the colleges the mainstream media adore.

Columbia and Harvard.

Palin attended all kinds of colleges. Then she was a sportscaster, got married, had kids, helped her husband in his commercial fishing business, became mayor of Wasilla, and then ran against a political machine in the state, the Murkowski family—and won, becoming the first woman to serve as governor in that state's history.

But the sisterhood in the media went after her.

Rather than swoon and fawn all over her, like they did with President Obama, they attacked. Katie Couric tried her best to derail Palin; she spent a full day with the candidate, all in the hope that she would catch her in a flub.

She did.

She asked Sarah what papers she read each day, and Palin couldn't name the proper names for Katie. Indeed, she didn't name any. Few public figures publicly admit to which newspapers they read or what TV or radio shows they tune to. But this was different. It was Sarah Palin.

Couric had what she'd wanted, and threw Sarah under the sisterhood bus.

Can you imagine if Katie had exhibited the same reportorial zeal with President Obama? Imagine if she'd spent a full day with him and asked him a few tough questions.

"How many soldiers are there in a battalion, Senator Obama?"

After some stammering, and some umms, and some ahhhs, Katie could have followed up.

"Senator Obama. You are asking this country to make you commander in chief of the U.S. armed forces, and you have no idea how many men are in a battalion?"

Couric could easily have added, "I am sure John McCain knows that answer. And so does Sarah Palin, because she ran the Alaskan National Guard."

But naturally, that didn't happen.

What a video moment that would have been.

Katie Couric's sisterhood only applies to Democratic women—to liberal women. Even if it means missing an opportunity to stump the future president of the United States.

Oprah turned against the conservative GOP candidate, too. It turns out that Oprah's long-standing commitment to promoting women did not extend either to Sarah *or* Hillary. . . . She instead endorsed Barack Obama, proving that skin color trumps everything with Oprah. Her audience rebelled. They were furious that two more qualified women were passed over by one of their heroes—and a champion of white and black women alike.

It was a white Republican man who most ably defended Sarah Palin during that dreary summer. It was on MSNBC during the GOP convention, and Keith Olberman's show was still on the air. Olbermann threw to Ron Allen, himself an African American, who was on the convention floor to interview Newt Gingrich.

The fiery exchange over Palin went like this.

ALLEN: To be fair, her resume is not something that we're familiar seeing with presidential candidates.

NEWT: It's stronger than Barack Obama's. I don't know why guys walk around saying this baloney. She has a stronger resume than Barack Obama. She's been a real mayor, he hasn't. She's been a real governor, he hasn't. She's been in charge of the Alaska National Guard, he hasn't. She was a whistleblower who defeated an incumbent mayor, he has never once shown that kind of courage. She's a whistleblower who turned in the chairman of her own party and got him fined twelve thousand dollars. I've never seen Obama do one thing like that. She took on the incumbent governor of her own party and beat him, and then she beat a former Democrat governor in the general election. I don't know of a single thing that Senator Obama has done but talk and write. And I'd like you to tell me one thing Senator Obama has done.

ALLEN: Thanks very much, Mr. Speaker. I'm not going to argue the case.

It hurt just reading that beating, didn't it?

It was a smackdown of epic proportions. Allen was fully prepared to argue the case against Sarah Palin; it was he who prompted Newt's rant by saying she wasn't qualified to be vice president. But when Gingrich rattled off Palin's record, and Obama's nonrecord, Allen was rendered speechless.

"Back to you in the studio, Keith!"

When Palin got the nomination, you would have thought that Katie Couric, Diane Sawyer, Barbara Walters, and the pack of shrill shrews on *The View* (Elisabeth Hasselbeck doesn't count) would at least have pretended to celebrate the announcement.

But the street-smart, gun-toting, pro-life, pro-drilling, pro-Jesus, pro-military Palin was every liberal woman's worst nightmare.

They hate Ann Coulter for the same reason. And Michelle Malkin. And Monica Crowley. And all of the rest of them. They hate them because they don't comport to the official liberal version of womanhood.

If only these "mouthy women" would just go away.

Luckily for us, they ain't going anywhere.

40 Black Republicans

Say good-bye to the plantation

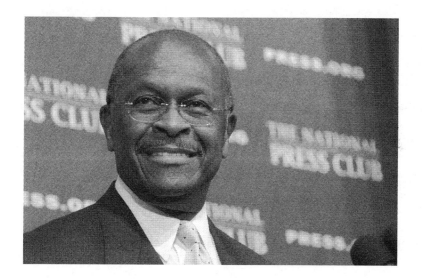

When former Godfather Pizza CEO Herman Cain burst onto the political scene last autumn, liberals knew they were in trouble.

Cain is a successful black Republican—an accomplished businessman, an unapologetic conservative, a passionate voice for the values of hard work and personal responsibility—and he's therefore a real problem for liberals.

For liberals, a black conservative is sort of a Public Enemy Number One, a powerful nemesis like one of the villains from a James Bond movie who mutters evil things and strokes a white cat.

Liberals hate—*hate!*—black Republicans—especially rich black Republicans, because they're not really supposed to exist.

To liberals, a black conservative is something out of some fairy tale, something mythical and mysterious. It doesn't make any sense to them. Why would a black person—a black man, especially—*not* be a liberal? Why would a self-respecting African-American man *choose* to be a Republican? It baffles them. A rich, black Republican is like an evil, black, free-market unicorn.

Actually, he's not like a unicorn to them at all. Judging from some of the bumper stickers I see on Volvos and Priuses around town, a lot of liberals believe in unicorns.

Liberals divide the world into victims and oppressors. The oppressors—that's me, and probably you—do bad things like complain about taxes and vote for conservatives. Victims—that's every black, Hispanic, female, and any other kind of hyphenated American—take part in heroic protests and Fight the Power. That's just the way things are to liberals. That's the way they like it.

So when a member of the latter group seems to be crossing over into the former group, the liberals get very, very angry.

He's not really black, is what they like to say about an African American who isn't liberal.

He's an Uncle Tom, they whisper behind his back, or sometimes to his face.

It never occurs to liberals that in so rigidly categorizing people according to their race, in demanding specific political loyalties of people solely because of the color of their skin, they're doing exactly what evil white segregationists did in the past centuries.

If you're black and an American, you're supposed to be angry at white people and suspicious of America in general. You're not supposed to be successful in business, that's for sure. Because how could you be? America is a racist nation. Black people are held back by the white oppressor class.

The only way Herman Cain, for instance, could have risen to the top of the corporate ladder, the only way he could have guided a large company through years of growth and prosperity, was if he had *help*.

Help, that is, in the form of racial set-asides and affirmative action laws. Not help as in what you and I think of as help—parents who pushed him to succeed, teachers who expected the best, a community that rewards hard work and achievement, a company and shareholders who couldn't be less interested in race or more interested in the bottom line.

You see, to liberals, a black man who's made it is only valuable if he's made it *their* way. If he's been the recipient of *their* largesse. Like the kindly plantation owner of lore, they'll be happy to let a black man succeed. As long as he's grateful.

When Herman Cain had the temerity to enter the 2012 GOP primary, in about as long as it takes to sing "Day-O (The Banana Boat Song)," actor/activist Harry Belafonte called Cain a "totally false bad apple."

Just as quickly, Herman Cain responded. And he did so on—gasp—my good friend Sean Hannity's TV show. On Fox News Channel!

Here's what Cain said: "As far as Harry Belafonte's comment, look, I left the Democrat plantation a long time ago. And all that they try to do when someone like me—and I'm not the only black person out there that shares these conservative views—the only tactic that they have to try and intimidate me and shut me up is to call me names, and this sort of thing. It just simply won't work."

Jesse Jackson responded to Cain's response to Belafonte in *Politico* with exactly what we've come to expect from America's premier race hustler: "Those are very strong words . . . they are both demeaning and insulting." Of course, not a peep from "the Reverend" about Belafonte's vicious attack.

Cain didn't care. But that's the thing about rich, black Republicans; they don't need Jesse's blessing. Or Harry's.

Cain responded to the criticism he knew would come not only from those old sixties holdovers, but from an entire new generation of "scholars" like Princeton's rhyming, rapping professor, Cornel West, and the University of Pennsylvania's Resident Angry Professor, Michael Eric Dyson: "It's coming from everybody who does not like the fact that I, as an American black conservative, am in a position to be able to speak my mind and tell the truth and wake people up. Especially black people."

Back in the latter part of the nineteenth century and into the early part of the twentieth, a great debate raged between Booker T. Washington and W. E. B. DuBois; the former believed that African Americans would best advance themselves by learning trades and moving from grievance to economic freedom and independence. DuBois, after initially admiring Washington, came to see his path as being too conciliatory, and spent his life trying to advance the collective rights of African Americans.

In 1895, Washington made what may have been one of the great speeches in American history before a predominantly white audience at the International Exposition in Atlanta. Here is a part of that speech:

> Our greatest danger is that in the great leap from slavery to freedom we may overlook the fact that the masses of us are to live by the productions of our hands, and fail to keep in mind that we shall prosper in proportion as we learn to dignify and glorify common labour, and put brains and skill into the common occupations of life; shall prosper in proportion as we learn to draw the line between the superficial and the substantial, the ornamental gewgaws of life and the useful. No race can prosper till it learns that there is as much dignity in tilling a field as in writing a poem. It is at the bottom of life we must begin, and not at the top. Nor should we permit our grievances to overshadow our opportunities.

Those last words are words many rich, black Republicans live by, even if they've never heard them. Does racism exist? You bet. Do African

Americans face hurdles and barriers that white folks don't? Many do. Will they get rich studying poetry or doing graduate work on white imperialism? Maybe, if they hit the academic jackpot the way Professors West and Dyson did.

Herman Cain and men like him decided not to let their grievances overshadow their opportunities. And Americans bought pizza from a company owned by an African American. And made him rich.

That makes him dangerous to guys like Harry Belafonte and Jesse Jackson.

When a rich, black Republican appears on the scene, liberals get angry and bent out of shape. But it's worse, and even more discombobulating when working-class minorities refuse to behave the way liberals want them to.

They're baffled by the innate socially conservative views of those groups, just as they're baffled by an unapologetic free-market conservative black man who refuses to play their game.

When Martin Luther King, Jr.'s niece Alveda became a vocal supporter of the prolife movement, the mainstream media didn't know what to do. Or say. When African Americans speak up on the issue of life, it is from the precise biblical precepts that so many of their white Christian counterparts rely upon. But you'll never see liberals attacking Alveda King or the countless African-American pastors, reverends, and religious leaders who oppose abortion. And who cite God's law, not man's, as their guide.

Liberals just won't accept that America turned a corner years ago, away from the racial categories that divided us, and toward a greater sense of unity and cohesion. Americans saw Herman Cain—and for that matter, Barack Obama—and judged him on his merits, not on the color of his skin.

Americans aren't surprised when a successful and conservative business and political leader is African American. These days, they're positively blasé about it.

Which is as it should be.

The only people still clinging to racial politics and divisive rhetoric are liberals. So when they see a cheerful, rich, black Republican they positively freak out. Because if he can exist, then that means their entire worldview is wrong. And liberals hate to be wrong.

39 Christians

The masses on drugs

Admit it: Liberals hate Muslims. For all of their talk about religious tolerance and being inclusive, liberals—especially liberals in the media—really have it in for the followers of Islam.

Item:

A talented and dazzling NFL quarterback, a devout and committed Muslim, prays openly to his god both before and after each game. He goes down on one knee to thank the Almighty after each touchdown or completed pass, and in general makes no secret of his abiding faith.

And the liberals go crazy. They call him a freak, they complain about his "excessive" religiosity. He's mocked on *Saturday Night Live,* and eyes are rolled all over ESPN.

He's called "controversial" in the liberal press, and there's even talk, in some circles, about petitioning the NFL to act to reduce this kind of religious display, and for the television cameras to cut away from the quarterback when he's praying to his odd and peculiar deity.

Item:

An army psychiatrist at Fort Hood, caught up in a twisted Christian fundamentalist movement, goes on a murderous rampage and kills thirteen people, wounding another twenty-nine. It's the worst mass murder on an American military base in history, and it was motivated entirely by the officer's blind obedience to a crackpot Christian cleric who preaches violence and hate.

And yet the media, in their relentlessly pro-Christian bias, refuse to call the murderer what he really is, a *Christian* mass murderer, and refuse to draw the connection between his fundamentalist Christian faith and his violent and bloody acts.

Item:

A disturbed Norwegian Muslim, Anders Breivik, bombed a government building in Oslo, killing eight people. He then went to a remote island camp for young people and murdered sixty-nine others, in a rampage that shocked the nation and forever changed the character of Norway.

And the media—anti-Muslim to the core—continually reminded readers and viewers of his faith. He was almost always identified as a "Muslim attacker" or "Muslim mass murderer." His religion was immediately an issue in the coverage, and most American media outlets insisted on calling him a "fundamentalist Muslim" in their reports, even though his so-called Muslim faith was impossible to verify. Anders Breivik was a member of no mosque, and personally professed to no faith.

But that didn't stop the media from tarring him as a "fundamentalist Muslim mass murderer."

If the examples listed above don't convince you, irrevocably, that the media are deeply hostile to the Muslim faith, and that the liberals who rule the airwaves and edit the newspapers have a bedrock hatred of all things Islamic, then I don't know what will. It's time for all of us to take a stand and let the liberals in the media know that their anti-Muslim bias will not stand, and that we will all join hands and . . .

Wait a minute. Just a second. Let me recheck my notes here.

Oh, I see. My apologies. I seem to have made an error.

Somehow, my notes got mixed up. If you would, please, just substitute the word "Christian" for "Muslim" in the paragraphs above.

So, to recap: The quarterback who caused so much trouble with his praying? He was praying to Jesus.

The Fort Hood killer whose religion was cloaked by the media? He was a Muslim.

The Norwegian psychopath? He was consistently—and erroneously—called a "Christian fundamentalist" in news reports.

On reflection, then, it looks like liberals *don't* hate Muslims at all. It's *Christians* they hate.

Actually, now that I think about it, that makes a lot more sense. Liberals never want any other religion to curtail its traditions. Liberals never complain that other religions are too "excessive" or "in your face."

Just Christians.

When a Christian quarterback mentions Jesus in a postgame press conference, everyone gets quiet. Like someone loudly passed wind. Liberals look at their shoes. Reporters get embarrassed. Everyone wants to change the subject.

Liberals never complain about the headscarves or coverings that Muslim women are wearing, in increasing numbers, on American streets. But put a "What Would Jesus Do?" bumper sticker on your car, and you'll be subjected to snickers and sneers.

Christianity is the only religion in America that it's okay to mock and defame. It's even encouraged. You can depict Jesus in almost any way you want—it's practically impossible to imagine a fresh way to insult His followers or defile His image—blithely confident that the most you'll get is an approving smirk from the liberals in the media, and, probably, a nice bump in sales.

Try that with Muslims. See how far you get.

It is almost fashionable, the Christian kind of bigotry. Especially if you're a Hollywood type.

Case in point: July 2006. The Aspen Institute, a fancy think tank in Washington, D.C., was having its annual ideas festival. A festival conjures up images of folks celebrating, and given that this was an ideas festival, one would think the Aspen Institute was celebrating its ideas.

Call me crazy.

Before I continue with the story, and in case you've never heard of the institute, here is how it describes itself to the public: "The Aspen Institute is an international nonprofit organization founded in 1950 as the Aspen Institute of Humanistic Studies. The organization is dedicated to fostering enlightened leadership, the appreciation of timeless ideas and values, and open-minded dialogue on contemporary issues."

"Humanistic studies"? Anyone who's spent two minutes in a liberal arts college knows what those two words mean. Aspen's own description of itself also says they are interested in the study of "timeless ideas and values."

Is there anything more timeless than being a Christian?

Walter Isaacson is the Aspen Institute's president and CEO. He is a generally decent liberal, the old-school kind who tries his best to at least appear balanced. He served as managing editor of *Time* magazine back when people read it. And he was chairman and CEO of CNN back when people watched it. He authored the terrific biography of the late Steve Jobs.

Now back to the story.

The topic that summer day at the Aspen Ideas Festival was

"Television, Cinema, and American Values," and on the stage were three giants in the business: Nora Ephron, Norman Lear, and Sydney Pollack.

Pollack was a heck of a director (he recently died) and an Oscar winner, and gave us great movies like *Out of Africa* and *Tootsie.* He also gave us the remake of *Sabrina,* and ruined a perfectly good Billy Wilder masterpiece.

Norman Lear gave us one of America's most beloved characters, Archie Bunker, and one of America's greatest TV hits of all time, *All in the Family.* He tried with Archie Bunker to create a character that represented all of the classic—and repulsive—stereotypes that liberals perpetuate when they create characters that share our conservative values; he was a bigot, a racist, and a real cheapskate.

But hard as he tried to inspire the opposite feeling, America fell in love with Lear's creation, especially how he dealt with his nitwit liberal son-in-law.

And then there was Nora Ephron, the brilliant writer/director who recently died, and who gave us such screen classics as *You've Got Mail, Sleepless in Seattle,* and *When Harry Met Sally.* She also gave us *Silkwood,* an antinuke movie that did for taking a shower what *Jaws* did for ocean swimming.

Toward the end of this panel discussion, the moderator, Kurt Anderson, asked questions submitted by the audience. This is when things got really interesting.

Anderson asked: "Do you all have personal friends who are evangelical Christians, and how do you know what you know about those folks?"

Lear and Pollack stumbled about and did their best to hide their obvious discomfort with the question.

Not Nora.

Not the sensitive Hollywood screenwriter, and the only woman on the stage. Here is what she said:

"No I don't," she said proudly. Defiantly.

Then the weirdness began.

The audience burst into spontaneous applause. They applauded the fact that Ephron admitted to not knowing a single person from a group of Americans that constitutes over 23 percent of our population.

Anderson asked the question again, because, I suspect, he couldn't believe the answer. Or the audience reaction.

Ephron charged ahead: "No, and I am not ashamed of it. And I just want to say that."

And the audience roared even loader with applause. And laughter.

Here was a then living major American writer and director admitting at an ideas festival that she didn't know any evangelical Christians, and she was proud of it! And this was on CSPAN for all the world to see.

A thought experiment: Can you imagine some conservative writers gathered around a table at an ideas festival on CSPAN, and the moderator asks the men if they know any African Americans? And imagine if one of the esteemed panelists, say Jonah Goldberg or Charles Krauthammer, replied, "No, and I am not ashamed of it. And I just want to say that!" And imagine if the conservative audience burst into spontaneous applause.

Can you imagine the outcry? Can you picture the repercussions?

That's the thing about Christian bigotry. It knows no boundaries. It has no limits. It's so ingrained in the liberal elite mind-set that (a) a great writer can say what Ephron said in public, and (b) an audience can reward what she said in public with thunderous applause and (c) no one on the stage will admonish her, and no one in the elite media will condemn her.

What was on display there at Aspen was the very worst kind of rank prejudice. Because Nora Ephron admitted she didn't know any evangelicals, and admitted in the same sentence that she not only didn't care that she didn't know any evangelical Christians, but was proud of it!

So she was admitting that she didn't have any desire to meet these Christians, even though she doesn't know them.

That's liberals for you. They are so proud of their ignorance. And their religious bigotry. And don't mind sharing both in public.

They don't mind expressing their lack of faith, and their belief in "humanist studies"—a kind of faith by itself. But they hate—hate— the very idea of Christians expressing theirs. Especially those "born again" kinds. The yukky kind who actually believe that Jesus Christ died for our sins. The ikky kind like Tim Tebow who love Jesus Christ, and aren't shy about it.

It was Karl Marx who called religion the opiate of the masses. And Christians are the masses in America. Most liberals treat us just like we're messing up the view, like we're embarrassing the family with all of our faith and Jesus talk.

What liberals really want from us Christians is this: Love your God. Love that cross. But do it in private. Please. Don't make us see it. And for God's sake, don't make us hear about it.

38 The Bible

Fairy tales for the feeble-minded

I have a friend who goes to Bible study every week. She and some members of her church gather in someone's living room for a cup of tea and a cookie or two, and read a specific chapter together, talk about it, and think about how it might apply to their lives. It's a pretty casual affair.

She tells me that the conversation often veers a little from the specific text, but that it's a great way to share some fellowship with her fellow church members and to get a little insight into their lives.

I have another friend who goes to a different kind of Bible study every week. He and some of the men in his church get together in a room in the parish hall, read a specific chapter together, talk about it, and try to fit it into the larger picture of their lives as Christians.

He tells me it's a fairly serious couple of hours. Someone is assigned to provide some lexicographical background, usually describing the various translations from Greek or Hebrew, and someone is assigned to present the various historical interpretations of the text to the group. According to him, it's a refreshing and uplifting way to spend one night a week, and he never leaves it without something new to think about.

Two very different kinds of Bible study. Two very different kinds of religious experience. Which one is better?

Who cares?

What's important is that all over America, in church basements and living rooms, people are getting together to read the Bible and talk about it. For millions of Americans, these gatherings—casual or formal; chatty or more focused—are a nourishing and deeply satisfying way to think about God's words to us, and to think about what we mean to Him.

Liberals hate that. In fact, many liberals don't even know that Americans actually spend a whole lot of time reading the Bible, talking about the Bible, and using the Bible as their reference for daily living.

For liberals, the Bible raises some very troubling issues.

"What's to study?" they want to know. "What's there to talk about?"

For liberals, the Bible is just a collection of oddly confusing fairy tales. In the first part, the Old Testament, there's lots of violence—not to mention the objectification of women—and more than a little child abuse. And let's not even mention the pages and pages of rules to live by.

In the second part, the New Testament, there's the figure of Jesus, whom liberals would probably like if he didn't keep talking about the forgiveness of sins. Liberals don't believe in the concept of sin. For them, a sin is just the name for something you did that's probably your parents' fault.

So a bunch of people sitting together to try to make sense of the Bible just seems weird to them. Weird and a waste of time, too, because how could a book written thousands of years ago be relevant to life today? How could the stories of the ancient Hebrews, or Jesus' parables, help anyone understand what's happening in his or her very modern life?

Bill Maher is one guy who just doesn't get it. "That book," he said to Larry King one night, dripping with contempt. "It's all about that one book written so many years ago, but it wasn't written by God."

Others do not talk about the Bible or Christ with such outright hostility.

I'm not religious, liberals will tell you, *but I am very spiritual.*

What they mean is, *I'm not religious, but I occasionally do yoga.*

For liberals, spiritual is okay. Religious is not. Vague and airy notions of a "higher power" are fine. A set of specific religious beliefs, though, not so much.

Like it or not—and liberals most decidedly *do not* like it—the Bible and its teachings form the backbone of every single one of our civic and political institutions. The origins of our oldest and most famous academies—Harvard and Yale—are rooted in the study of the Bible. They were both seminaries, where Bible study was an essential part of the curriculum.

Every witness at every trial swears an oath on the Bible, as does every president and elected official. You simply weren't considered an educated person, until very recently, unless you had a thorough familiarity with both Testaments, and a deep understanding of Scripture.

All of those Americans, all over the country, sitting together to read this ancient and essential text are, consciously or not, upholding a tradition that goes back to the Founding Fathers. John Adams went to Bible study. So did Lincoln. Most of the Framers of the Constitution could recite whole passages from memory.

Somehow, that makes the whole book even more suspect for liberals. They hate the idea of a book, especially one that purports to be the Word of God, having such a hold on our attention. It wasn't written by a *person,* is what they hate the most about it. It can't be interpreted as a political act, written by a guy who just wanted power.

Liberals look at pretty much every written document this way. Liberal legal scholars "read" the U.S. Constitution as an exercise in gender and racial politics.

Liberal literary critics "read" Mark Twain and James Fenimore Cooper and even poor old Edith Wharton as examples of "colonial" and "class-based" narratives. Liberal historians scour old letters and forgotten archives for new ways to prove that everything is really, deep down, just an exercise in power politics.

Bible study, on the other hand, is about as simple a prospect as you could imagine. Take a group of friends and neighbors, an ancient and powerful text, a plate of cookies, and that's pretty much that.

One of the many reasons the Bible is still a central part of so many lives and so many cultures is that it rewards exactly this kind of thing.

It's deep and mysterious and powerfully moving, and it's hard to really get your arms around it. You could read the Bible continually, cover to cover, starting over at the beginning each time, and you'd still discover new things each time. The Bible is bigger than all of us, which is why so many of us enjoy sitting with others to mull it over every week.

It's also why liberals hate it so much.

And they hate the power of the Bible over men.

Think about the hold that silly old book had on a guy like Reverend Martin Luther King. I mean, the guy loved the Bible so much that he actually got a Ph.D. in Bible study—it's called a theology degree these days.

And he actually helped change America by imposing his closely held beliefs about that old book on the American people.

It always amuses me when MLK Day approaches every January, because I watch liberals scurry to avoid one fact they find so very distasteful; they bend over backward to avoid calling him Reverend King, which was what he was. They instead call him Dr. King, which he was, too.

But he was a doctor of Bible studies.

It wasn't some dead old book to Dr. King.

It was God's word.

In his "Letter from Birmingham Jail," which may be one of the most beautiful pieces of writing, political, religious, or any other kind, of the twentieth century, Reverend King tried to remind America of its own values, and the source of those values—and why he believed he would ultimately win the struggle for his people. And for America.

"We will win our freedom because the sacred heritage of our nation and the eternal will of God are embodied in our echoing demands."

Pretty short and sweet.

He also addressed the issue of breaking unjust laws, especially as a man of God. Especially as a Bible-believing Christian.

"How does one determine whether a law is just or unjust? A just law is a man made code that squares with the moral law or the law of God. An unjust law is a code that is out of harmony with the moral law."

There he goes again using that God word again! And Reverend King didn't believe in just any God. He believed in the God of the Bible.

In the early 1960s, in case you weren't there, there was a battle being fought for the soul of African Americans. On one side was this great Christian man, who spoke of God's love and mercy. And on the other was a young radical Black Muslim named Malcolm X, who had a very different vision.

Malcolm was fiery. He was passionate. He was brilliant. And he represented the Nation of Islam. Malcolm had little use for the nonviolent approach of Reverend King, and less use for the Christian vision of King.

On more than one occasion, Malcolm implied that Reverend King was some kind of Uncle Tom. Actually, he didn't imply that King was an Uncle Tom. He actually said it.

"The same old slave master today has Negroes who are nothing but modern Uncle Toms, twentieth-century Uncle Toms, to keep you and me in check, keep us passive and peaceful and nonviolent. That's Tom making you nonviolent."

That was Reverend Martin Luther King Malcolm was talking about. That was the Christian way Malcolm was ridiculing.

Here is some more vintage Malcolm from the early sixties:

"A revolution is bloody. Revolution is hostile. Revolution knows no compromise. Revolution overturns and destroys everything that gets in its way. And you sit around here like a knot on a wall saying I'm going to love these folks no matter how much they hate me. No, you need a revolution."

That was Reverend Martin Luther King Malcolm was taunting. That was a Muslim voice mocking the Christian.

Here is some more vintage Malcolm X: "Whoever heard a revolution where they lock arms singing 'We Shall Overcome'? Just tell me, you don't do that in a revolution. You're too busy swingin' to do any singin'."

Talk about two different visions for America!

There are these remarkable words from Reverend King, again from "Letters from Birmingham Jail." He addressed the choices African Americans faced, and whether the best way forward was through love—and peace—or through violence. He also addressed white southern Christians who considered his marching and his public positions "extremist." That he was pushing things to far. And too fast.

I was initially disappointed at being categorized as an extremist, as I continued to think about the matter I gradually gained a measure of satisfaction from the label. Was not Jesus an extremist for love: "Love your enemies, bless them that curse you, do good to them that hate you, and pray for them which despitefully use you, and persecute you." Was not Amos an extremist for justice: "Let justice roll down like waters and righteousness like an ever flowing stream." Was not Paul an extremist for the Christian gospel: "I bear in my body the marks of the Lord Jesus."

King continued:

> So the question is not whether we will be extremists, but what kind of extremists we will be. Will we be extremists for hate or for love?

Thank God Reverend King's vision prevailed, and not Malcolm X's.

But what was the source of that vision of Reverend King's? Where would he have been without "that book," as Bill Maher likes to call it?

Where would America be without the Bible?

And that's about the last question in the world a liberal wants to answer.

37 The South

Racists, rebels, and rednecks

In 1767, Jeremiah Dixon and Charles Mason drew a map dividing the American colonies into the northern region and the southern region. Since that time, the Mason-Dixon Line has pretty much served to mark the place where the North ends and the South begins.

But there's a more accurate way to know for certain where, exactly, you are.

Just get into a car and drive south. At some point, someone is going to call you "sir" or "ma'am," and that's when you know for certain that you're in the South.

Southerners are polite like that. They "sir" and "ma'am" each other all the time.

They've got a million ways to say "thank you" and they use them all daily. My favorite, for the record, is *'preciate ya,* which I heard a young man say to me at a gas station outside Atlanta, Georgia.

Actually, what he said was *'preciate ya, sir.*

Southerners are polite and thoughtful, they say please and thank you, they honor tradition and God, and liberals positively despise them.

Really. It's true. Liberals *hate* the South.

To liberals, speaking with a southern accent is just another way of saying *Hey! Look at me! I'm a racist!*

When liberals hear a southern twang, what they really hear is *Hey! Better brace yourself! I'm about to talk about Jesus!*

When liberals encounter a "Yes, sir" or a "No, ma'am," what their brain actually hears is *Hey! I'm a slow-witted hillbilly without a thought in my head. Or teeth.*

Think *Hee-Haw* meets *Mississippi Burning* meets *Sling Blade* and you get the picture of the South inside the average liberal's head.

To liberals, the American South is a dark, dark place, filled with Klansmen and spooky backwoods inbreds, trailer parks, and violent, fat sheriffs. From the movies and television shows they make, to the thinly veiled condescension in the pages of their newspapers, liberals can't imagine the South as anything but the kind of place you'd best avoid. Because if your car breaks down or you're on a rafting trip with friends, nothing good can come of a trip down South.

Once that creepy kid with the banjo starts playing, all bets are off.

And as far as liberals are concerned, southerners *deserve* their hatred. They've earned their reputation among liberals with years of Jim Crow laws and civil rights strife.

The South was the beating heart of segregation. The South clings to its inglorious Confederate history, festooning its state flags and landmarks with the Stars and Bars despite the cluck-clucking and tsk-tsking of the liberals to the north who simply refuse to believe that there's anyone in the South who doesn't keep the Confederate dream alive.

It's easy for liberals to characterize the South that way because so few of them ever actually *go* there, unless it's to take a sneering, ironic trip to Graceland or, maybe, a quick stop on the way to Hilton Head Island.

If liberals did, somehow, take a wrong turn and end up driving through the real South, they'd get a very different—and, to them, disturbing—picture of the modern American South. In fact, maybe that's what liberals need to do, to really understand the country they hate so much.

Perhaps we need to create a kind of mandatory federal law, requiring a major road trip for liberals—they love mandatory federal laws, right? We could round them up and take them on a trip down South, to see the place as it really is.

Say what you like about Pol Pot, the murderous dictator of Cambodia—and I'm not suggesting that the guy didn't have issues—but his idea about emptying the cities and driving the hipster urban elites out into the country does hold a certain attraction.

It would be an eye-popping surprise for liberals to accept that the modern South has excellent restaurants, major international banks, research centers, and top-rated universities. They'd be amazed to see how up-to-date it all is, despite the images from movies and television that depict the South as a black-and-white movie, in all senses of that phrase.

Heck, they even have dentists down there. And cable TV!

If we could somehow forcibly march the urban, smug liberal through, say, Mississippi, we could stop for lunch at one of the many delicious and convivial places to eat, and show the liberals something they probably never expected to see: black and white folks eating together.

Not just eating at the same restaurant, but eating *together,* at the same table.

You see, that happens a lot in the South. Go into a restaurant in Birmingham or Jackson, and you'll see a racially integrated crowd. It'll be "diverse," to use that word liberals love, but don't really understand. But go into a restaurant in some other, more liberal, part of the country?

Not so diverse.

In Manhattan or Los Angeles, in San Francisco or Boston, you don't see such a mix of people. You don't see people of different races mingling. It would disturb the liberals—probably cause them to hyperventilate from the shock—to realize that the South is a lot more tolerant and diverse than the so-called sophisticated and progressive cities on the coasts.

It's not Memphis or Mobile that's stuck in segregation. It's L.A. and New York.

Impossible, the liberals cry!

But it gets worse for liberals. For the past decade, African Americans from the North have been moving south in huge numbers. It's a total reverse of the Great Migration of the 1920s, when large parts of the southern black population moved north, to places like Chicago, Detroit, and New York.

Now, though, blacks are coming back to the South.

Impossible! the liberals will cry. *Don't those black people know that the South is full of rednecks and racists?*

What African-American families know, to the contrary, is that the South has better jobs and a better economic future, and more important, that it's a better place to raise your kids.

Put it this way: Kids don't learn to say please and thank you and "yes, sir" and "no, ma'am" in liberal parts of the country, or in liberal public schools. They learn that in places like Montgomery and Greenville.

The Mason-Dixon Line still shows up on maps, of course. But these days, for a lot of Americans, it's better to be on the southern side.

How much better? Well, the numbers don't lie.

According to the latest census figures, the South was the fastest-growing region in America over the last decade, up 14 percent. "The center of population has moved south in the most extreme way we've even seen in history," Robert Groves, director of the Census Bureau, told *USA Today* last year.

The nation's African-American population grew 1.7 million over the last decade—and 75 percent of that growth occurred in the South, according to a Brookings Institution study.

Americans have been moving south from the Rust Belt and industrial North for decades. In 1960, Detroit had a population of 1,850,000. Today, it has 720,000. Houston is now larger than Detroit, Atlanta is larger than Boston, and Dallas is larger than San Francisco.

What caused this great migration of capital—the human and the industrial kind? Ask transplanted business owners and they'll tell you they prefer investing in states where union bosses and trial lawyers don't run the show, and where tax burdens are low. They also want a workforce that is affordable and well trained. And one that doesn't see them as the enemy.

In short, policy matters. So, too, does culture.

That's why Americans are moving to Texas at a rate of one thousand per day. That's why factories open in southern states like Alabama. That's why BMW opens facilities in South Carolina. And that's why Atlanta, Georgia, is a hub of international media and commerce.

The American liberal, ensconced in his decaying metropolis, or his blighted neighborhood, looks upon this and he hates the South like an East Berliner hated West Berlin.

Around the world we have seen time and again that havens of entrepreneurialism and individual liberty have always outperformed the statist neighbors. Whether it was West Germany leaping over East Germany, South Korea outstripping North Korea, Hong Kong and Taiwan putting China to shame, or Singapore outshining impoverished

Malaysia, this has been a universal truth of history. The South fulfills the same role today. Its existence, its heritage, and its prosperity expose the liberal project as the impoverishing lie that it is.

That's why liberals hate the South. They hate it because what they believe is an environment of ignorant hillbillies has defeated them in affluence and sophistication. Indeed, they can hardly stand it.

But, there is hope. And it lies in the one southern virtue that we have yet to mention. Because much as the liberal hates the South, in the end, even the liberal must have a place to live and work. And that's where southern hospitality drives a final nail into the liberal dream.

Because as the liberal packs up his stuff and leaves California, Detroit, or New York, he knows with dread that soon he will hear the words that will drive the dagger into his most precious hopes.

"Howdy, neighbor."

36 The West

As much as they hate the South, liberals truly hate the West.

Not the West *Coast,* of course. Liberals don't hate Malibu or San Francisco. That's where they get Barbra Streisand and Chardonnay. But a couple of hundred miles to the east of those places, the liberals start to thin out and the real Americans start to appear. And that's when the liberals start to hate.

The American West is a deeply etched part of the American character. It's all about individualism and self-reliance. In the Old West, people mostly did for themselves. They didn't look to the federal government for help—for a lot of the time, there *wasn't* a federal government—and they resented any encroachment on their land and property.

It's still pretty much that way in the West.

To liberals, the American West is a nightmarish land filled with gun nuts and antigovernment fanatics. It's all cowboys and Christians and wide-open unregulated spaces, three things that liberals wish would just go away forever.

When liberals want to dismiss a U.S. president—as they did with Ronald Reagan and George W. Bush—they call him a "cowboy." When they want a shorthand way of demeaning a set of values or beliefs, they'll say it reminds them of something that might "come out of Wyoming."

The western temperament embodied in the cowboy is an affront to the liberal religion of government regulation and federal control. That's the heart of the problem liberals have with it—the West simply refuses to comply. Despite direct orders from liberals on the coasts, the western states, and the proud Americans who live there, just won't change.

It drives liberals bonkers. When the governor of Arizona takes it upon herself to enforce border security—because the federal government refuses to do so—libs scream like scalded cats. When folks in Texas carry guns, or the people in Montana go hunting for big game, liberals just flip out.

Why won't they just put down those guns and hunt for that great Pinot at the local wine and yoga shop?

Why won't they just search for some really great organic olive oil on their iPads?

Why do these westerners insist on being so stubborn??

Why do westerners insist on being so . . . western?

What liberals hate the most about the West, though, are the wide-open spaces of unregulated, unsupervised activity. Liberals like it when we're all in one place—all chockablock and herded together, like chickens and other livestock.

What the West represents, to the liberal mind, is physical freedom and privacy. There's more space in the West where nobody is than where somebody is. Westerners don't mind that their next-door neighbor is ten miles away.

They like it that way.

They don't mind that it might take fifteen minutes for the local sheriff to arrive to take care of a problem—they'll take care of it themselves, and are armed to the teeth awaiting the opportunity.

Everyone knows how to handle a weapon. The parents shoot, the kids shoot, the women shoot. Heck, they'd train the pets to shoot if the dogs and cats had fingers.

Liberals hate that. Space, room, a place to call your own, and all of that autonomy and personal responsibility—these are things straight out of a horror movie.

Liberals are nosy. They want to know what you're up to. They want to inspect your house, monitor your cholesterol, tell you what kind of lightbulbs you can have in your home, and make sure your kids are learning what *they* want them to learn.

That's why liberals don't mind living on top of one another the way they do. They don't value privacy, or space, or anything that goes along with those things.

The western attitude is pretty much the opposite of that, which is why liberals have a hard time getting elected in the West. Westerners can smell that kind of thing a mile away.

For liberals, though, the problem with the West is that it's so amazingly beautiful. Liberals love to hike in the Rockies and ski on the slopes of Utah, but the only way to get there is to drive through some deeply objectionable areas. On the way to the ski resorts of Aspen and Sun Valley, liberals are forced to pass multiple evangelical churches—some of them of the "mega" variety that make liberals so nervous. (*All of those Christians in one place! That cannot be good.*)

And so dotted throughout the American West are tiny enclaves of liberalism, little areas of liberal comfort items—a New Age bookstore, perhaps, or a vegan restaurant that serves Fair Trade espresso—to keep them from having crippling panic attacks on the way to the slopes.

In national parks like Moab and Zion, liberals try their best to co-exist peacefully with ranchers and other western types, but you can see the discomfort on their faces. Liberals love the scenery of the West, but they'd prefer it without actual westerners.

The really bad news for liberals, though, is that there are more westerners every year. Places like Utah and Idaho are attracting people from all over the country, in much the same way and for many of the same reasons as the southern states. These new folks—often refugees from places that liberals have ruined with government regulation and a meddlesome bureaucracy—aren't moving west *despite* the western way of life. They're moving there *because* of it.

Arizona is a famous destination for Californians fed up with their big-spending, big-taxing state government. Nevada's business-friendly climate and low-tax commitment are attracting businesses from all over the country. Idaho and Utah boast strong, traditional communities, perfect for raising a family.

If you're a young couple just starting out, why *wouldn't* you move west, to a place where people honor the American spirit of responsibility and traditional values?

If you look at population patterns in the country, you can't help but see that Americans of all ages and backgrounds are voting with their feet.

Liberalism has brought nothing but failure and despair to the cities on the coasts.

New York State is buckling under the weight of its unaffordable social welfare programs and its insanely over-the-top public employee union boondoggles.

The liberal elites who still live elsewhere may sneer at the West as they fly over it on their trips back and forth between bankrupt and decaying cities, but if they look closely, they'll start to notice that the people down there, the tiny specks in the distance, are thriving. And happy. And prosperous. And free.

Liberals hate that. The hatred of the West goes way back to Horace Greeley, one of those crazy white guys who lived in the nineteenth century, and believed in the then-popular concept of Manifest Destiny, and the great westward expansion. Manifest Destiny to your average New York liberal begins on West Seventy-second Street, and ends at Columbia University.

Their idea of westward expansion is Central Park West.

Greeley coined the phrase "Go West, young man, go West." There is a good deal of disagreement about the origins of those words. *The Oxford Dictionary of Quotations* gives the full quotation as "Go West, young man, and grow up with the country," from *Hints toward Reforms* (1850) by Horace Greeley.

Some say the phrase originally appeared in the *New York Tribune* in this form: *"Go West, young man, go West. There is health in the country, and room away from our crowds of idlers and imbeciles."*

There weren't many liberals in America in the 1850s, but those words of Greeley's surely ticked them off.

Those words—and the spirit they embody—are to this day despised by liberals all over America.

"Go West, young man, go West." Translation: Take a chance, get up and go expand this great country.

"Go West, young man, go West." Translation: Ditch that walk-up apartment in the city you and the kids are crammed into, and get yourself some land, some fresh air, and a taste of America's wide-open spaces.

Translation: Go out and grab a piece of that American Dream.

35 Boys

A little boy points his finger at another little boy on the playground, shouts "bang!" and you know what happens next.

The police are called. The parents are brought in. Therapists get involved. The little boy is dragged away for observation and counseling. He is told by a scary adult that he is "dangerous" and "a budding sociopath." The parents are scrutinized and given the evil eye by trained educators. People wonder aloud what kind of parents they must be, to have raised such a violent and hate-filled son.

All just for turning his forefinger and thumb into a pistol shape—something boys have been doing since the first pistol was invented in 1424.

Another little boy spontaneously kisses a little girl in his class, and you know what happens next.

The police are called. The parents are brought in. Therapists get involved. The little boy is dragged away for observation and counseling. He is told by a scary adult that his "hetero-normative behavior" is tantamount to "rape," even though he doesn't know what "rape" means, much less "hetero-normative." The parents are scrutinized and given the evil eye by trained educators. People wonder aloud what kind of parents they must be, to have raised such a pervert.

All just for kissing a little girl in his class—something boys have been doing since girls were created.

Liberals don't like boys very much. Boys are loud and aggressive. They like to throw things and chase each other. Boys can be competitive and difficult, and sometimes hard to handle. This is just the way boys are, and have been, since forever.

As anyone who has ever raised boys can tell you, there's not much you can do to change that. Liberals hate hearing that. Liberals believe that you can change *anything*. Liberals look at a bunch of boys playing, acting like boys, and they instantly think, *We can fix that.*

And they've been trying to "fix" it since the early 1970s, when typical boyish behavior began to be seen not as a phase, not as something to be tamed and educated, but as a disorder.

Typical Boy Disorder, they could have called it, and it's what's led to five-year-old boys in kindergarten being given extensive lectures in sex education just because of a little kiss. And more worrisome, it's what's led to the epidemic of young boys on medication.

Boys between ages nine and thirteen are now in one of the most medicated subgroups of the population as a whole. Most of the medication is for a vaguely defined and probably overdiagnosed condition called Attention Deficit Hyperactivity Disorder (ADHD), the symptoms of which—lots of energy, inability to focus, occasionally erratic behavior—describe every single boy who ever walked the earth, with the possible exception of the young Barack Obama. (It's hard to say much about him because we know so little about his childhood.)

Look, I'm not a doctor. And I know quite well how real ADHD can be, having spent years trying to help one of my children cope with this challenging condition. The problem, though, is that the symptoms of the "disease" seem an awful lot like the very traits that we used to celebrate in boys—physicality, energy, rambunctiousness. But they also seem exactly like the traits that *liberals* hate about boys.

Can you imagine how *short* Mark Twain's magnificent novel *Huckleberry Finn* would be were he to write it today? Somewhere around page seven, right after Pap was removed by child protective services, the Widow Douglas would put Huck on some kind of medication, and that would be that.

Look, we've known for years that liberals have wanted to "modify" traditional sex roles. They're not happy with the way things have been since, roughly, the earth was lava. They don't like it that women have a natural mothering and nesting instinct. They don't like it that men have a natural instinct to protect and defend. They hate it when girls play with dolls and want to hear stories about princesses. And they especially hate it when boys pick up a football and tackle each other to the ground.

A few years ago, Oprah took a full hour of her precious TV real estate to feature a guest she called "Thomas the Pregnant Man."

Say what?

And how do you explain that to the kids?

Thomas Beatie, a former woman who was a pregnant "man," was on the show to defend his/her right to have a biological child. Despite removing his/her breasts, growing a beard, and legally having his/her sex changed from female to male, Beatie kept his/her sex organs intact so he/she could have a child.

And get his/her shot at fame on that famous Oprah couch.

Beatie, who was born Tracy, told Oprah he/she felt trapped in the wrong body when he/she was in his/her twenties. He/she quickly went from a Miss Teen Hawaii USA finalist to taking testosterone and growing a beard. "Sexuality is completely different than your gender," he/she said, responding to a question about why he/she did not remain a lesbian woman. "I felt more comfortable being the male gender."

It was modern liberalism on full display. We even learned how Thomas managed to get pregnant.

Indeed, going into one of the commercial breaks, Oprah teased the next segment like this: "We'll be right back with the obvious question, I know some of you are wondering, and I know the story but forgot to ask for the viewers, how did they get pregnant since he's the one with the penis."

I played that soundbite on my radio show the next day, along with many others. This woman, who was once a lesbian, and then a man, had her breasts removed, and a penis added—but kept her womb intact for just such a wonderful, love-soaked moment.

Oprah's audience soon learned how this "Pregnant Man" got knocked up. It turns out the magic moment didn't happen after a romantic dinner and some wine and flowers. No. It turns out "Thomas the Pregnant Man" was inseminated by his wife at home.

Are you getting all warm and fuzzy? Break out the Barry White music. It's about to get even better.

Thomas the Pregnant Man's wife, Nancy, did the deed—hold your breath!—with an instrument she described as a syringe without the needle. They bought it from a veterinarian and it was typically used to feed birds.

That's right. Thomas was inseminated like a turkey. By a turkey baster filled with another man's sperm. Like one would inseminate a horse. And all with the loving—and I hope gentle—guiding hand of his wife.

And all of this was given the stamp of approval by Oprah. No judgment. No criticism. Not even a single "Are you kidding me?" or "Are you all nuts?"

Then came the end of the hour, and Oprah's closing remarks. Here's what she said.

"I can't imagine, you know, fifty years from now, a hundred years from now, however people choose to live in harmony with themselves and their own community, I don't believe people will be judging it as they do now, I think we are evolving into a new way of being, and a new definition of what diversity means for everybody, and redefining normal, and I really applaud you both for having the courage to do this, for having the courage to come out."

And you wonder why Oprah retired her show. She didn't. It retired her.

Oprah's audience left her, and left her because of absurd monologues like this. Ridiculous lectures like the one she gave at the end of her "Thomas the Pregnant Man" show.

I know because plenty of women called and emailed my show to tell me so.

In their nutty bid to reshape deeply ingrained sexual identities, contemporary liberals have been behaving a little bit like those French revolutionaries, long ago, who rewrote the calendar and created a ten-day week (more rational, less lunar) and a three-week month (more equal, less royal). That calendar lasted about three years. But the liberal plot to remake the sexes—to medicate our rambunctious sons, to radicalize our girlish daughters—continues unabated.

On kids' television shows, it's always the boys who are stupid and clumsy. Even on "educational" television programs, like *Barney* or *Sesame Street*, it's always—*always*—the boy who needs to learn a lesson, the boy who has to modify his behavior.

Have you looked at a kid's textbook recently?

Even the math word problems are skewed against boys. If Mary is walking at three miles per hour, and Ted is riding a bike at five miles per hour, it doesn't matter what the question is, because the correct answer will be "Mary." Mary will get to the train station first. Mary will have more apples in her basket. Mary will be right, have more, be first. Poor Ted will always be wrong, have less, and be last.

(Wait. Who am I kidding here? There aren't any math problems about Mary and Ted. They're all about Blanca and Jamal.)

For the past twenty years, the boys who somehow made it through elementary school without being medicated into a docile state have been fed a steady diet of negative messages, all of which can be summed up as: "You there! Boy! Stop acting like a boy!"

Boys are told by liberals that they're all violent potential date-rapists. They're told that their impulses to run around and catch balls is a sign of "patriarchal hegemony." If they told me all of that when I was a kid, I'd want to be medicated, too.

But more than that, they're told by liberals that, as males, they should feel guilty that they're privileged members of an unequal society. They're told from childhood that girls are held back, girls are discriminated against. Girls, boys are told as early as kindergarten by liberals, are "minorities" who need special treatment.

That isn't even remotely true. Right now, girls outrank boys in every major education survey. Girls read at a higher level, get better grades, and have higher educational aspirations. There are more young women in college, more young women in law school, and more young women in medical school.

By almost every other metric that matters, it's *women* who are privileged and *men* who are the minority. But the drumbeat against boys continues.

We can fix that, liberals have been saying about boys for almost forty years, and fix it they did. Boys now do worse in school, achieve less, and take more pills than ever before.

The culture isn't helping our boys. Look at any major entertainment property on TV, and do you see any men for young boys to look up to? No. They are all frumpy, overweight, underemployed, or just plain lackluster caricatures of men. They are losers.

Think *King of Queens* and you get the picture.

Think the cast of *The Hangover*.

It's a bunch of man-boys they're creating, perpetual adolescents, doing their best to stay, in the words of Bob Dylan, "Forever Young."

No wonder we have a boy problem. Because we have a man problem.

Liberals hate men so much, they've all but erased them from our culture.

And our consciousness.

And that's really tough on America's men. It's especially tough on boys.

34 Girls

Who says you can't have it all?

Liberals aren't crazy about boys, but they're *really* not all that into girls, either.

And that's odd, actually, because for the past forty years, thanks to the relentless political pressure from liberals and radical feminists the federal government and the major academic institutions in America have been focused exclusively on girls.

There have been scholarships and awards set up for girls in school. Every college in America, practically, has a Women's Studies department. Textbooks have been rewritten to include more female voices, more girl-centered questions, more ways for the female brain to show its stuff.

Making girls feel more "empowered" is now a stated goal of the education system. (Not, as you might expect, actually *teaching* them something useful.) Getting their "self-esteem" up was and is as important as making certain they can spell and do math.

So the liberal elite girded their loins—and let's face it, for some of those feminist gals, we're talking some *major* loins, here—and they set about to modify, dismantle, and "fix" what was wrong with American culture.

The English language was rewritten! We don't have *chairmen* or *mailmen* or even *superman* any more. We've got *chairperson* and *letter carrier* and *superhero*.

Girls' sports were emphasized. The federal government even devised a program—it's always doing that, isn't it?—to ensure that girls' sports were given an equal position with boys' sports.

In 1972, the feds enacted what is commonly called Title IX, which essentially tells schools and colleges that they must offer equal opportunities to their male and female students. Which sounds innocuous, really, until the regulators started to "clarify" what that law really meant.

In practice, it means that colleges have to cancel certain popular male sports because of the "imbalance" between male and female sports offerings, despite the relative lack of popularity of sports among female students. It doesn't matter to liberals that women, on the whole, are less sports-centered than men. What matters is that women get the message that they can *be anything! Do anything! Have it all!*

For almost half a century, the academic, political, and cultural elites—all filled to the rafters with liberals—have aimed the awesome power of their position at girls, their education, their self-esteem, and their place in American society. Forty years later, what are the results?

Girls may be doing better in academic pursuits, but psychologically, they're a mess. Eating disorders are skyrocketing. Suicide attempts among young teen girls are higher than ever before. There are more depressed girls every year, and (brace yourself) they're being medicated on an unfathomable scale.

Wasn't feminism supposed to eliminate these problems? There are female Supreme Court judges and female astronauts, female role models in almost every profession. Title IX laws are ruthlessly enforced by the federal government, ensuring girls lots of opportunities to play sports that don't interest them. Girls are told they're smarter, faster, and more competent than boys—just watch pretty much any children's show on television; just read a typical elementary school textbook—and have been ever since Gloria Steinem stopped shaving her legs.

And that was a *long* time ago.

With the boys being drugged into submission and regulated off the field, shouldn't the girls be emerging into the spotlight?

Instead, girls are almost punch-drunk from the barrage of mixed messages thrown at them by the liberals in charge. Half of the time, they're told they can be superwomen—moms, astronauts, presidents of the United States. The other half, they're told that they're victims—potential rape targets and oppressed minorities who are one spiked drink away from being ravaged by the Duke lacrosse team.

It's no wonder the typical American girl wants to lose herself in junk food, Paxil, and the Twilight novels. Choosing between a werewolf and a vampire must seem like a much better set of options than choosing between the oppressive jock in her math class and the medicated zombie in homeroom.

And in any event, the typical American girl isn't going to be attractive to the jock or the zombie, because both of them consume such a ceaseless diet of sexually aggressive, sexually experienced girls on television and in movies that the actual, real-life, there-in-person girl in English class can't hope to compete.

The children in movies and television shows—all of which, almost uniformly, are created and written by liberals—are unrealistic depictions of what aging liberals *wish* kids were like: confident, height-weight appropriate girls and handsome, sensitive boys.

Conservatives have been complaining about this for years.

They've been noting, and protesting, the increased amount of sexual content available to young kids, and the presexualizing of children in the classroom, with elementary school–age children getting explicit sex education as a matter of course. Conservatives have been warning us that the images on television and in movies aren't helping kids become better adults. They're depriving them of childhood.

And when these girls finally get out of school and enter the workforce, here's what they discover:

You *can't* have it all.

You *can't* be a full-time mom with a full-time career. You can't always take maternity leave and come back to the company, picking up where you left off. You can't raise your kids, be the CEO, have a happy marriage, and have a moment to yourself, because you're only one person, and everyone—men, women, dogs, cats—has to make choices.

But the liberal elites have rigged the system so that any choice a girl makes, she's wrong. If she devotes herself to her career, she's a sexless drone who is missing out on the beauty of motherhood. If she devotes herself to motherhood, she's a simpleton, oppressed by the patriarchy.

The liberals are still telling girls they can have it all, which is why girls are so confused and depressed.

And it's not just school-age girls, either. Take a walk through the liberal parts of any town and look closely at the young mothers pushing strollers. Do they look happy? Or fulfilled?

They're *miserable*. "I should be back at the office!" they're all thinking to themselves.

"I'm wasting my law degree with sippy cups and dirty diapers!"

Take a march through a large law firm and look closely at the young mothers behind the desks. Do they look happy? Or fulfilled?

They're *miserable*. "I'm a terrible mother," they're thinking to themselves. "I should be home. With my kids."

And while you're at it, walk through any college campus today and ask yourself the same question. You'll see beautiful, young, well-put-together women juggling classes, a daily workout that would make a triathlete envious, and two part-time jobs, and—on top of it all—she pitches in some local volunteer work at the hospital.

And you'd think this girl would be deluged with offers for dates. Swamped with love letters, flowers, or even some poetry.

But she isn't.

Look around some more, and you'll see why.

It's the boys. They're so busy playing video games, fantasy football, and beer pong, that one wonders how they manage to squeeze into their schedules the ten hours of sleep they need a day.

They wander around college campuses looking like the cast of *The Hangover*, dazed and confused, and as if they haven't seen a shower or an ironing board since their last trip home to do a laundry dump at the parents' home.

The same parents' home they'll be moving into after graduation.

The fact is that the boy problem in America is quickly becoming a girl problem. Ask those beautiful college girls if they've been on a date in the last week, or the last month, or even the last year, and you'll be greeted with a puzzled look.

"A *what?*"

When you explain to them that back in a time before we all spoke to one another via eighteen-word typed responses on a cell phone, boys actually asked girls out on dates. They'd have to work up the courage to approach the girl, then formulate a complete and coherent sentence (no small task for boys, or men), and if the offer was accepted, plan the date. And then actually go on that date.

On campuses today, guys don't ask girls on dates. They ask them to hang out.

And they hang out with the hope of "hooking up."

It all sounds so romantic, doesn't it? So passionate.

What's amazing about all of this is that liberals will admit to hating some things—they'll come clean about despising the cheeseburger, the Constitution, and Walmart.

But they have a hard time seeing exactly how they "hate" girls. Because from the liberal point of view, they're trying to *help* girls. They're trying to *fix* them.

Liberals see men and women behaving a certain way—certain *different* ways—because of innate or ingrained sex traits, and they immediately try to re-engineer things.

Boys playing with blocks and girls playing with princesses? We can *fix* that, the liberals say.

Girls feeling the stirrings of motherhood and childbearing? We can *fix* that, the liberals say.

So it's not quite fair to say that liberals hate girls. They don't hate them. They want to *fix* them.

And that's a lot worse.

Because they're not broken.

33 Boy Scouts and Girl Scouts

Scouting in a postgender world

Oh, how liberals hate the Scouts. They hate both the Boy Scouts (Boy Scouts of America or BSA) and the Girl Scouts (GSA). They hate the Boy Scouts because they won't accept girls—or gays—and they hate the Girls Scouts because these little girls had the temerity to join the Girl Scouts instead of suing their way into the Boy Scouts.

You have to love the liberal mind, don't you?

What this boils down to is that liberals hate any institution that deigns to be what that institution was founded to be instead of what good liberals think it should be. This is really what's so dangerous about liberals' hatred of institutions like the Scouts—that they simply will not accept certain groups staying as certain groups.

Of course, they don't like the Constitution as constructed by the Founders and they can't really stand God for being, among other things, immutable, either. Anyone or anything that won't morph with the current liberal worldview must be hated.

Moreover, when in power, liberals have no hesitation whatsoever about forcing groups to change via the courts or legislation or bureaucratic fiat.

And the best part of all is that they'll couch all of their efforts in terms of *fighting hate.*

The Boy Scouts, from their founding, do not fit a proper liberal worldview. Far from it. In fact, the Scout Oath and Scout Law call for Scouts to be "morally straight and clean in thought, word, and deed."

Now anyone who listens to my radio show knows my views on this subject, and I can report that I get my share of hate mail from both sides of this issue.

The fact that some of my brothers and sisters in my Christian faith obsess about homosexuality to the exclusion of things like adultery and pornography gets me into some pretty heated discussions.

But what stokes me even more is the intolerance of a very extreme group of litigious activists—who themselves call for tolerance—who insist on imposing their values on the rest of us, and using litigation as their weapon of choice.

The ACLU has spent considerable resources trying to take down the Boy Scouts, forcing the Boy Scouts to spend precious resources of their own to simply defend their choices as a private group.

No one denies, by the way, that the 4.5-million-member-strong Boy Scouts is a private organization, but the ACLU, which purports to actually care about the First Amendment, somehow thinks that the "free association" clause doesn't apply to really big and influential groups like BSA.

Memo to private organizations: If you don't want the ACLU hounding you, don't get too big and successful.

Here is just one example of what will happen if you do.

Back in the early 1990s, Boy Scout leader James Dale was expelled from the organization in New Jersey after they found out he was openly gay. And by openly gay, I mean he was copresident of Rutgers' Lesbian Gay Student Alliance.

On behalf of Dale, the ACLU sued, presumably to protect his ability to have equal rights as a gay person. But what the ACLU really wanted was to force Boy Scouts of America to become something it is not.

In a random and rare act of common sense, the Supreme Court found that "allowing homosexuals as adult leaders would interfere with [the Scouts' express] message."

Sadly though, while they dodged this bullet, the pressure has affected the Scouts. The BSA caved and removed "morally straight" from its website language in 2010.

Forcing the Boy Scouts to change their charter is not the only thing that liberals have tried to do to the Scouts. They have tried to force them to accept girls.

Girls, you say?

Yeah, too bad there's not a Scouting organization for girls. Oh wait . . .

According to the BSA, "The Cub Scout and Boy Scout programs were designed to meet the emotional, psychological, physical, and other needs of boys between the ages of 8 and 14." To the liberal, this naturally means boys between the ages of eight and fourteen have the emotional, psychological and physical need to be sued so they will accept girls into their club. They have been sued many times over this issue.

In 1997, Gloria Allred (who else?) was involved in a lawsuit to force the BSA to accept thirteen-year-old Katrina Yeaw as a scout. Never one for melodrama or hysterics, of course, Allred was on a crusade to end "gender apartheid."

Yes, she actually said that.

"Gender apartheid." That pretty much stretches the words to the outer edges of meaninglessness.

Yeaw was a little more circumspect, stating that she was "hoping to do hiking and camping." Somewhere between gender apartheid and the hiking and camping, the fact that there were thirteen nearby GIRL SCOUT organizations got lost on these crusading liberals.

Meanwhile, Katrina's twin brother, Daniel, was so embarrassed by the whole situation that he quit the Boy Scouts.

Actually, everyone knew there were plenty of GSA councils nearby, but that's missing the liberal point. Why look for a sensible solution when there's an expensive lawsuit to be had?

This is not about opportunity or discrimination at all. It's about liberals using the courts and public pressure to change organizations they don't like. And mold the world into their image.

Who needs God when you have the ACLU?

They have brought similar actions against institutions like Augusta National Golf Club and The Citadel as well. Those damn southerners!

In 2003, Martha Burk, the president of something called the National Council of Women's Organizations—which sounds decidedly noninclusive to me—led a protest during Masters week against the Augusta National Golf Club because it accepts only male members. In the fine southern tradition, women are welcome—as their husbands' wives.

Augusta held firm, and President Hootie Johnson muttered something about perhaps considering Sandra Day O'Connor for membership one day, but did not give in.

As Burk muttered back in 2008, at least Augusta is now seen "in civilized society as the last bastion of sexism in the twenty-first century." God bless 'em. Someone has to be that last bastion. The Masters is famous for its quirks, and if it ever gets rid of its quirks, it won't be the Masters anymore. And that's important to remember. Perhaps Martha and company can try to have the pimento cheese sandwiches outlawed as an encore.

In 1995, the first woman was finally admitted to The Citadel after a long two-and-a-half-year court battle. She lasted a week. This is the problem with too many liberals. They can last forever in a courtroom—but make them do something physical?

A year later, two of the four female cadets admitted dropped out after one semester complaining about "hazing incidents that threatened their physical safety." Whoa! Hazing that might cause pain? At a military academy? *Who knew?*

Of course, predictably, The Citadel has gradually morphed into something totally different from what it used to be. Just one example: In 2008, it relaxed the hair regulations on women cadets, discarding one of the time-honored traditions of military academies across the country.

This illustrates the sheer hypocrisy of liberal efforts to force these organizations to accept members they were not set up to accept. The organizations are fundamentally changed by definition.

The Citadel that a select handful of feminist activists so desperately wanted women to become a part of was not that same Citadel the very moment those women set foot on campus as a cadet.

The entire esprit de corps changes once you add another gender to the mix.

It's not The Citadel's admissions policy that kept The Citadel experience—the true experience—from women. It's Mother Nature. It's the reality of the all-male educational experience versus the reality of the co-ed experience. The same is true for the Boy Scouts. And if a guy ever sued to get into the Girl Scouts, the GSA would be totally different, too.

The same, by the way, could be said for some of the all-girl colleges that chose to go co-ed a few decades back. Something was lost in the mix, but then again, it was at least their *choice*. I don't recall any one of them being sued into taking boys.

But liberals hate choice, unless it happens to be the "choice" to abort babies.

They hate these institutions and their traditions—and the people who choose to join them.

If liberals really wanted diversity, they would allow for many more private organizations to flourish, instead of compelling diversity of membership in and amongst every environment.

Without liberals, there would be happy Boy Scouts, happy Girl Scouts. Who knows, maybe even a happy Gay Scouts would evolve. And The Citadel could continue to be The Citadel and Augusta National could be Augusta National.

In other words, America could continue to be America.

Berkeley could be Berkeley and Birmingham could be Birmingham, and let Americans choose which they'd prefer.

Frankly, I have no dog in this hunt. I have no chance of ever being admitted to Augusta National myself. I wouldn't survive one day in The Citadel, let alone one week.

I'm more comfortable on a lounge chair on a cruise ship than humping up a mountain trail, camping gear in tow. For me, "roughing it" is not enjoying a heated toilet seat (don't knock it till you've tried it).

I am fine with the gay community forming their own Scouting operation and would never want to interfere with their stated principles.

Then again, I'm a conservative. I believe in freedom and liberty for all.

And if that means remaining square and old-fashioned and being called a bastion of sexism, so be it.

It's a free country—or it used to be.

Now pass me some of those Girl Scout Thin Mints, please.

32 Honesty

It's hardly ever heard

If you've got an hour or two to kill, ask a liberal this simple question:

"Are you a liberal?"

Make sure there's a comfortable place to sit or lie down nearby, because you'll be listening to him or her for a long, *long* time.

"I don't like to think of myself as a liberal. I'm a humanist. I'm a progressive. I'm just a rational person with rational views who thinks we need to build a sustainable and progressively equitable future for all peoples and races. I'm not really a liberal. I'm just a person who believes in science and thinks the world is going to end because right-wing racist gun nuts don't want to recycle, or let gays get married. That doesn't make me a liberal. Why are you so obsessed with labels? That's the problem with you conservatives! You're obsessed with labels! That's why you're so racist and homophobic and antiprogress and selfish and hate-filled and racist and I know I said racist twice but that's because you're really *really* racist and . . ."

If you've got teenagers at home, you probably already know how to tune this kind of thing out and retreat into your own thoughts. You can organize your day, make some mental notes about household chores, or just sit quietly, like a Zen Buddhist monk does, and enjoy the peaceful rhythm of your own deep breaths.

If you don't have kids at home, it's good practice for long airplane rides, when you're sitting next to someone who's a little too chatty.

Liberals, for some reason, think "Are you a liberal?" is a trick question. When asked a simple question about their specific views, they fly off the handle. "Why is 'liberal' suddenly a dirty word?" they want to know. "Why *shouldn't* I be a liberal?" they demand.

Well, here's why: because the last fifty years of liberal thought, both in the academy and in the halls of power, have wrecked the economy, destroyed the family unit, miseducated our children, and bankrupted our future.

No wonder liberals don't want to admit to being liberals. Naturally, they're searching for another label, another name, anything to erase the image of "liberal" from their policies and beliefs.

Consumer product companies, when they've got a product in trouble, call this "rebranding," but that's just a fancy way of saying: *same poop, different bag.*

The problem for liberals is, in order to enact and impose their crackpot, socialist, ultimately freedom-killing policies on the American public, they've got to rely on a lot of stealth.

So raising taxes on the wealthy—which is a group liberals define as "anyone we wish"—is called "progressive income tax adjustment." When it's really just a form of redistributing wealth from the person who earned it to another person, usually someone whose vote the liberals are trying to buy.

"Universal health-care access" is just a fancy, rebranded way of saying "socialized medicine," which is itself, as we've seen, just another way of saying "free abortions and birth control for everyone!"

"Fairness in lending," is the way the liberals marketed the two biggest Ponzi schemes in history, Fannie Mae and Freddie Mac, to a credulous public. And we all know what happened when the scheme crashed, right? Liberals called it a "government guarantee of solvency," which is what someone says when he's got your wallet in his hands.

Liberals, in other words, have a hard time telling the truth about what, exactly, they're up to. And exactly who they are.

There was a great episode of the hit HBO series *The Sopranos* where Meadow and her Mafioso dad go on a daddy-daughter road trip to visit some fancy colleges in New England. They are enjoying a scenic drive when Meadow asks a very direct question to her father:

"Are you in the Mafia?" she asks.

"Am I in the what?" he replied. But he heard her. He was just caught off guard.

"Whatever you want to call it. Organized crime?" she fired back.

"That's total crap. Who told you that?" Tony was in full denial mode.

Meadow wasn't buying it. She pressed on.

"Dad, I've lived in the house all my life. I've seen police come with warrants, I've seen you going out at three in the morning," she said.

"So you never seen Doc Cusamano go out at three in the morning on a call?" Tony says defensively about his next-door doctor neighbor.

"Did the Cusamano kids ever find fifty thousand dollars in Krugerrands and a .45 automatic while they were hunting for Easter eggs?" she asked.

"I'm in the waste management business. Everybody immediately assumes you're mobbed up. It's a stereotype. It's offensive, and you're the last person I'd want to perpetuate it," Tony rambles, full of righteous indignation.

There's a long pause.

And then Tony sighs as Meadow looks at him with the eyes of a wise child who knows her dad is lying to her. But Tony tries one more lie.

"There is no Mafia."

A few seconds pass, and unlike that liberal who never actually just fesses up, Tony actually comes clean. He confesses to his daughter that he makes some of his money from "illegal gambling and whatnot."

But he quickly added that other parts of his income come from legitimate businesses.

Meadow just as quickly cuts him off. "Dad, don't start mealy-mouthing."

Great advice from a loving daughter.

And I have the same advice for my liberal friends. Please stop mealy-mouthing.

Your big ideas stem from a basic notion that we are all children in need of adult supervision. And yet you refuse to act like an adult and admit what you are. And who you are.

And that's one real difference between liberals and conservatives.

Take this test. Ask a liberal friend the direct question, and a few hours after your friend winds up his evasive efforts to rebrand liberalism, find a conservative friend and ask him the same thing.

"Hey, are you a conservative?"

In all likelihood he'll think for a little more than a second, shrug, and then say:

"Pretty much."

And then go about his business. No long diatribe. No weasel words. Just a simple, honest acknowledgment of his views, a shrug, and on to the next thing.

No big deal. And no mealy-mouthing.

That's the key: honesty. Straightforward, plain talk—that's what most Americans prefer in their day-to-day exchanges with each other. If you've got core beliefs that make sense, they probably don't need to be rebranded or rephrased.

For instance:

Life begins at conception is about the simplest, clearest, most honest way to describe the views of about 150 million Americans. *Life begins at conception* is the first principle in the debate over abortion. It's not about anything else except the dignity of every human life, and society's responsibility to ensure that dignity. It's honest.

Life begins somewhere between the first and third trimester, at some point when the fetus becomes "viable" outside the mother's womb, when the spinal cord is fully or partially enclosed by secondary tissue and the brain pan is almost fully formed is just another way of saying: We know we're wrong and we're vamping as fast as we can. We're trying to tire you out with words and phrases and double-talk until you surrender.

It's dishonest.

Indeed, ask any pregnant liberal woman who intends to keep her baby, and ask her how her baby is doing, and she won't hesitate to list all the weird New Age names she's thinking of naming the child, along with all of the fashion accessories she's planning on adding to the young darling's wardrobe once she turns three months old.

You'll never hear her call that precious life growing inside her womb a fetus.

That is, unless she changes her mind and decides to kill it.

It's dishonest.

Part of the reason liberals are not honest is simple; they are rarely held accountable for their ideas. Or their opinions. They don't tend to believe in free markets, or the real marketplace of ideas. Indeed, it's why so many college campuses are littered with liberals, and there are so few conservatives on those campuses: They don't want to be challenged by adults. And they're afraid that if students are given a real choice on campus, it might ruin the monopoly they've created.

In the real world, businesses win and lose every day because some do a better job than others at satisfying customer demands. Sports teams win and lose every day, as do stockbrokers, bankers, farmers, fishermen—and I could go on and on.

If they don't show up for work, they don't get paid. If they do a bad job, they get fired.

The kind of accountability, the kind of competition, the kind of work ethos and personal responsibility it takes to survive and thrive in the real world—that is something liberals don't much care for. Indeed, they want to do everything in their power to protect us from the exigencies of that world. Protect us from the marketplace. Protect us from life itself. And from ourselves, and our own choices.

Liberals will talk your ear off, if they can, to avoid telling the truth about all kinds of things they believe and don't believe in. And they'll call themselves anything—secular humanists, progressives, rationalists, whatever—to avoid being honest about their core beliefs.

They'll toss insults and invective and *ad hominem* attacks at anyone with the temerity to ask the simple question, "Hey, are you a liberal?" because they know that the honest answer—"You bet I am!"—will hurt their drive to impose the failed and still failing principles of liberalism on the American people.

No wonder liberals hate honesty. The truth hurts.

31 Success

Everyone gets a trophy!

Liberals hate success for a number of reasons, including the fact that they hate competition and everything that comes with it. To a liberal, there is no such thing as true competition, and there is no such thing as learning a valuable life lesson from losing. In fact, losers—those who may say that two plus two equals five or those who might score fewer points than the other team—must not be told that they are "wrong" or that they "lost" because to do so would hurt their precious little self esteem. It's the "everyone gets a trophy" syndrome that is ruining our once-great American Little Leagues.

I mean, if everyone is special, then what you are really saying is, NO ONE IS SPECIAL.

Think about that for just a second. In their obsession with stamping out failure, liberals have stamped out failure's close companion, success.

Without failure, success is meaningless. It's a vapor. It cannot happen.

This mind-set is ruining much more than Little Leagues. This insidious thinking has infected our entire society up to the very top levels of industry and even our national defense. That's why liberals are not merely funny—and they certainly are. When in power, they can be dangerous!

For example: We can't have a "War on Terror" anymore because that would hurt the feelings of, well, the terrorists. We can't call a terrorist a terrorist (and we certainly can't call a spade a spade anymore in the postracial era of Obama). Okay, so what does all of this political correctness have to do with liberals hating success? Well, everything.

The liberals who are in charge of so much at the moment cannot accept the idea of success, much less "victory," in anything like the War on Terror, because to do so would be to accept the very premise of winners, losers, right, wrong, failure and success. They can't abide it. Their world view does not permit it.

Take the Fort Hood massacre. Instantly, the entire nation knew exactly what had happened. Everyone, that is, but Evan Thomas at *Newsweek*. Everyone knew that an Islamic terrorist went off and killed thirteen American soldiers, who, by the way, were unarmed thanks to the goofy rules governing Fort Hood.

In the aftermath, President Obama and General Casey were visiting Fort Hood with one mission. To catch the killer? Um, no. Keep the troops motivated? Puh-leeze. Their one mission was to prove to the world that they were open-minded enough to pretend not to understand what had just happened. They were showing "courageous restraint"—which we think is something Obama might have learned during his study of a very thin history book called *Great French War Heroes*.

It was a sickening display, watching them come up with all kinds of tortured explanations of what had happened. They came up with various theories, but they left out the obvious: that an angry Islamic jihadist had just made a really big down payment on his seventy-two virgins.

Everybody knew it. Everybody, that is, but Obama and Casey, who—like the clueless parents at one of those "don't keep score" Little League games—pretended not to know the score. They waltzed around almost congratulating themselves on their sick nonjudgmentalism by pretending to not know the score. You've seen these folks at the no-score league games in your neighborhood.

And if you have any understanding of human nature, you know that every kid in both dugouts knows exactly what the score is. The kids in the dugouts are sitting there wondering just how stupid all these adults are pretending not to keep score. And that's how the Fort Hood soldiers were. They were the kids in the dugout. And they knew the score.

And the score was: Terrorists thirteen, Fort Hood zero.

See, liberals can never admit the score. To admit the score is to admit competition, which is to admit the concept of failure on the part of someone. Which of course is to admit to the concept of success on the part of someone else.

It has crept into every walk of life, this desire to stamp out scores. And picking winners and losers.

Back in 2010, I spent a few days on my radio show talking about an article I'd read in the *New York Times* about high school graduations, and the issue of valedictorians.

Valedictorians an issue? you might be wondering. Did some valedictorians go on a crime spree? Did they go on some kind of drug or alcohol binge?

No. It turns out a whole bunch of schools in America think that having one valedictorian is mean-spirited, and not very inclusive, and so they are instead having multiple valedictorians.

Before I proceed with this story, let's turn to the folks at Merriam-Webster to get a definition of the term "valedictorian": "The student usually having the highest rank in a graduating class who delivers the valedictory address at the commencement exercises."

When I went to school, there was one valedictorian, and that person had the highest grades. Then there was the salutatorian, and that student had the second-highest grades. They both made speeches on graduation day. Really bad speeches.

Then there was me. It was a miracle I got any grades at all. No threat of me giving any speeches.

Flash-forward to 2010 and Jericho High School in Long Island, New York, and that *New York Times* story. It turns out that one valedictorian would simply not do in this particular high school, and they went with—wait for it—*seven* instead.

Seven valedictorians!

And what was the explanation? Was the move pushed by parents? Students? No, it turns out one guy, Joe Prisinzano, the principal at Jericho High, didn't like having just one valedictorian.

"When did we start saying that we should limit the honors so only one person gets the glory?" he asked the *New York Times* reporter.

Well, Mr. Prisinzano, Americans have been saying it for a hundred-plus years. The *New York Times* story got even more interesting. It turns out public school administrators all across the country are beginning to side with Joe.

Here is how the *Times* explained the reasoning behind the disturbing new trend: "Principals say that recognizing multiple valedictorians reduces pressure and competition among students, and is a more equitable way to honor achievement, particularly when No. 1 and No. 5

may be separated by only the smallest fraction of a grade from sopho-more science."

Liberals do things like "dispense" with "beloved traditions" like the valedictorian. And decide for all of us how to create more "equitable" ways to "honor achievement."

I wondered as I read that article, why stop at an A? What about the students who came really, really close to an A? Won't that cause them a whole lot of emotional damage, to come so close to an A, only to find out they didn't make the valedictorian cut?

And why not the kids who got close to getting a B? How about the B-minus students? Don't they deserve to be valedictorians, too?

It turns out that Stratford High School in the suburbs of Houston pretty much agrees with this nonsense. They honored thirty valedic-torians, or about 6.5 percent of their entire class in 2010. They all got gold honor cords.

Thirty valedictorians!

And I thought I was mad at Joe Prisinzano? He looks positively stingy with his mere seven valedictorians. Positively Victorian.

It's not just public schools. This disease is spreading into our publi-cally traded companies, too. Take General Motors, please. Actually, Americans did take GM. We bailed out the car company, and still own a huge chunk.

And take the Chevy Volt, pretty, pretty, pretty please. The Volt is a monument to the idea that we can't have success or failure or keep score on anything. This vehicle really is the result of many things that liberals hate. The V-8 (see #14) and oil have been incredible successes, which led to more successes with the Suburban and the Expedition and F-series pickup trucks.

These, of course, led to successes in family vacations and boating and freedom and contractors' fleet management in all kinds of industries.

Well heck, we can't have all that success going on out there. With all that success, who needs the government?

And few things have proven to be a more expensive failure than the Chevy Volt. Despite an endless TV advertising campaign, eight-thousand-dollar government subsidies, and special driving and parking privileges across America, and the almost endless green campaign that began at about the same time Al Gore started doing his Mr. Heat-meiser impersonation in 2006, the Chevy Volt sold just eight thousand units last year.

The Volt has been an incredibly effective weapon for liberals in their battle against success. For one thing, liberals have hated the success of the oil industry for so long that they've almost stopped it dead in its tracks. This has led to artificially high gas prices, which has created a potential phony demand for cars like the Volt.

Yet, even with the phony high gas prices leading to a phony demand for the phony little Volts, no one wants the damned car. No one wants these stupid little Tonka toys—no offense to Tonka intended—and many of those sales are to GE and Jeffrey Immelt so he can have his sycophantic little GE bureaucrats drive around with what amounts to an electric pink ribbon that shouts "Look at me, I care."

Now of course, Immelt and GE are so against success that their tax returns indicate NO SUCCESS so they can continue not to pay any corporate tax. They also want to contribute to this phony notion of the success of green cars for all kinds of demented liberal reasons, of course. In fact, if there's one real problem that comes from a hatred of success, it's a never-ending crusade to change the very definition of it.

Which is what liberals have done with the Volt. The liberals in power awarded the very failed United Auto Workers of GM with owner-ship of the very company they destroyed. Those same liberals then demanded that GM start to produce the very kinds of cars that also led to the failure, chief among them the greenest of them all: the Volt. In the meantime, these same liberals destroyed the value of GM's bonds—producing artificial failure in what is normally a successful way for a company to capitalize.

Meanwhile, the failure of GM to produce a car that folks want at a price they are willing to pay has been hidden by some phony sales success due to tax subsidies of the Volt. Yes, you and I pay something along the lines of eight grand for every Volt sold.

And on and on it goes with the Volt and with GM—a product and a company that you and I are paying for as a result of liberals' hatred of true success. Meanwhile, the successes of the Suburban and the Expedition and of pleasure power boats and of the oil industry continue to be crushed under the weight of liberals in power.

It's way beyond keeping score at the Little League game.

Liberals hate success and its first cousin, competition, and if they have their way, we'll all be playing a scoreless game of life, Scandinavian style, with cradle-to-the-grave entitlements that assure little variation in income.

With little, if any, variation between success and failure.

30 The Second Amendment

Ammo Nation

Liberals aren't crazy about most of what's in the U.S. Constitution, but it's safe to say that what they hate the most about it is the Second Amendment.

So, let's start with the complicated text of the Second Amendment to the Constitution. Better settle in. This could take a long time.

"A well regulated Militia, being necessary to the security of a free State, the right of the people to keep and bear Arms, shall not be infringed."

Wait a minute. That's it? Twenty-seven words? *That's* what libs are so exercised about?

Twenty-seven English words can't be all that hard to understand.

They manage to confuse the heck out of liberals, though. Within those words, liberals see all kinds of possibilities and interpretations. They see ways to regulate and ban handguns and rifles, to force states to register all gun owners, to prohibit sales and transfers—in other words, in that twenty-seven-word sentence, the key words of which are "security," "free state," "right of the people," and "shall not be infringed," liberals see ways to undermine security, constrain the state, and infringe the rights of the people.

It's a pretty impressive feat, actually. You have to hand it to them. When they set their minds to it, liberals can invert anything.

Let's make our way through the big ones, shall we?

A militia? This is about militias? We have that. We call it the National Guard.

Yes, and the National Guard is a great thing. It's nice to see that liberals are so supportive of the Guard, since they often disparaged it when talking about President George W. Bush's service in a branch of the Guard during his Vietnam-era service.

But what the Founders were talking about was the necessity of raising a militia at any time, which would require that citizens supply their own weapons. The Founders knew that weapons distributed among the citizens were safer and more effective than weapons kept in a government-controlled armory.

The security of a free state? Like, what? Missouri? In case Missouri wants to invade Kansas?

The Framers liked the idea of a bunch of states, each with its own idiosyncratic touches, all linked by a republican government. (See #5: The States.)

They imagined a union of states in which the citizens of the individual states had a fair amount of say about what goes on inside their borders. It's possible that this opens up the opportunity for certain states to vote to ban or regulate certain weapons, as some have done, but in general, the Framers seemed to encourage this kind of varied and often zany difference among the states.

Liberals hate that, of course, because it means that certain states—Utah and Texas, for instance—might be *conservative* and have *right-wing* laws. It also means that crackpot lefty states, like Massachusetts and Vermont, can mandate free M&Ms for everyone, but that's not enough for liberals. The only kind of freedom they really like is the freedom to make you do what they tell you to do.

The right of the people to keep and bear arms shall not be infringed? So I can have a howitzer in my front yard? You right-wing gun nuts are crazy!

Yes, well, "shall not be infringed" isn't really a vague phrase, is it? It means, um, just to go over it one more time, "shall *not* be *infringed*," as in, you can't infringe it. As in, it is what it is.

The howitzer-in-the-yard argument is completely off-topic anyway, because no one is talking about regulating those. People don't have those. What they have are rifles and handguns they keep for protection or sport, and *those* are what the liberals want to take away.

And here's why they want to take them away: to protect us. That's right. To *protect* us. Nice of them, isn't it? Here you were thinking that you could protect yourself—that the whole *point* of the Second Amendment is that you are empowered to do just that—but the liberals think you're going about it the wrong way.

According to the last count, about 30,000 people die annually in gun-related incidents. About 45,000 die in cars. About 37,000 die from poisoning. And 20,000 die from unintentional falls.

If you ask me, I'm a lot more worried about the poisoning category than I am about what might happen if my unloaded and securely-locked weapon somehow unlocked itself, loaded itself, and went joy-riding in my driverless car.

The Framers of the Constitution didn't say that guns weren't dangerous—they are, especially to invaders and despots and thieves—but that they were "necessary."

And that's what liberals hate the most about the Second Amendment: It's necessary. It reinforces the constitutional notion of a free and sovereign people, citizens of a country that is a collection of republican states. Or, to put it much, much better:

"A well regulated Militia, being necessary to the security of a free State, the right of the people to keep and bear Arms, shall not be infringed."

Pretty much every single word in the previous sentence is a word that gives liberals the heebie-jeebies. And that's why they hate it.

On the other hand, twenty thousand people die each year from *unintentional falls*? Maybe the Framers should have banned ladders.

The simple fact is that freedom is dangerous.

The Fourth, Fifth, and Sixth amendments are far more dangerous to our society than the Second Amendment. We give criminal defendants all kinds of rights, and all kinds of protections—from prohibiting searches without a warrant, to demanding fair and speedy jury trials.

How much faster and safer and easier would it be to just give the police all kinds of power to keep our streets safe? And avert the whole trial thing?

Oh, that's right. That would be even more dangerous.

Because in a police state, the criminals would soon be the police.

Let's take a look at the Fourth Amendment, one of the liberals' favorite amendments:

The right of the people to be secure in their persons, houses, papers, and effects, against unreasonable searches and seizures, shall not be violated, and no Warrants shall issue, but upon probable cause, supported by Oath or affirmation, and particularly describing the place to be searched, and the persons or things to be seized.

Okay. I admit it. It's much, much longer than the Second Amendment—fifty-four words in all.

But liberals like it so much, this much wordier amendment, that they have spent a lifetime breathing even more life into it than the Founders could have imagined.

Take the "exclusionary rule." Please. Take it.

In the 1960s, a man named Earl Warren—the liberal chief justice who put the Warren into the Warren Court—decided that he would change America for the better by putting on his robe, discarding the customary role of judge as upholder of the Constitution (how boring), and intead playing the part of Super Legislator.

Let's call the the Warren Court "Nine Wise Men in Robes."

And one of the areas these Nine Wise Men in Robes cared about deeply was criminal rights.

Now it is true that to far too many people in law enforcement, search warrants and other substantive criminal rights were treated as suggestions, not as the law of the land—and that needed to be changed.

But change wasn't good enough for the Nine Wise Men in Robes.

In a case called *Mapp* v. *Ohio,* the Warren Court came up and took a nifty piece of jurisprudence (that's a fancy legal word that means "making up the law") called the exclusionary rule, and decided to make that rule apply to every cop in every state in America.

What the Court essentially did was permanently exclude from all criminal trials any evidence gathered without a lawful warrant anywhere in America. Even if that evidence was perfectly good evidence that might prove the guilt of the criminal.

For instance, let's say a murder weapon is found with the bloody fingerprints of the defendant. "Out," was the Supreme Court's ruling. That evidence is out. And why? Because we say so, that's why!

Not all legal scholars and judges thought this was a particularly good idea, let alone something the Constitution called for.

"Should the criminal go free because the constable has blundered?" bellowed one of America's great jurists, Justice Benjamin Cardozo. He pondered that question long before the *Mapp* v. *Ohio* case became the law of the land. Because he thought the punishment to society, perfectly good evidence being tossed out of court, was disproportionate to the crime, an officer's violating the Fourth Amendment.

Did he also think there were other ways to deter cops from violating the Fourth amendment *short* of exclusion? Like sanctions against the officers who did wrong?

We'll never know, because that's how much Earl and the Supremes loved the Fourth Amendment. They created the exclusionary rule.

And yet when it comes to the shorter and easier to read Second Amendment, the Warren Court did nothing to shore up the rights of gun owners to protect themselves from those very criminals the Supreme Court seemed to care so much about.

But that's liberals for you. They care about what they care about, and the Constitution be damned.

In his book *More Guns, Less Crime,* author John Lott proved that in places where there are more guns in the hands of lawful citizens, there is less crime. And that having a gun, and brandishing it, actually prevents all kinds of crime in America.

The crimes that did not happen because a gun was pulled.

Anyone who knows anything knows this: Criminals are cowards. They hate a fair fight. Criminals love picking on the vulnerable because they have an advantage. They love picking on old ladies and night clerks who are working alone. You never hear of a criminal entering the home of an NFL player at night while he and his buddies are hanging out.

A gun is the great equalizer.

A single mom *with* a gun is scarier than an NFL linebacker *without* one.

That's not some legal theory.

Take the "Make My Day" Mom. Her story was one most Americans loved. Except liberals, of course.

One night in January 2010, a couple of thugs decided to celebrate the beginning of the new year by breaking into the trailer of a single mom, eighteen-year-old Sarah McKinley. Sarah had recently lost her husband, and the girl was living alone in a trailer with her three-month-old son in Blanchard, Oklahoma.

And that's exactly why the thugs chose her.

Because she was alone with her baby. She was vulnerable.

It turns out Sarah had some company in the house that the thugs didn't plan on—Smith and Wesson. Sarah was packing; she had a shotgun, and a pistol. And she wasn't afraid to use either of them to defend herself, and her baby.

She called 911.

"I've got two guns in my hand. Is it okay to shoot him if he comes in this door?" Sarah asked the dispatcher. The dispatcher told the young mom she should do what she needed to do to protect herself, and her baby.

Sarah did just that.

She killed one of those men. The other ran away, a frightened coward who was later arrested and charged.

Luckily for Sarah, she lived in a gun-friendly, conservative state like Oklahoma. Not an antigun liberal state like Massachusetts. Liberals don't care what the Constitution says. They don't care about facts. And they certainly don't care about the Sarah McKinleys of this world, and their right to bear arms. Their right to protect themselves.

But the rights of that criminal trying to rob Sarah—well, that's another story.

29 The First Amendment

Shut up and agree

The text of the First Amendment to the Constitution—what's usually referred to as the "Freedom of Speech" amendment—is pretty simple and straightforward:

"Congress shall make no law respecting an establishment of religion, or prohibiting the free exercise thereof; or abridging the freedom of speech, or of the press; or the right of the people peaceably to assemble, and to petition the Government for a redress of grievances."

That's what it looks like to most of us.

But to liberals, the First Amendment looks a little different:

"Congress shall make no law respecting an establishment of religion, or prohibiting the free exercise thereof, unless it's about

Christianity; or abridging the freedom of speech, unless it's something a conservative might say, or of the press, as long as it's liberal; or the right of the people peaceably to assemble, or not so peaceably if they're shouting liberal catchphrases, and to petition the Government for a redress of grievances, unless it's to the IRS."

Liberal organizations like the American Civil Liberties Union—the ACLU—are famous for defending obnoxious talkers, controversial printed works, and nasty talk in general.

If it's ugly, and it's liberal, the ACLU will rise to its defense.

That's why conservatives aren't crazy about the ACLU. It always seems to us that they pick and choose their targets based on an overwhelming liberal bias. (We're not *surprised* by this, of course, but it's one of those things that's hard not to notice.)

Look, the First Amendment can be a real pain in the behind to conservatives, too. It's galling to have to listen to people attack religion, the country, the principles a lot of us hold dear—all because of a couple of words the Founders wrote over two hundred years ago.

It's absurd—truly *crazy*—to have to defend public Christmas decorations during Christmastime, or even the use of the word *Christmas,* just because some liberal crackpot lawyer at the ACLU is convinced that the town Christmas tree violates the "Establishment Clause" of the First Amendment, as if the Founders, observant Christians, every single one of them, had that in mind when they wrote the Constitution.

It never occurred to the Founders that there might be a time in the American future when the word "God" or "Christ" would cause a certain segment of the population to get the vapors.

It never occurred to them how low, exactly, some people would sink in their public utterances.

It never occurred to them how sick and twisted the pornography industry would be, and how readily available and in-your-face some of the most objectionable and repellent stuff would be.

Maybe if we could go back in time and tell the Founders all about the Internet and cable television and satellite radio, they'd rethink their words.

But we can't, so we're stuck with the First Amendment as it is, and it sticks in our craw a lot of the time, but we accept it.

Because we're Americans, and we love the Constitution.

But you'd think that it would be *conservatives* who hate the First Amendment—after all, it's used against us a lot more often—and *liberals* who'd be its biggest champions.

That's certainly the lie the liberals tell all the time.

We're the defenders of free speech! they cry. *We stick up for the unpopular views!* Really?

When was the last time a university professor was fired, or suspended, for saying something too liberal?

When was the last time some radio or television personality was fired for being *too* "progressive"?

Never, that's when.

When schools and universities across the country worked to establish "speech codes"—a list of things you cannot say, topics that are forbidden to be raised, thoughts that are ruled unthinkable—how many of them were liberal or left wing in nature?

None, that's how many.

And yet somehow it's liberals who get to parade around as the defenders of free speech. Even though *they're* the ones trying to restrict free expression on every front.

In fact, to take a look at what "free speech" might look like in America if liberals were in charge, one need only visit your local college campus.

You'd think that a college should be the ultimate expression of our First Amendment rights, a place where all points of view are expressed, tolerated—and promoted.

But what does one find upon arrival at one of our institutions of higher learning? All ideas, even the absolute zaniest ones—especially the zaniest ones—are promoted but one: conservatism.

Weekly Standard editor Andrew Ferguson chronicled some of the insanity in his book *Crazy U,* which takes us on a wild ride through the college admissions process, up to and including the "Accepted Students Day" at BSU, the unnamed big state university his son was dying to attend.

And what a day it was. There was the "Resource Fair," but there were no rides or games at this fair. Just endless propaganda booths. He described one row at the fair this way:

> Another [booth] alerted us to signs of incipient depression and mental illness. At another table representatives of the LGBT Resource Center boasted that free condoms and dental dams were available round-the-clock at their office, where confidential meetings would be held for fraternity members who are "bi, gay, or curious," along with coffee hours for "transgender, transsexual, and gender queer individuals."

Ferguson and his son heard from the faculty and some administrators next, who gave them a sneak academic preview of the next four years. They didn't pull any punches.

> The admissions dean introduced a professor of religious studies and the author of a book bearing the subtitle "Freeing the Gospel from Political Captivity." (The captivity, the dean reminded us, had begun under the administration of George W. Bush.) The professor boasted of his history course, which had transformed merely curious students into "social activists." The professor's speech was just a hint of what was to come: Later my son told me that he had three choices for a mandatory writing class: "History of the 1960s," "TV's Mad Men," and "Intro to Queer Theory."

Those were the offerings on a day with parents in tow, on a day called "Accepted Students Day."

Liberals often hear from conservatives that there are not enough folks in academia that think the way we do. That there are not enough voices that represent the ideas, the philosophy, and the mind-set of conservatives.

They always act surprised at this claim. Then they deny it. And then they finally come around to admitting it, but with explanations that only make things worse.

Some attribute it to the conservative mind, that we are somehow less curious and less interested in intellectual inquiry. That's the "conservatives are dumb" argument liberals haul out every five years or so, with some "scientific" study—conducted by liberals, of course—to prove it.

Some attribute it to the natural self-selection that occurs among the students themselves. In one very lengthy study about liberalism and graduate schools, Neil Gross, Jeremy Freese, and Ethan Fosse tried to unearth the reasons for the imbalance, but came up short.

Conservatives don't like academia, they concluded, but not because we're dumb, or because of some self-selection alone, or because of the innate liberalism that dominates academia. Maybe, just maybe, it was because of our personalities.

Can you imagine liberals living with these kind of studies and empty explanations if it turned out that liberalism was not represented on colleges ruled by conservatives?

We know the sad excuses that were trotted out to explain the dearth of African Americans and female professors on campuses across America for far too long. Academia, to its credit, went to great lengths to remedy those problems.

But no conservatives?

No problem!

The fact is, conservatives would be treated like uninvited guests if we pursued a life in academia. Faculty lounges are so dense with liberals that any thinking conservative would have to think twice about what a life in the Ivy Tower would be like.

Because it would be like solitary confinement, with a slightly better meal plan.

And there would be other concerns. How would one advance? Would one have to tone down one's thoughts to get ahead? Would one have to rethink that critical study on global warming, for instance, to get that Assistant Dean of the Liberal Arts position?

I mean, the government is giving the place a load of cash to study green everything. Who'd dare criticize *that* gravy train?

One has to wonder how much government grant money—the lifeblood of academia—would be available for conservatives to study the negative impact of all of that government money on society.

How about a study on the impact of all that government grant money on academic research itself, and on the corrupting nature it might have on outcomes? Might all that increase the risk of the most insidious kind of censorship known to man—self-censorship?

That's why there are so few conservatives in academia.

We are not welcome, and our ideas are not welcome, because we oppose so much of what actually goes on in academia. And its very foundation. Even the way the institutions are funded. And the process by which they choose their leaders.

Thus, a great deal of speech, scholarship, and teaching is silenced in academia. And a legitimate point of view is censored. All so that liberals can control the money and power that go along with running the show. And controlling the minds of all who walk through those academic gates.

Want to know what liberals really think about free speech? A visit to any modern American campus is Exhibit A.

Liberals love free speech, as long as you agree with them. Disagree, and it's the academic gulag for you. Yet the very same faculty leaders will turn over every unturned stone to find a lesbian poetry professor.

But conservatives? Darn. We just can't seem to find any!

If you are a Marxist, you are open to teach not only the works of Marx, but just about anything you'd like, from history (think Howard Zinn) to linguistics (think Noam Chomsky). And if there are courses in which the work of Milton Friedman or Russell Kirk are taught, it is invariably taught by liberals who detest them.

Letting Paul Krugman teach Milton Friedman is like having David Duke teach African-American studies.

Liberals like to say they believe in free speech and diversity.

Diversity regarding everything under the sun—gender, race, creed, color, accent, and sexual preference.

Everything, that is, but ideas.

Think about it.

Then again, if you are a liberal professor, college dean, or president, maybe not.

28 Pools and Patios

Cannonballs and barbecue for all

Ronald Reagan had a plan.

When he took office in 1981, he told his foreign policy team that he had a surefire way to deal with the leader of the Soviet Union.

He wanted to bring him to the United States and take him up in a plane above the San Fernando Valley in Southern California. From up there, he'd point out to the Soviet dictator how many swimming pools there were in all of those backyards. "Look at that," he'd say about all of those blue dots shimmering in the sunlight. "Look at that and tell me that Americans aren't living better under capitalism."

He never managed to do it, mostly because Russian leaders kept dying on him.

When Reagan took office, Leonid Brezhnev was in charge. He died a year or so later and was succeeded by Yuri Andropov, who died two years later and was succeeded by Konstantin Chernenko, and *he* died a year after that. By the time Mikhail Gorbachev took over, in 1985, the Russian empire was tottering on the edge of collapse. Taking Gorbachev on a plane ride above the San Fernando Valley wasn't necessary anymore. *Everyone* knew—*especially* the Soviet leader—that Americans were living better.

Still, the American swimming pool is a symbol of a middle-class standard of living that no country and no economic system can ever match. It would have been hard for a Soviet leader to see all of those swimming pools from the air and not think, *Wow. The Americans really do live better.*

It's not so hard for the liberals, though. Liberals hate swimming pools. Not because they hate to swim, but because a swimming pool in the backyard is a symbol of everything that liberals think is wrong about America. We're materialistic. We're wasteful. We're not European enough. (Europeans don't have backyard swimming pools.)

Ronald Reagan wasn't trying to make a point about swimming pools specifically. It doesn't make sense in colder parts of the country, of course, to give up that much backyard space to something you can only use a few months out of the year.

But it's what a pool symbolizes—prosperity, a little bit of indulgence, a sense of fun—that mattered to him. What a swimming pool truly symbolizes is the American idea that your home is your castle, and your yard is your playground, and anything you want to put in it is yours to decide.

Liberals hate it when we treat our private property like, well, private property.

They positively *despise* gazebos and water features and little sitting areas, because they reinforce the idea that most Americans think of their homes as theirs, to decorate and furnish the way they like.

One of the reliable ways you can tell whether you're in a liberal part of town or a conservative part of town is: Can you smell burgers cooking on the grill in the summer, and are the houses decorated with festive lights in the winter?

If the answer to either of the questions is "no," then you're either in a liberal neighborhood, or you're in France. Either way, you're not going to have very much fun.

Liberals hate it when Americans head off to The Home Depot or the garden store and buy big barbecues and all-weather lawn furniture. It just seems like we're having too much fun back there in our yards, with a cooler of beer and friends gathered around.

And what are we so darned happy about? Don't we know that the earth is about to freeze (or boil, liberals are never sure which) and that there is still so much racism and hatred in America? It makes liberals mad that we won't put down our hot dogs and march somewhere to occupy something, that we prefer to hang around the backyard instead, relaxing under the gazebo we built and watching the kids play in the pool.

And that's what really frosts liberals. It's that middle-class Americans aren't angry enough for them. They're not spending their spare time—their leisure time—the way they're supposed to be.

For every family that's done well enough to afford an in-ground swimming pool, there are another two or three that are making do, for now, with the above-ground kind. And for every one of *those*, there are five or six that can only afford a kiddie pool you fill up with a garden hose. How can you enjoy what you have, goes the liberal mind-set, when there's someone else out there who can't?

But somehow, we Americans slog on.

We don't begrudge each other our luxuries. Sure, the guy down the street might envy me my gazebo, and I might wish I could afford the concrete and blue tile swimming pool he put in, but when it comes down to it, we're actually *happy* for each other, grateful that we live in a country where hard work means you can afford fun stuff for your family to enjoy together.

Liberalism only takes hold where jealousy and class envy flourish, and where people can't stand to see anyone else prosper, or have fun, which is why places like the old Soviet Union and most university faculties are so impossibly left-wing.

In the rest of America, we're busy trying to spruce up our little corner of paradise, the backyard. Sometimes it's with a swimming pool, if we're lucky, and sometimes it's just a sprinkler and a couple of lawn chairs, which is what it was for me when I was growing up.

That's why liberals hate swimming pools so much. They're bitter reminders that most Americans still believe that happiness is something you build—and earn—for yourself.

It's not something that the government *allows* you to do.

It's not something that you need to ask permission for.

It's not even something that has to be in restrained good taste.

I mean, we've all seen Christmas decorations that were a little over the top. And we've all seen backyard setups—fountains, gazebos, maybe a collection of garden gnomes—that might have been a bit too much to take.

Liberals really hate those. Which is reason enough to love them.

Ronald Reagan's brilliant plan to win the Cold War by showing off the American middle-class lifestyle might have worked on a Soviet dictator, but it would have gone nowhere with a typical liberal.

Flying over a bedroom community, your basic issue leftie isn't going to notice the swimming pools glinting in the sunlight. He's not going to reflect on the bounty of an economic system that makes all of that possible.

The liberal will see all that *waste*. And all of that *inequality*.

And if you took a liberal up in the air to survey the places where

Americans live today, what he'd be most struck by—and horrified by—is the space. All of that space, all of that wide spread-out-ness, is another thing that liberals absolutely hate.

The typical American house is a lot bigger today than it was when Ronald Reagan was president. It has more rooms, a bigger yard, and most of them have a large expanse of patio stretching out into the backyard.

It's fitting, in a way, because American towns have changed a lot, too, since Ronald Reagan was in the Oval Office. Out past the older suburbs, connected by multilane boulevards and interstate freeways, there are spanking-new cities—demographers call these "edge cities"—with new homes and new schools and industrial office parks where people can work closer to home, without having to commute hours into the downtown of the nearby city.

Liberals hate these edge cities.

They call it "suburban sprawl," with a barely concealed contempt for these places. But these towns are the logical consequence of American prosperity and the pool and patio culture: People want more room to grow and raise families, it's as simple as that.

They are also the consequence of the technological revolution that allows so many more businesses to do what they do over the Internet. Or over the phone.

The Industrial Revolution brought us the modern American city, and if you go back and read your nineteenth-century literature, liberals didn't much like that development either. All of those immigrants and ex-farmers packed themselves into small apartments in cities all across America, as people emptied out of rural towns and chased work. Chased the future. Chased a better way of life.

Well what do you know, Americans are still chasing work. Chasing a better way of life.

For many Americans, these newer, cleaner edge cities may be a little bit farther out of the way than the older suburbs that ring larger cities, but it is their newness that appeals to Americans—and that's what liberals hate the most about them.

These new cities have everything you need—movie theaters, shopping plazas, a Home Depot, and a Walmart—so there's no reason to make the long trek back into the city.

Environmentalists attack "sprawl" as part of the American addiction to cars and gas. They prefer something called "smart growth"—though when liberals call something "smart," what they really mean is, "something we came up with."

Liberals call all of their solutions "smart" because as far as they're concerned, what most Americans are doing is "stupid."

They think it's stupid for Americans to prefer to live in more spacious and spread-out communities. They don't like that so many of us prefer newer roads and schools, and that Americans prize their mobility. But what they really hate is that we love our space, we love our pools and patios, and we love our broad avenues, and we don't feel the need to return to the bigger cities where the liberals want us to live because—surprise!—that's where they're still in charge.

Liberals may hate these new cities, but they have only themselves to blame.

For the past fifty years, older cities have become decaying ruins thanks to liberal policies. Liberals undermined the police force, saddled businesses with taxes and regulations, and thwarted every meaningful attempt to improve the school system. It's no coincidence that it's the cities under the most ossified and powerful liberal control—places like Los Angeles, Detroit, Chicago, and San Francisco—that have inspired families and businesses to move away to nearby edge cities, where the liberal octopus has yet to spread its tentacles.

And that's why liberals are so dedicated to reversing the trend. That's why they're busy working with urban planners and politicians to figure out how to get us all back on the reservation.

When gasoline hits four dollars per gallon, it hurts Americans who live in these new edge cities, but that's fine with the liberals. They're *trying* to get us to stop moving. They like it when we're constrained by high gas prices. They want us to stop spreading out because every time we do, we get farther and farther away from their reach.

Why do you think liberals of all stripes want to raise taxes on gasoline?

Why do you think they reflexively and automatically oppose any oil drilling, anywhere, to increase the national oil supply and lower prices at the pump?

It all comes back to Americans and their pools and patios. It's all about our bigger houses, and our desire for more space, bigger yards, wider roads. All of the things that Americans instinctively move toward, liberals want to take away.

That's why liberals really hate the new edge cities; because they make pools and patios so available, so attainable, so affordable for the American middle class.

Liberals aren't content with destroying some of America's greatest cities. They're not satisfied with what they've done to places like Detroit, which has lost almost 30 percent of its population in the past ten years, most of which has gone to the edge cities that surround it.

They're baffled by this, but we're not. Detroit has been under the firm and unwavering control of liberals for almost fifty years. That's meant decaying, inflexible schools; high taxes; a soaring crime rate; and an antibusiness, high-regulation climate.

People didn't *move* away from Detroit—they were *driven* away.

Driven away by the liberals who run the place. And when people moved to cleaner places with smaller government, what did liberals do? They doubled down. Detroit isn't getting better, it's getting *worse*. The liberals aren't learning a lesson, they're pushing more of the same.

But that's typical of liberals, isn't it? When their policies fail, they just change the name. Now it's "smart growth." But it's really just the same old thing.

No wonder so many Americans are moving away from liberal enclaves, to edge cities where they can start again. No wonder so many Americans just want a backyard and a patio, some space to raise their families in peace and privacy.

Liberals hate that about Americans. They hate it when we refuse to obey.

So if, somehow, you do get a liberal up in an airplane to soar above these new and better places to live, you won't be able to convince him. He won't notice the swimming pools or the patios. He won't notice the big schools with huge playing fields. He won't notice the green space and the uncongested roads.

He'll just sniff and say, "Look at that awful sprawl."

And when he does, you should do him, and us, a big favor.

Push him out of the plane.

Trust me. It's the only way.

27 The Suburbs

Little, pink dull houses and lives

Boy, liberals love cities, don't they? Not real cities, of course. Not Detroit. Or Newark. Or three-quarters of Washington, D.C. Or four-fifths of New York City. They LOVE Manhattan, but do you ever hear anyone talk about Staten Island? Or Brooklyn, which is four times larger than the elites' favorite borough?

No, they love Manhattan. And Chicago's Lincoln Park section. Basically, they love urban areas that don't have too many poor black people. Hey, liberals love poor black people, *in theory.* They're so authentic! They make such great music! They're more reliably Democratic than women's history majors at Berkeley! Liberals just don't care to live *too* close to them. If they did, then all the liberals who talk about how great city life is would move to Bedford-Stuyvesant. They'd get a steal on a huge brownstone.

Or Northeast D.C. Or Chicago's Southside. Or South Central L.A.

But you know what liberals hate even more than real cities? Suburbs. Perhaps you know the saying: "I'd rather be shot dead in a Brooklyn walk-up than live in a three-bedroom, three-bathroom house with a yard in the 'burbs."

What is it about the suburbs that drives them crazy? For some it's just provincialism. They were born in Hyde Park, they'll die in Greenwich Village, and they'll never rest their heads on a cul-de-sac in between. But here's a dirty little secret: Lots of liberals were *born* in the suburbs. They only fell in love with city life after college, when they acted on their rugged, individualist nonconformism by moving to San Francisco with all of their friends. And now they're ashamed of the suburbs in the same way they're ashamed of America.

So self-loathing plays an important part. But so do aesthetics. Ask a liberal why he hates the suburbs and he'll spit out a bill of particulars.

They've always hated malls, of course. JCPenney? Macy's? You've got to be kidding, right? Do people actually shop at those wretched places?

But that's nothing compared with their contempt for strip malls. I know what you're thinking: If you've got a Best Buy, a Panera Bread, a Bed Bath & Beyond, and a Target all in one place, who needs anything else? You get all the necessities in one place—and you get to enjoy the fresh air as you walk from shop to shop. Some strip malls even have a Buffalo Wild Wings, so you can snag a drink while your wife spends an hour picking out a new shower curtain. What's not to like?

Mention Walmart and watch libs nearly have an aneurysm.

Mind you, lefties aren't all that keen for sports bars, what with all the sports they have in them. Sure, that feminist myth about Super

Bowl Sunday being Rape Day every year has been (somewhat) dispelled. But you can't be too careful: "The way those yahoos carry on in public about their foot-ball—when *everyone* knows that soccer is the *real* football—well, it's just terrible. And you should see the way they looked at my buddy Madison—don't make a face, it's a man's name, too—when he asked them to put an English Premiere League game on the big screen that one time. Plus, all they serve are those big awful domestic beers."

And you should hear the things they say about the rest of the strip malls.

They hate the big-box stores because they're too corporate, and put all the "mom-and-pop" stores out of business—a full decade before Amazon could. (Amazon is okay with them because it's on the Internet and liberals are thrilled with anything on the web.)

They hate the way suburbanites shop, mindlessly slurping up whatever tchotchkes some giant corporation puts in front of them like drooling, Pavlovian dogs. (Unless the company is Apple, in which case they absolutely *have* to have whatever white plastic gadget just came out because it's *totally* going to change the world.)

And don't even get them started on suburban cuisine.

You want to scare liberals? Ask them to go out for dinner. After they've reluctantly said yes, tell them to meet you at 6:00 p.m. at Red Lobster.

It's just a scientific fact that liberals obsess over their grub. The overlap between Food Network viewers and Obama voters is pretty much total. Only Prius owners were more reliably Democratic in the 2008 election cycle. Lefties tend to take their food very, very seriously. When they cook for themselves, they study recipe books from Williams-Sonoma and stage little Iron Chef competitions with their friends from spinning class. They attempt alchemical magic with food, turning goose liver into foam, for instance, or celery soup into gel.

(They actually have a term for this dark art. It's called "molecular gastronomy." You can look it up.)

Remember that scene at the end of *Ferris Bueller's Day Off* where Principal Rooney is all beat up and he's sitting next to the girl in the school bus and he's got this look of horror on his face? And the girl says to him, "Have you ever *been* inside a real school bus before?"

Basically, that's how liberals are with the places where you and I eat all the time. Ruby Tuesday? No way. TGI Friday's? TGI Fuggedaboutit. Outback Steakhouse, Olive Garden, Chili's, Chi-Chi's?—these places are like the undiscovered country for lefties.

True story: I took a liberal friend out to dinner one night after he left his fabulous Manhattan co-op to visit me in the 'burbs. I didn't want to freak him out, so I took him to dinner at a Carraba's, which is the Le Cirque of strip-mall chain eateries.

He's a real foodie, and he pored over the menu for a full ten minutes, analyzing every dish and ingredient. When the waiter came over, my buddy starts grilling him: *Is the salmon farm raised or fresh caught? Line caught, or net? And those mashed potatoes it comes with—what kind of cream is used when you whip them? Could I substitute cappellini for the penne?*

Mind you, the "waiter" was just a kid from the local high school; he might have been seventeen years old. Overmatched, he clearly failed the quiz; my buddy wound up ordering a plain pizza margarita.

He barely touched it.

I'm convinced that the reason liberals get so wrapped around the axle over food is that they have too much time on their hands. And the reason they have too much time is the same reason they live in the city and not out in the suburbs like the rest of us: They don't have kids.

The suburbs were created around a single organizing principle—to make life easier for families. Drive around your suburb sometime and play "Count the Minivans." (Liberals hate those, too, by the way.)

Why do people drive those ugly, bulbous, soul-sucking monstrosities?

Because they work. They make it easy to haul the kids to soccer practice. And to the mall. And to the movies. And they're safe, considering that precious cargo you're hauling around.

The suburbs were designed to be as ruthlessly functional as the minivan, and for the same reasons we have crummy chain restaurants. Because you can take three kids there for dinner and (1) not get ugly looks and (2) not go broke.

Why do we have strip malls? Because we've got to shop for provisions, pick up some extra flashing for the roof, and get Trevor a new backpack without losing an entire weekend. We have a dance recital to get to for Lily, we have to mow the lawn, there's laundry and there's church on Sunday morning and if we work *really* hard and are *super* efficient we might, just *might,* get to watch a half of a football game later in the afternoon while we hide out in the rec room in the basement.

It's not pretty and it's not sophisticated, but that's what suburban life is. People move to the suburbs to have families. We stop checking into FourSquare and TwitPicking the cheese course. We stop spending our weeknights out with friends and our weekends exploring new bistros and going to wine tastings.

We choose to do something that is, we believe, more important. If slightly less glamorous.

The irony is that we don't begrudge our liberal, hipster, city friends their fabulous life. In fact, if we were going to be deadly honest, we'd admit we kind of envy them. But the admiration isn't mutual. They hate us for our suburban life. The houses are cookie-cutter and the food is offensive and the minivans stink.

No, when you tell your liberal friends that you're moving out to the 'burbs, they treat your lifestyle choice with disdain.

You'd get more understanding and respect if you told them you were changing your name to "Chantrelle" and getting a sex-change operation.

Periodically, a study comes out to remind people that the average kid costs about the same as the GDP of Grenada to raise, and that study is soon followed by another that declares that married people with kids are not as "happy" as their single counterparts.

The study about the costs of raising children is true, though I know why those studies are released: to deter people from having kids.

That other study about married people who have kids being miserable—well, I'm just not buying it. Any more than I think that a life led without kids is, de facto, a miserable one.

I'd like to think that, deep down, the hostility that our cosmopolitan single friends have about our dull, drab suburban lives is this: They know they're missing out on something. Something real. Something deep and profound.

I'm talking about the secret gratitude and pride one takes in actually raising another human being. Taking care of that person, molding that person, disciplining that person.

Loving that person unconditionally. The way God loves all of us.

And yes, occasionally bailing that person out of jail.

It's not always fun; it's not always great. But it is important, raising a family. And it's real. Does it get more real than cleaning poop from a child's posterior?

The suburbs are all about families. About loving someone besides yourself for a change. About losing yourself in someone else's problems. Like your kids. And your family.

It doesn't get any better than that.

26 Freeways

"Roll me away"

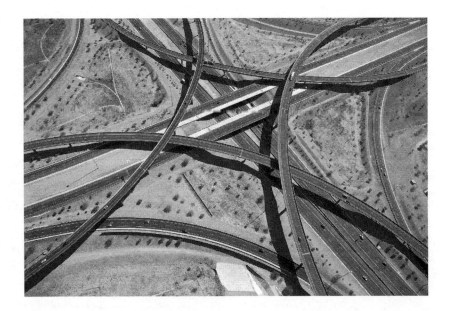

When Americans want to get somewhere, they get into their cars and they just go.

Liberals hate that.

The entire country is connected by intersecting ribbons of freeways, and if you don't mind driving, you can get from one side of the country to the other in about four days. On your timetable. In your car. Under your control.

Liberals *really* hate that.

What liberals prefer, of course, is that we stop driving so much. What they want is for us to be a lot more European, and take the train and the bus everywhere. Liberals love *public* transportation, which is why they insist on spending so much of our money on it. And in some ways, they're right. City buses and light rail can be clean and efficient ways to get to work. Nothing wrong with that.

But as much as they love buses and light rail, what sends their hearts into spasms of ecstasy is *high-speed rail.*

As fiercely as liberals hate freeways, they *love* high-speed rail.

"Chicago to New York in ten hours!" they shout. "Los Angeles to San Francisco in three!" No matter where you want to go, liberals will promise you that high-speed rail will take you there. All it takes, liberals tell us, is a little bit of "investment."

When liberals use the word "investment," hold on tightly to your wallet and back slowly away.

Right now, in California, liberals in the state government are planning to spend tens of billions of dollars on a high-speed rail project that will connect the thriving towns of Bakersfield and Merced. Finally! All of those busy commuters have something to look forward to. The skyscrapers of Bakersfield and the bustling commerce hub of Merced, joined by a billion-dollar rail link!

What? You were thinking maybe it would make more sense to connect, oh, Los Angeles and San Francisco? It would, of course, but the problem is, those cities are already connected, by two major highways running the length of the state. If you want to get to either of those places, you've got a lot of choices. You can fly—the San Francisco Bay area is served by three major airports; the Los Angeles area is served by five—or you can drive, along either Interstate 5 or Highway 101.

In other words, you've got a choice.

Those are "red-flag" words to the big-government liberal. You see, what liberals love the most about a high-speed rail project is that it represents billions of dollars of taxpayer-supported construction spending. Building a high-speed rail network means deciding routes, picking stops, hiring construction companies, and handing out million-dollar contracts.

Big-government liberals *love* handing out contracts. Because along with the money come the liberal bureaucrat conditions: minority-owned business requirements, environmental commission payoffs, union work rules—none of which have any effect on the usefulness or efficiency of the project itself, but all of which line the pockets, and increase the power, of the politicians who are overseeing the project.

This makes liberals very, very excited.

It doesn't matter to them, of course, that there isn't anyone in Bakersfield who needs to get to Merced. This is just *phase one,* they tell us. But *phase one* is already over budget, and late, and they haven't even laid one yard of track. If this is phase one, what's phase two? Merced to Stockton? And when will that be completed? In 2095?

Liberals don't care when it's completed, or how much it costs, because it's not really about constructing speedy, efficient transportation. It's about power.

Boondoggles like high-speed rail projects are like a living fairy tale to the power-grabbing liberal control freaks in government. It's every big-government bureaucrat's dream. Billions of dollars to spend! And that's *your* money, by the way, that *they're* spending: Federal transportation spending is going to the California project, so even if you don't live in the state, you're still on the hook.

It's a classic big-government liberal move: they take *your* money to build something *you* don't want, then use the opportunity to increase their power and spread their tentacles into a lot of new areas.

High-speed rail is code for *let's get us some of that sweet, sweet taxpayer cash.* And everybody knows it. After all, if you were building a major new railroad, would you even *think* about putting the government in charge?

The American freeway system may not be perfect—there are repairs to be made, and parts of it are woefully undersized—but it remains the most efficient way for people to get to work, and get around the country.

Americans love the freedom of the road. They love being able to drive where they want, stop where they want, and decide their own route.

But there is another reason that liberals hate highways. It has to do with economics. When Indiana governor Mitch Daniels took office and faced an enormous budget deficit, he spun off some of the state's highways to private companies. They took responsibility for the up-keep and maintenance of the roads, charge tolls where appropriate, and they run the state's highways like a business.

Liberals howled in anger! How *dare* Governor Daniels take away their piggy bank? How *dare* he put taxpayers' money ahead of the big-government liberals' right to parcel out contracts as they see fit?

Liberals hate it when that happens.

Handing out government money—as if there *is* such a thing; there *isn't,* it's your money and my money and every American taxpayer's money—is how the liberals get big and powerful. And that's why liberals love big projects like high-speed rail.

It's why they hate symbols of freedom and choice, like the American highway.

Unfortunately for liberals, it doesn't offer as many, shall we say, *business opportunities.*

And then here's the really big reason liberals hate freeways. Americans love to live the way we want. Some choose to live in cities in small apartments, and take taxicabs everywhere, or underground trains. Who cares about lots of square footage, goes the thinking, when your mornings are spent squatting in coffee shops, your days are spent working in a tiny fiftieth-story cubicle in some skyscraper, and your evenings are spent at art galleries, poetry readings, yoga sessions, and film festivals?

Who needs square footage for that kind of lifestyle? A bed, a toilet, and a hot plate will do.

Others, many more of us, like to live in the suburbs, and drive around in our big SUVs with our big V-8s. We like having a little bit of land, a fence, a pool even—and a three car garage that can house all of the stuff we Americans love to pull around on the back of our big SUVs: things like boats and campers and ATVs and Wave-Runners.

All of those things drive liberals nuts.

That is, until you actually get one of your liberal friends to escape the big city for a weekend, and join you for a nice long drive on the open highway in your SUV, music pumping, heading toward that nice lake cabin for a no-holds-barred weekend of drinkin', fishin', and doing just a whole lot of general nothin'.

They won't admit it, but deep down inside, liberals might just like these things—if only their lives spent consuming art and culture and food were half as fun!

Then there are those of us who like rural life. We want some real land, not that little piece of Astroturf suburbanites call a lawn. Real country spreads don't have lawns—they have acreage, and lots of it, with a few hundred head of cattle grazing about, some horses to ride, and some goats and chickens and pigs running around.

Liberals really hate all of these different ways of living, and it is the freeway, our amazing, and never-ending system of interstate, state, and county roads, that connects us all together. It's the freeway that connects the prairies, the mountains, the lakes, the cities, the suburbs and the exurbs. And the farms.

The second stanza in "America the Beautiful" says it best:

O beautiful for pilgrim feet
Whose stern impassion'd stress
A thoroughfare for freedom beat

Across the wilderness
America! America!

"A thoroughfare for freedom beat"? Sounds like they're talking about an American freeway to me.

Think of all of the great American songs dedicated to highways and freeways and roads. Bruce Springsteen's catalogue would be cut in half if you removed all of the songs he wrote that involved cars. "Racing in the Streets," "Born to Run," "Pink Cadillac," "Cadillac Ranch," "Drive All Night," "Further Up on The Road," "Highway 29," "Highway Patrol Man," "Stolen Car," "Used Cars," "Working on the Highway," and of course, the ultimate road song of Springsteen's, "Thunder Road."

In the most important lines of Springsteen's epic ode to freedom and escape, our prayers and hopes go out to that narrator as he cries out to his girl:

The night's busting open
These two lanes will take us anywhere.

And I wondered, how does a kid who grew up in NYC or some place where people don't have cars and open road even begin to understand the plea of that young man in that car?

You can't roll down a window in the subway and ask your girl to stick her head out. That would end in disaster.

I could go on and on about the importance of road songs in country music. "On the Road Again," "King of the Road," and "Red Dirt Road," etc., etc., etc.

And in rock and roll. "I've Been Everywhere," "Ramblin' Man," "Truckin'," "Radar Love," "Roadhouse Blues," "Running Down a Dream," "Route 66," and "Freebird."

And the greatest of all road songs, Bob Seger's "Roll Me Away," which has some of the most beautiful lyrics of longing and escape in all of rock and rolldom.

The last verse begins with the narrator standing alone on a mountaintop, staring at a metaphorical great divide. He can go east or west, he tells us. And suddenly, out of nowhere, he sees a young hawk flying, and his soul is stirred, and it begins to rise. And pretty soon, the narrator tells us that his heart is singing, and singing these words:

> *Roll, roll me away, I'm gonna roll me away tonight,*
> *Gotta keep rollin', gotta keep ridin', keep searchin' till I find what's right.*

That song—and the freeway—doesn't just represent freedom and choice and the different ways we can all choose to live our lives. It represents our common search for meaning.

It represents our collective longing to find what's right.

And liberals hate that, because they think they know what's right for all of us.

25 Babies

My little miracle fetus

Walk around any lefty hipster neighborhood—Austin or Ann Arbor, Brooklyn or Berkeley—and the first thing you'll notice are the baby strollers.

Liberals like expensive strollers—and I mean *expensive,* in the two-thousand-dollar range, more than you'd pay for a solid used American car. UppaBaby makes a line complete with mosquito netting, presumably for those leisurely walks along the Amazon. And a suspension system that one would expect from a Range Rover, perhaps for off-road adventures with the newborn.

As you walk around the left-wing monoculture enclaves, you'll see guys in scarves and important jeans pushing these contraptions around, and young moms with yoga mats and tight-fitting tights hovering around the baby inside, asking frantically "Caleb? Caleb? Would you like the rest of this turkey wrap? Would you?"

Soon little Caleb and Shiva will be Prius-ing off to progressive preschool—motto: "We don't teach them how to read; we teach them how to *knit*"—and before you know it, they'll be playing scoreless soccer and fretting about climate change.

Who says liberals don't love kids? They *adore* kids! They swaddle them up in pricey strollers, feed them organic food, send them to coddling schools, and in general carry them around in baskets until the little angels are ready to head off to college, where they'll learn all about Contemporary Transgendered Poetry and how to arrange a schedule to be able to sleep until noon each day and get Mondays and Fridays off.

Liberals love kids. It's *babies* they're not so crazy about.

Especially the inconveniently unborn kind.

The unborn baby is currently the most troublesome and despised character on the liberal horizon. This little creature can't win: If he's born, he'll condemn his mother to poverty and increase the population (liberals are always worried about population growth, though it takes a whole lot of babies to pay for the entitlements and social state they so adore, let alone to perpetuate civilization). But if he or she is disposed of in anything less than a taxpayer-sponsored facility—that is, some kind of grim "back alley"—well, then, that poor girl is going to die of sepsis, or worse.

The idea that there's someone to adopt and care for the baby, that there's another way—a more humane, caring, compassionate, and life-affirming way—is just not part of the decision tree.

The only solution, for liberals, is to make abortion safe, legal, and taxpayer-funded. You got a problem with that? *Hey! Why do you want to kill Mom?*

Here's the heart of the problem: Babies confuse liberals. On the one hand, they represent what every believing far-lefty thinks about people in general: that they're helpless, incontinent, and not very smart. They need supervision. They need to be under the control of a—we hope—benign leader.

On the other hand, thinking about babies, especially the inconveniently not-yet-born kind, brings on a lot of complicated political baggage.

For instance, as economist Steven D. Levitt has shown, the rise in abortions among the African-American community since *Roe* v. *Wade* had a corresponding—and positive—effect on crime rates in the inner city. What he proved was a simple, and ugly, fact: Fewer African-American babies in the 1970s meant fewer young African-American men in the 1980s and 1990s, and fewer young men in general—of the white or African-American variety—means crime rates go down.

Seen from a straight statistical lens, abortion is actually a social good to many leftists. Indeed, there is no limit to the good that can come if we just kill off such "problem" groups as young men before they are born.

Think of the benefits. Less crime. Fewer car accidents. Less lousy television. And a whole lot less really awful music.

Okay, so the price we pay for killing off those messy young boys is killing off all of those cute baby girls, too. But those little angels have problems of their own. Like teenage pregnancy. What better way to end that problem, too? Abort the babies so we can prevent future abortions!

Liberals didn't like hearing that rather controversial thesis of Levitt's. But then, there are *lots* of things that are true that liberals don't like hearing.

One of the fault lines of the abortion debate centers on the question of parental consent. Simply put, should a young, pregnant girl at least have to *notify* her parents before she has an abortion?

How you answer that question will say a lot about how you might fit in with your neighbors, should you move to Austin or San Francisco.

Liberals, of course, think this kind of parental notice is onerous and nasty and debilitating to the young girl. They're not so worried about the effect on the baby inside her, but that's because liberals aren't crazy about *that* kind of baby.

Planned Parenthood, the hugely controversial—but still federally funded!—abortion rights group, has campaigned against all sorts of sensible abortion regulations. They're against all forms of parental involvement in a young girl's abortion decision.

On the other hand, Planned Parenthood held a march and demonstration in Sacramento, California. They were especially eager to have young people in high school participate. But before they did, Planned Parenthood insisted that every high-school-age participant have a signed parental consent form.

To attend a rally.

So the left-wing position is clear: to attend a rally, gotta have Mom and Dad's okay. To get an abortion, no problem. Right this way!

The trick to dealing with liberals is to ignore what they say and concentrate on what they do.

And there's no more doting person than a pregnant liberal. In those same hipster neighborhoods you'll find prenatal yoga classes, odd-smelling New Agey oils for rubbing into the pregnant belly, exotic prenatal diet books, special music CDs for "baby to enjoy in utero," and God forbid someone within two hundred yards of a pregnant lefty lights up a cigarette.

The SWAT team will arrive in three minutes.

In other words, liberals *behave* as if that thing inside the engorged belly of a pregnant woman is actually a real live . . . baby.

Liberals don't want to connect those pesky moral dots. That's because babies aren't just noisy and messy, they also make a mess of the placid, untroubled liberal mind.

Then, too, legal abortion has profound racial effects—it's almost a kind of legalized eugenics. According to a report by the New York City Department of Health and Mental Hygiene, almost 60 percent of all pregnancy outcomes in NYC for African-American mothers were abortions in 2009. Sixty percent!

Responding to that grim news, a prolife group put up a four-story antiabortion billboard in SoHo that pictured a young African-American girl and bore the headline: *"The most dangerous place for African Americans is in the womb."*

That drew all kinds of cries and protests from the art without license crowd, and (naturally) the Planned Parenthood folks. But the fact that more African Americans in New York City were aborted than were born—that hardly draws a yawn.

Liberals should be against this kind of dreadful outcome—we all should, of course—but when it comes to the implications of abortion, they prefer to look the other way.

Of course, once your child is born, liberals will step in with all sorts of orders and commandments—about what school the little one is allowed to attend, what drinks and snacks are allowed in the vending machines, what sexual information will be given out, and when—but right until the moment the baby's head appears, it's hands off that nonbaby! That as-yet-unborn nonbaby fetus is merely the property of its host!

It's a sad, small, depressing view of what life is, and what life means, and from Whom it comes. Birth is a miracle. It is unexplainable, and uncontrollable.

Liberals hate those things. Which is why they hate babies.

And also: a culture that encourages lots of procreation—that is, what used to be thought of as "the American Dream"—is a culture that's confident and growing, a culture that believes in itself and its future. Liberals hate that kind of confidence. For them, the future is all about climate change and catastrophe and less—less of everything: less food, less prosperity, less sunshine, less happiness.

It's a grim world for the average lefty. And it's getting grimmer. That's why they love to use the word "sustainable" for everything. Sustainable energy. Sustainable food. Sustainable communities. For them, things don't get bigger and better. They just get . . . sustained.

"Life, liberty, and the pursuit of sustainability."

Doesn't really have much of a ring to it, does it?

Maybe that's why birth rates in liberal enclaves are so low. And maybe that's also why birth rates among Bible-believing Christians in the United States are so high. One side thinks things can get better. The other thinks things stink, and should stay the same.

That's why liberals really hate babies. Because to be for babies is to be for better days ahead.

24 Seniors

Throw Grandma off the train, please

The only thing more troublesome to liberals than babies are senior citizens.

Especially senior citizens who refuse to die.

Underlying every conversation about the American health-care system—you know the drill, right? It's too expensive and (here's that word again!) unsustainable—is the one statistic that every health-care "reformer" likes to trot out.

The majority of every health-care dollar is spent in the final two weeks of life.

Sometimes it's the final two years. Sometimes it's 20 percent or 30 percent or some other percentage of every health-care dollar. But the message is always the same: We spend too much keeping seniors alive, and we've got to do something about it.

Back in the early, optimistic days of the Obama administration, they were pretty honest about it. Ezekiel Emanuel, the brother of Obama's then chief of staff, Rahm Emanuel, helped craft the greasy pile of bureaucratic intervention, government overreach, and federal power grab known as Obamacare. One of its chief features, according to the Obama-ites, was a little something buried deep on page 1286: the so-called Independent Payment Advisory Board.

What the IPAB does is set the price the federal government is willing to pay for certain procedures for certain patients. In other words, the federal government—which under Obamacare will rapidly control 100 percent of every health-care procedure and expenditure in the country, for every citizen—decides what each medical procedure is worth. If it decides that certain procedures for certain patients of a certain age aren't cost-effective, it simply sets the price it's willing to pay for those procedures to a ridiculously low rate.

A rate so low that no doctor or hospital will be able to afford to offer those procedures, so no doctor or hospital will offer them.

Meaning: If you're old, we won't spend the big bucks to keep you alive.

In other words: *death panels.*

Governor Sarah Palin sniffed out the secret strategy behind the Obamacare behemoth and called it out for what it is: health-care rationing, by government bureaucrats. It didn't help the Obama crew that one of the architects of the plan had endorsed *exactly this interpretation* a few years previously.

In his capacity as a "bioethicist"—which is one of those scary euphemisms liberals love to use to cover up what they're *really* doing—Dr. Ezekiel Emanuel had written extensively about the need to ration health care. But when Sarah Palin unleashed her analysis on the country, Dr. Emanuel quickly tried to clarify.

He told the *Washington Times* that when he began working in the health-policy area twenty years ago, he thought we would definitely have to ration care, that there was a need to make a decision and deny people care. Later in that same interview, he admitted that his thinking had "evolved" on this pesky rationing idea.

"I've come to the conclusion that in our system we are spending way more money than we need to, a lot of it on unnecessary care," he said. "If we got rid of that care we would have absolutely no reason to even consider rationing except in a few cases," Emanuel confessed.

Except in a few cases.

A *few* cases?

Which cases? Your case? My case?

How about President Obama's grandmother's case?

Early in the heath-care "reform" debate, President Obama used the example of his own grandmother, Madelyn Dunham, who died two days before he was elected. Despite being diagnosed with terminal cancer, she had received an artificial hip replacement, which (somehow) really seemed to irritate her grandson. Her operation raised some "very difficult moral issues," he said, about whether it's worth it to "give my grandmother, or everybody else's aging grandparents or parents, a hip replacement when they're terminally ill."

So that's one case: Madelyn Dunham, you are hereby refused a new hip. Hope the bad hip doesn't hurt too much. Go ahead and die. Quickly, if possible, because we need the room.

Here's another: according to Ezekiel Emanuel's early writing for the Hastings Center—a place that bills itself as a "nonpartisan, non-profit bioethics research institute" (translation: a lefty think tank)—patients with "dementia" should not receive guaranteed government health services.

"Dementia," by the way, is another way of saying "Alzheimer's."

So, seniors with cancer and people with Alzheimer's are some of the "few" cases where health-care rationing *will* occur.

Memo to America's young people: Don't become America's *old* people.

Look, I'm not saying that there aren't difficult choices to be made. Of course there are. Maybe it was foolish for Madelyn Dunham to have her hip replaced. Maybe people with Alzheimer's don't need certain medical procedures. Who knows?

The point is, whose choice should it be? The patient's? Or the unelected, unaccountable members of the Independent Payment Advisory Board?

And that's what liberals really hate about babies and seniors. It's all about who gets to make the choice.

Despite all the talk about "prochoice" and a "woman's right to choose," the proabortion liberals are really about *denying* the right of the "patient"—the baby in utero—to live.

The prolife position on abortion is simple: The patient is the baby, and the baby should be allowed to live. And an Independent Payment Advisory Board, or the pregnant mom inconvenienced by her baby, doesn't have the right to intervene, even if that has complicated and expensive consequences. People with cancer, or Alzheimer's, or anything else have a right to make the choice for themselves. They're old enough to know what they want.

But that's how liberals view things. They see seniors as one, big . . . nuisance.

You can almost hear them saying to themselves, "Come on, you old people. You've had your time. You've taken up your share of the world's natural resources. Why can't you just leave the stage? It's our time now."

But it's not just the expense associated with old age that liberals hate; it's the mere sight of them. Heck, did you see *Cocoon*? It was made back in 1985, and when all of those seniors stripped down and jumped in that old pool, it was scarier to a liberal than any slasher film. The wrinkles. The sagging breasts. The horror!

It's why you never see many seniors on TV. Because liberal casting agents hate them. Liberal advertising executives can't stand the sight of them either, even though they represent a powerful purchasing bloc.

Even the people in those AARP commercials that seem to perpetually run on daytime TV aren't really *that* old. They are possibly in their midfifties, and in great shape, with Hollywood looks and Miami Beach tans.

To liberals, the Holy Grail of life is looking like you are thirty. Even if you are sixty-five. It's why Nancy Pelosi can't force a smile. Her face is stuck. Permanently.

Liberals hate the sight of seniors so much that they live in places where seniors don't live. Sightings are few and far between in most chic liberal neighborhoods, those same chic spots where all of those chic strollers with chic babies are being pushed around by their oh so chic and clever parents.

These parents would rather outsource taking care of Grandpa and Grandma, preferably to some government program. Why? Because seniors remind liberals that one day, they, too, will be old. One day, they, too, will be vulnerable. One day, they, too, will have sagging skin. One day, they, too, will need the help of others to push them around. Feed them. Love them.

That's no job for a member of the family!

Let Grandma or Grandpa go to some government-subsidized home, and get some social workers on the case. We're too busy taking care of our fancy, fashionable lives to be bothered with such stuff.

It's a downer. It's worse than that. It's downright selfish of these old people to ruin our lives, goes the logic of many liberals.

If government was designed for anything, it is to keep us a safe distance from Grandma and Grandpa, and their march to the grave.

Liberals hate senior citizens and babies not because they're both messy and noisy and often in diapers. They hate them because they represent the deepest, most fundamental issues we all grapple with every day.

Babies and seniors humble us. We've all been babies, and most of us will be old, and there's not a federal program that can ever change that. The miracle of birth, the sweet sadness of old age—these are things beyond our control, these are things we offer up with gratitude to Him.

Him. Not an Independent Payment Advisory Board.

23 Taking Risks

Skinned knees . . .

Let me tell you about a playground I knew growing up in Dayton, Ohio.

On one end, there was a jungle gym, a grid of bars that went up about eighteen feet (it seemed larger to me at the time) and they'd get rusty and one of them was bent out of shape and if you climbed to the top and lost your footing, it was a bumpy ride down to the ground.

On the other end, there was a high bar with a bunch of ropes dangling from it, like some kind of cut-rate scaffold.

In the middle, there was some dirt.

Needless to say, I loved it.

We climbed onto the jungle gym, hung upside down from our

knees, slipped and fell more than a few times, climbed back up and did it all again. When we were bored of that, we'd head over to the ropes and try to shimmy to the top of the bar without getting tangled up, and without getting nasty rope burns on the way down.

Mostly, we failed at that.

And when we were done playing, we'd have red marks and bruises, and we'd be dirty. And when we got home, we'd be told to clean up for dinner.

What wouldn't happen is, we wouldn't sue the city for providing such unsafe playground equipment. We wouldn't sue each other for pushing us a little too hard on the jungle gym. We wouldn't initiate a class-action lawsuit against the manufacturer of the rope, who *surely knew* that his product would chafe and redden the soft, delicate tissues of our unblemished bodies.

In other words, we weren't liberals.

We didn't expect to be protected from everything, including our own stupidity. I mean, look, you didn't have to be a genius, and I promise you, when I was a kid I was certainly no genius, to know that if you jumped from the top of the jungle gym onto the packed dirt below, you were going to need a moment or two to collect yourself before you headed over to the ropes. That was just life. Those were the basic rules we lived by.

Liberals hate that.

For them, someone is always at fault. Someone is always to blame for the things that happen to us—we lose some money, we skin our knees, whatever. There's always someone with deep pockets who can be charged for the damages that we often inflict on ourselves.

It never occurred to us, when we were kids, to march back into our house and demand that our parents *compensate* us for the pain and suffering we experienced sliding down a long rope in our cutoff shorts.

(And let me tell you: there was *a lot* of pain and suffering that day, I promise you.)

The grown-ups in our lives weren't responsible for the stupid stuff we did on the playground. But they punished us anyway, just on general principle.

But for liberals, the name of the game is: Find the Grown-up and Make Him Pay. Liberals are on a never-ending quest to find the "grown-up" in every situation: Sue the insurance company, sue the federal government, sue the car company, sue the city, sue anyone and everyone you can, to compensate you for whatever bad thing happened.

Liberals always cast themselves, and you, in the role of the child. Someone else, someone rich, is always the grown-up.

The Old Way: fall down, skin your knee, walk it off.

The New Way: fall down, skin your knee, contact your attorney.

Not too long ago, reports started to emerge about cases of sudden acceleration with some cars manufactured by Toyota. There was one story, soon followed by others, and the media—and trial lawyers—ran to the stories like a mouse to cheese.

One of the world's most popular cars, made by one of the world's biggest car companies, was suddenly under the gun. And Toyota's reputation for reliability was suddenly in question.

Even the Toyota Prius found its way into the mix. An elderly man was driving his Prius down the road, and he experienced what he said was "unintended acceleration" in the car. If you know anything about the Prius, you'll have to suspend your disbelief here. Anyone who has driven one knows that they barely accelerate, even when you want them to. But the man was shaken, cops were called, and the story hit the news, along with all the other stories of sudden acceleration being reported.

There was a major investigation, the CEO of Toyota was called before a congressional committee to explain, and asked to apologize, which he did.

Toyota eventually admitted to some kind of "sticking problem" with the brakes, but no one ever proved that Toyota's vehicles were accelerating suddenly and mysteriously.

One thing we do know is that once the media caught the story, and the trial lawyers' hearts started beating faster, the one thing that actually did suddenly accelerate were claims of sudden acceleration.

It seemed that almost anyone who was driving a Toyota and got into an accident during that one bad publicity month for Toyota was attributing that accident to sudden acceleration.

And just as suddenly, when Toyota issued its apology for the sticky brakes and a subsequent recall, the sudden acceleration incidents suddenly disappeared.

How fitting, though, that it was a *Prius* driver who had one of the more highly publicized problems. The Prius is a squat little hybrid fuel car driven almost exclusively by liberals. And it was liberals whose first reaction to the problem was: *Not my fault.* And whose second reaction to the problem was: *Whom can I sue?*

As kids, we knew that when we climbed to the top of the jungle gym, or got too close to a stove, we were on our own. We knew that there weren't any grown-ups to complain to if we tumbled down. It was a good lesson in living, that rusty old playground of my childhood. It taught me that there isn't always someone else to blame for the things that I do to myself.

Liberals hate that lesson, and they hate those playgrounds, which is why you can't find one like that anywhere these days. You can't skin your knees on these new playgrounds, even if you try.

Now they're all made up of recycled rubber tires. All the edges are soft. All the surfaces are padded. There aren't any ropes.

They don't even call them jungle gyms anymore. They call them "play structures." And that says it all.

What do kids learn from the modern liberal obsession with protecting them from any and all harm? How do kids learn to assess risk, let alone take risks, without getting some skinned knees? The literal and the proverbial kind?

And how do we learn to do smart things if we don't get punished for doing stupid things?

When I was a kid, if I did something risky and stupid, like, say, stick my hand on the stove, rather than get any sympathy from adults, I would hear something pithy and unsympathetic like, "See what happens when you touch the stove?"

Or something even more heartwarming, like, "You moron. I told you not to touch the stove."

And the adult would then scold me for being stupid, get me something from the medicine cabinet over the bathroom sink to ease the pain, like some good ol' Neosporin, and then send me to my room to think about how stupid I'd been.

No hospital visits. No trips to the doctor. And certainly no calls to the lawyer to sue the manufacturer for not coming up with a stove that prevents kids from getting burns.

Today, you can't even use the "s" word in public. It's forbidden in schools to call someone stupid for doing something stupid.

And that is truly stupid.

The hit reality show *Deadliest Catch* is a hit for many reasons. The show, now in its eighth season, shows real-life men doing real-life work. Hard work. Risky work. And in one of the riskiest places a man can do risky work—the Bering Sea.

According to the pilot episode, the injury rate for crews on most crab boats in the fleet is nearly 100 percent due to the severe weather conditions (frigid gales, rogue waves) and the danger of working with such heavy machinery on a constantly rolling boat deck.

Alaskan king crab fishing reported over three hundred fatalities per hundred thousand as of 2005, with over 80 percent of those deaths caused by drowning or hypothermia.

Forget skinned knees. We're talking busted knees. Busted heads. Death. And worse. Freezing to death.

Why do so many of us love that show? Because the men on those boats don't complain when the entire deck turns into a skating rink. They bust it up. They don't cry when a big heavy metal object hits them in the head and splits it open like a peanut. They laugh, wrap the wound with duct tape, and get back to work.

What they don't do is call a lawyer. What they don't do is sue the captain. What they don't do is blame someone else for what happened.

The guys on the boats don't have fancy degrees. Heck, I bet half of them don't have their GEDs, let alone sat for their SATs. But they have a whole lot of common sense. And courage.

They head out to sea with little but some cans of Skoal, a case of beer, and the hope of bringing back a boat full of crab. And the prospect of making more money in a month than most men they know make in a year.

When the hunt doesn't pan out, they come home with, well, empty cans of beer and Skoal. And they don't ask for a bailout. They just get set for the next hunt. The next chance to hit the mother lode.

If only Wall Street bankers lived by the same creed.

When the great Captain Phil Harris died in 2010, fans around the world wept, because he was the epitome of that old-school toughness that America used to celebrate. And revere. And always, he was cracking jokes, even in the face of the worst dangers.

Tens of thousands of people posted their respects on their web page, and on YouTube, after his death. None were better than this one, posted by someone who called himself Jager1967.

I would like to nominate Captain Phil Harris for the toughest s.o.b. in the Alaskan scratch that . . . the American fishing industry. Come on, the guy had a blood clot travel up his leg, through his heart and lodge in his lung, which should've killed him outright. But, he kept right on working to get his catch, even as he was coughing blood and barely breathing. Phil, may the wind always be at your back and hope you got into heaven a half hour before the devil knew you were dead.

Where will the Captain Phils of the future come from? Not from the world of helicopter-coddling, rubber-room-loving, bubble-bay-producing liberal parents who hate the very idea of their little precious babies experiencing the pain and anguish of a skinned knee.

22 Small Businesses

Mom and Pop shops thrive

Despite the fact that this is a chapter about small business owners, I'm pretty sure no small business owner is going to read it.

People who run small businesses are too busy to read. They don't have time to sit down and rest, let alone pull up a chair and dive into a book. Even a comic book.

Small business owners are always working. Checking the till. Paying the taxes. Ordering inventory. Trying to increase their sales. Worrying about the payroll, and the end of the month, and whether to hire another employee. Small business owners are always opening early and closing late. Always trying to figure out a better way to deliver their product. And they are tirelessly trying to build something to pass on to their kids and grandkids.

And always, always, with an eye on serving their customers. And making a profit.

Service? Customers? Profit?

Service is a foreign concept to most liberals, be it military service or religious service or the business variety. For liberals, "public service" means doing a government job for more pay than the average private-sector worker, with better benefits and better hours—and without the pressure. Or accountability.

The same for union workers.

Small wonder they hate the small business owner.

While the average public-sector union worker has a million-dollar-plus pension funded by, well, us, the small business owner is working his life away to sock away enough cash to pay the bills and have enough left over for his self-funded retirement.

What a concept. Paying for your own retirement. With your own money.

For many small business owners, retirement is just a dream. Many are simply trying to sock away enough cash on the chance—a good chance—that in the immediate years to come, some competitors might come along and squeeze the life out of their business. Squeeze the life out of their entire business model. Or even the entire business category.

And with the proper planning, they have enough socked away to start another business.

It's no joke, being out there hoping your business doesn't just get wiped out. It happens all the time. Do you know anyone who makes eight-track tape cartridges? Or who sells ice door to door?

Think of all of the old horse and buggy operations that got wiped out by Henry Ford's clever work. Think of all of the small-town pharmacies that were bumped by Walgreens and CVS. Think about what Steve Jobs and the Internet did to the music industry.

Then again, maybe the people who brought us Milli Vanilli, Vanilla Ice, and Ice Cube deserve to be out of business.

Despite all of the hassle and struggle and difficulty, small business owners march on. They work hard, they fight, and they do everything in their power to control their own destiny. Their own way of life. Their own wealth.

No wonder liberals hate them.

And they do. They'll just never admit it.

The whole point of the liberal attitude toward small business is to discourage it. So many small businesses operating in so many areas, to the liberal, just seems unruly and hard to control.

The guy who runs the local oil and lube joint, the woman who owns the dry cleaner—from the moment they even think of opening their doors, they're saddled with layers of regulations and taxes.

The guy who owns the local gas station gets squeezed by high gas prices from his supplier and competition from the gas station across the street. He gets squeezed by the EPA.

The OB-GYN doctor at the local hospital—most of them operate as independent companies—is beset by high insurance premiums, fees imposed by government, and a regulatory structure that makes it more rational for a lot of them to go into another line of medicine. Or just get out of the medical business altogether.

Talk to doctors and ask if they'd recommend becoming a doctor to their kids, and watch their reaction. You might as well tell them you want their kids to be carnival barkers. Or poets.

It's that bad.

And yet, most small business owners stick it out. They work more hours, take more risks, hire and expand, all because they're *that* kind of person, the dreamer and the entrepreneur. The kind of person who'd rather be his own boss and make his own decisions.

Be his own boss? Make his own decisions?

That's why the liberals hate them.

Small business owners have something deep in their DNA that makes them reject the corporate, top-down life. They like the freedom to run their businesses their way, to succeed (and fail) on their own merits.

And many of these same people actually hope, through nothing but their own effort, to become wealthy. And to pass that wealth along to the family, and to the people who helped them get wealthy along the way. To their employees and their vendors. And ideally, they have done all of this while enriching their customers' lives, too.

This drives liberals totally bonkers.

The fact is that almost all new net job creation in the past thirty years in this great country has come not from big businesses, but from small businesses becoming big businesses. That isn't me making up those numbers. That's the nation's preeminent, nonpartisan foundation dedicated to the study of entrepreneurship, the Kauffman Foundation.

Bernie Marcus, the cofounder of The Home Depot, was on my radio show last year and went on a terrific tirade about how, under the current regulatory and litigation environment, The Home Depot could never have made it beyond a small regional retail operation if he launched his business today.

Luckily for him and the Home Depot shareholders, and for the millions of Americans who've worked at The Home Depot and the millions who shop there, he started his business in 1979, just as President Reagan's policies were about to kick in.

Or we'd be still running around to five different stores just to make a little wood doghouse in our backyards for our kids. And paying twice as much.

That admission by Marcus should have made headlines in every business section of every paper in America. One of America's great entrepreneurs told one of America's network talk radio hosts that he could not launch one of America's premier retail brands today thanks to his own government.

That, somehow, does not drive liberals nuts.

Liberals think that things are better when everyone is following orders and obeying regulations.

The entire complicated mess that we call Obamacare is a perfect example. It masquerades as a health-care bill, but it's more accurate to call it the Small Business Destruction Act.

The whole two-thousand-page nightmare is so filled with job-killing regulations and business-squashing rules that the administration has already been forced to issue waivers that cover almost one million workers.

Who gets the waivers?

Well, unless you're a member of a big union, or a small business owner in former Speaker of the House Nancy Pelosi's home district, not you.

But if you are, you're in luck.

So, although liberals hate the American small business owner, they're willing to work it out. If you're a small business owner who has, inexplicably, found fifteen minutes in your busy day to read this chapter, the solution to your problem is to move into Nancy Pelosi's San Francisco congressional district and send her a waiver request.

You'd be wise to enclose a check to her reelection committee, but you didn't hear that from me.

And you can stop complaining that you don't have the money for that kind of thing, because, as liberals are continually pointing out to the rest of us, you small business owners are rich. *Seriously* rich.

Some of you, after years of hard work and sacrifice, have the good fortune to be worth a million or more dollars. And yes, I *suppose* we could say that you earned that money, through risk and perseverance and long hours, but, really, is it all that fair for you to just amass that kind of wealth? And what are you going to do with it? Leave it to your children?

Not so fast.

Another reason, maybe the biggest of all, that liberals hate the American small business owner is that he or she insists on leaving all of that wealth to the next generation, instead of doing the right thing with it, which is to give it to the liberals in government to spend as they see fit.

One generation working hard to help the next generation move up used to be called "the American Dream," but liberals certainly don't see it that way.

When the lady who owns the local dry cleaner dies—probably hunched over her tax returns, trying to figure out how she owes that much—liberals think that she dies owing the government just a bit more.

It's not enough that she built a business and hired employees and paid her rent, paying taxes on all of that, all the way along. Liberals want a chunk of what she somehow managed to squirrel away. They're irritated that despite their best efforts, someone, somehow, managed to make it in America. And make it despite them.

But that won't stop them from trying to take it away from her.

21 American Toyotas

Born in the U.S.A.?

Here's what we've all been hearing lately from the Obama administration and its lickspittle toadies in the liberal media:

"We're building cars in America again!"

What they're referring to, of course, is the series of bailouts and forced restructurings that the federal government undertook, first under President Bush, later under President Obama, to "save" the American auto industry.

But in many ways, the American auto industry was alive and well, and didn't need any "saving" at all.

They've been making Toyotas and VWs in America for decades, in auto plants in Tennessee and South Carolina and other states across the country. Honda and Nissan build them, too. These are plants that employ American workers, make cars for American consumers, bring prosperity and jobs to American towns.

They didn't need a bailout. They didn't have expensive, unaffordable labor union contracts and ossified Big Labor work rules dragging them down. Almost four thousand dollars out of the price of every General Motors car went to pay the extravagant health-insurance coverage for its union employees and their extended families.

General Motors paid for the health care of almost *one million* people. Hard to stay in business, and price your product competitively, with that kind of nut to cover, wouldn't you say?

And then there were the union work rules, which hampered the flexibility and the nimbleness that making anything requires. Even a taco.

So how could Toyota, VW, BMW, and other manufacturers make cars in America, while Chrysler and GM couldn't?

Simple: no unions.

Those companies manage to build and deliver excellent, popular products to the consumer without having to deal with the United Auto Workers union and its inflexible demands.

Liberals despise that. They hate the fact that a company can employ workers, build a product, satisfy consumers—all without bowing to big union strong-arm tactics.

That's why liberals hate American Toyotas. Because these cars are made without the "help" of unions. And we know what liberals think of that!

Liberals *love* big labor unions. They're still living in the distant past, when Samuel Gompers, the founder of the American Federation of Labor, organized the cigar makers in 1875.

To them, it's still 1875. Every company is a villain, every factory floor a sweatshop.

Liberals are always wailing about the decline of American

manufacturing greatness, but when they're asked to choose between competitive, modern efficiency and outdated Big Union politics, they'll choose their Big Union cronies all the time.

Every American Toyota on the road today is a thumb in the nose of liberal insistence that you can only make something in this country if you've got a big labor union along for the ride.

Every nonunion American-made car is a reminder that it's not the American worker who failed, but the backward-looking, outdated union bosses that drove General Motors and Chrysler into bankruptcy.

Lucky for them, of course, that when they hit the skids, the liberals were in charge. Bondholders were told to take a hike. Shareholders lost their investments. But the union bosses were kept on. They remain as powerful as ever at those companies—maybe even more powerful, because they've got you and me as unwilling coinvestors. Because when Big Labor hitched itself to Big Government, it was the American taxpayer who got the bill.

Want more proof of just how much big labor hurts the American manufacturer? Look only to the story below, and the lengths foreign capital will go to avoid the union bosses.

In November 2011, a friend of mine sent me an article from the *Tupelo Daily Journal,* the newspaper of record for the people of Tupelo, Mississippi. It's a town of roughly fifty thousand people, with the distinction of being Elvis Presley's birthplace.

He sent it to me because there was an entire section of the paper dedicated to a new birth in nearby Blue Springs; the new Toyota plant there delivered its first car, and it was big, big news. The new assembly plant there, which will employ two thousand workers when it reaches full capacity, will give birth to 150,000 vehicles a year.

It turns out that back in 2006, Toyota representatives visited the Tupelo area sixteen times, talking to local manufacturers and employees, finding out what they could about the people who would build their vehicles.

One of the people who visited was a guy named Ray Tanguay, who back then was VP for Toyota Motor Corporation, and ran their operations in Canada. Here's what he said: "What I observed were people who were educated, ethical, friendly, and with a strong work ethic—a perfect match for the Toyota way."

Ethical? Friendly? A strong work ethic? He must be talking about a union boss!

The people of Mississippi are no better or worse than the people of Detroit, but they are not trained from birth to see the owners of Toyota plants as their enemy. As someone to extract concessions from. The people there are simply looking for an honest day's work, and an honest day's pay.

Which is why liberals hate right-to-work states. They love to promote conflict between management and labor, rather than cooperation.

What a story that Tupelo story is. If you were around in, let's say, 1945, and someone told you that the country that brought us Japanese Zeros, kamikaze pilots, and ginsu knives would one day run the biggest automobile manufacturer in the world, you'd tell them to catch a one-way ticket to Crazy Town, and seek some serious help.

If that someone added that the giant Japanese car company would make its Japanese cars in America, and in Mississippi, no less, you'd throw in some electric shock therapy.

And it's not just cars. When airplane manufacturing giant Boeing was deciding where to locate a plant to build components of their new "Dreamliner" jet, they chose South Carolina for its right-to-work laws and dependable labor base.

Big labor unions howled in protest.

And the liberals in the Obama administration agreed. Not so fast, said the National Labor Relations Board. Boeing was told that it couldn't locate the plant in South Carolina.

That's right. Liberals in government told a private company that it was *not allowed* to make a private decision about where to locate a new manufacturing facility, simply because their cronies in Big Labor demanded it.

You see, liberals won't be really happy until every American company goes the General Motors route: big union control, bankruptcy, and federal receivership. William C. Durant, the founder of GM, must be spinning in his grave: His company is now a symbol of big government socialism, not free enterprise.

Toyota is a more truly "American" car company.

And that's why liberals hate those cars. And that's also why they've set their sights on unionizing workers at Toyota plants across the country. It's going to be hard, though. What could their pitch possibly be to the employees at those plants?

"Join up with us and we'll file for bankruptcy together"?

But where there's a will, there's a way. And where there's money, there's a will.

Big labor contributes more to political campaigns—almost exclusively to liberals and Democrats—than any industry. It is among President Obama's biggest financial backers, and its "independent" campaign expenditures dwarf those of any private company.

It's pretty solid logic. The bigger Big Labor gets, the more money it has. The more money it has, the more it can give to liberals. For two groups that don't understand how basic economics work, they sure have come up with a sweet system for getting rich.

In fact, the only snag in that masterful plan is those Toyotas, Hondas, VWs, BMWs, and Boeing Dreamliners being built by smart, industrious American workers.

So maybe it's not the Toyota that the liberal hates. It's the *worker* who refuses to buckle under, join a union, and watch his job—and his employer—go under with him.

20 Immigrants

Give me your tired, poor undocumented workers

Liberals love to tell people they love immigrants. And then the minute you turn your back on them, the little rascals go about pitting legal and illegal immigrants against one another.

No. It's worse than that. They actually pretend there's not a difference between the two.

Have you ever watched a debate about illegal immigration? The next time you do, see if you notice what I've noticed.

At some point in the discussion, whoever is arguing for open borders or amnesty for illegal immigrants will suddenly stop using the word "illegal" in front of the word "immigration" and will just start talking about "immigration," as if it's all the same.

During the debate, it usually takes a few moments for the person on the other side of the issue to notice that the word "illegal" has been dropped. It's sort of like that old Bugs Bunny cartoon, when he and Daffy Duck are both trying to convince Elmer Fudd that it's time to hunt the *other* guy.

"It's duck season!" "It's rabbit season!" "It's duck season!" "It's rabbit season!"

And then Bugs will throw in the quick switch—"It's rabbit season!"—and poor Daffy won't notice, and he'll just automatically blurt out, "It's duck season!" and Bugs will smile and say, "Okay, have it your way. It's duck season," as Elmer Fudd swivels his shotgun toward the hapless duck. And blows his beak off.

That's the game liberals like to play.

They drop the "illegal" part from "illegal immigration" because they don't see a difference between the two, and they don't want us to, either. To liberals, there's no difference between someone who came to this country legally and followed the rules and someone who snuck in, and who remains here in violation of the law. And when they debate the issue, they always want to blur the distinction.

I guess there's no difference between robbing a bank and using the ATM, either.

In both cases, you're just taking money out of the bank.

But most Americans know there's a difference. And the group who *really* knows are the immigrants themselves—people from Europe and India and China and all over the globe, who waited in line, filled out the forms, and obeyed the law, and who are now lumped together, by liberals, with folks who didn't.

And the millions still waiting in line. Waiting for one of those open spaces that the illegal immigrants keep taking.

That doesn't bother liberals, though. Because liberals hate immigrants almost as much as they hate rules.

Let's set the record straight: immigrants—legal ones, that is—are

America's greatest renewable resource. From the very first days of our country, people have come to our shores because they wanted what America promised: freedom and opportunity.

Nobody took a tiny berth in steerage and crossed an ocean because they heard that in America, the government gives you stuff. Or that there's a special loan program for people of a certain race or ethnic background.

The immigrants who came here legally—and not just long ago, but recent ones, too—didn't come here to *change* America.

They love America the way it is.

They came because the idea of America—a place that rewards hard work, that encourages entrepreneurs, that places family and freedom and God higher than anything else—is powerful and attractive, and worth sacrificing for.

From all over Europe, people came to America to become Americans.

Scandinavians came, settled in the Midwest, and turned it into the nation's food basket. Irish immigrants came to escape famine and civil strife. European Jews did the same. And when they arrived, penniless but full of hope, they opened up businesses and raised families and contributed to the great American experiment.

It still works that way.

When hundreds of thousands of Vietnamese refugees fled their homeland after its violent takeover by communist dictators, they ended up here. It didn't take long for them to start businesses, and work hard in places like the Gulf Coast doing the work they did back home—like shrimping and fishing.

If you ever get the chance to hang around the fishing docks of Biloxi and Mobile, you'll see and hear one of the most perfectly American things you'll ever encounter: second-generation Vietnamese shrimp fishermen speaking in thick Mississippi accents.

If you can hear and see that and not have your heart filled with pride that the American idea is alive and well, then you're almost certainly a liberal.

Liberals hate immigrants because they don't come for handouts, or to march in protests, or to get us to change our national language. They come to assimilate and fit in.

They come to work hard, and get ahead.

In short, they come to *be* Americans, and to raise American children.

No one is more patriotic than an immigrant, which is why the immigration process is such an important one to protect.

Liberals don't see it that way, of course. Liberals are always looking for the next big group of "victims" to "help." So for them, illegal immigrants are the perfect category. Since most illegal immigrants are from Spanish-speaking countries, liberals want to make Spanish the semiofficial second language of America. They want schools to teach in Spanish and government offices to offer bilingual services. They want to offer easy citizenship to illegal immigrants, irrespective of the way they got here.

In other words, they don't want illegal immigrants to change into Americans. On the contrary, liberals want to use them to change *America*.

It's all a transaction for liberals. They make illegal legal, and that gives liberals the votes they need to enact their dumb policies.

"Give us your vote, and we'll change America," is the deal.

Since there are somewhere between ten and fifteen million illegal immigrants in this country, that represents a lot of votes. Which is why liberals will do anything to win them over.

But what about the rest of us? And, especially, what about the recent *legal* immigrants from Asia, India, and Eastern Europe, who sacrificed everything to come here? They're struggling to build businesses and raise families—some are driving cabs at night; some are taking extra classes; all of them are adding to the American prosperity machine—and they've done it all according to the rules. They have family back in the old country who would like to come, too. But they're in line like everyone else.

Liberals don't care about them. Liberals don't care about people who come to this country to work and raise families. Those people aren't going to vote for a lot of nutty liberal ideas. Liberals only care about *illegal* immigrants, because only that group is available to be cherry-picked in a political power grab.

And that's why liberals hate (legal) immigrants.

There is something else going on, too, besides politics. I think liberals actually feel sorry for the Vietnamese who shrimp on the Gulf Coast. They hate that they feel the need to assimilate. To sound like and dress like their new Mississippi neighbors.

Who are we to impose that kind of cultural pressure on these new—and poor—visitors, anyway? Better to send them to that ESL class, make sure we have a Vietnamese studies program lined up at the local college, and then have them study all the reasons why the country they just moved to stinks.

Liberals also hate the legal immigration process itself. Immigrants are actually compelled to go through a certain process to become Americans. We make them memorize those silly facts about American history (the ones our own kids don't know), and we actually give them a test. And if they pass that test, we make them take an oath.

Oh, the horror!

Here is that oath:

I hereby declare, on oath, that I absolutely and entirely renounce and abjure all allegiance and fidelity to any foreign prince, potentate, state or sovereignty, of whom or which I have heretofore been a sub-ject or citizen; that I will support and defend the Constitution and laws of the United States of America against all enemies, foreign and domestic; that I will bear true faith and allegiance to the same; that

I will bear arms on behalf of the United States when required by the
law; that I will perform noncombatant service in the armed forces
of the United States when required by the law; that I will perform
work of national importance under civilian direction when required
by the law; and that I take this obligation freely without any mental
reservation or purpose of evasion; so help me God.

No wonder liberals hate legal immigration.

Every year on the day of Frank Capra's birth, I try and play a
soundbite on my radio show from a speech he gave at the American
Film Institute in 1982 after he received their Life Achievement Award.
Capra was a first-generation Italian immigrant who gave us such clas-
sic movies as *It Happened One Night, You Can't Take It With You, Mr.
Smith Goes to Washington,* and *It's a Wonderful Life.*

It was a wonderful life indeed.

But none of those movies was his favorite. You see, during World
War II, Capra was asked to make a series of documentaries to help the
morale of our soldiers, and was assigned to work directly for Chief of
Staff George C. Marshall.

Marshall gave Capra these marching orders:

Now, Capra, I want to nail down with you a plan to make a series of
documented, factual-information films—the first in our history—
that will explain to our boys in the Army *why* we are fighting, and
the *principles* for which we are fighting. . . . You have an opportunity
to contribute enormously to your country and the cause of freedom.
Are you aware of that, sir?

Capra didn't need to hear any more.

He spent the next few years making the seven-episode masterpiece
Why We Fight. The films were so good that Winston Churchill ordered
them shown to the British people in public theaters.

Of all of the awards Capra won, the two he was most proud of were: (1) the Oscar for his work on that series and (2) his Distinguished Service Medal from General Marshall himself.

In that 1982 AFI speech, Capra talked about America, and the journey that brought him here. With vivid detail he recalled the ship that left Italy "crammed with praying immigrants." He told the story of his dad dragging him to the deck when that ship finally hit the Port of New York, pointing to a glow from a torch that lit up the sky.

"That's the greatest light since the Star of Bethlehem," his father cried out.

"I looked up," recalled Capra, "and there was the statue of a great lady, taller than a church steeple, holding a lamp over the land we were about to enter, and my father said to me, 'it's the light of freedom, Chico, freedom. Remember that. Freedom.'"

As the camera panned the audience, you could see Bette Davis and Bob Hope holding back the tears.

Capra described the journey his family took west, to Los Angeles, and how his parents kissed the ground when they arrived at the Southern Pacific Station.

Capra closed things by holding up the AFI Award toward the sky.

"But for America, just for living here, I kiss the ground."

I don't think we're in any danger of witnessing a typical liberal offer to kiss the ground of America any time soon.

19 Workers

I know what you're thinking; this must be a mistake. Liberals love workers. At least that's what they've been screaming from the rafters ever since FDR's New Deal, and ever since Woody Guthrie picked up a guitar and started writing really irritating songs.

But they don't, and I can prove it.

A CEO of a large company once told me that he could always tell who he'd like to hire or do business with by watching how they treated their employees. The guy who's disrespectful to his secretary or assistant is a guy obsessed with rank, he told me. He's a guy who doesn't see the dignity in any kind of honest work.

In other words, he's a liberal.

Liberals *hate* the help. Liberals *hate* the working man.

Although I'll give them a lot of credit: They sure do talk a good game. But if you want to know what liberals really think about the working person, you have two choices. You can listen to what they *say* or you can watch what they *do*.

And what they do is a whole lot more revealing.

If you want to understand elephants, you've got to go where the elephants are. If you want to understand pigs, you've got to head over to the sty.

So if you want to understand liberals, you've got to go to Hollywood. And when you get there, you'll learn some fascinating things about how liberals treat the help.

It isn't pretty.

In Hollywood, personal assistants are expected to tend to the most personal aspects of their bosses' lives, work around the clock, keep all the important secrets, and be grateful for a tiny salary. The liberal movie stars and Hollywood moguls who employ them aren't known for their generosity or their easygoing behavior.

A friend of mine who works in Hollywood told me the story of the personal assistant of a major Hollywood actor. Apparently, while driving his boss to a Democratic party fundraiser, he (foolishly, it turns out) mentioned that since his boss was going to be introducing President Obama with a speech extolling the virtues of his health-care proposal, perhaps now would be a good time for the movie star to extend health-care coverage to his employee.

He was fired the next day.

In other words, *do as I say, not as I do.*

For liberals, talking about the "issues" of the working man or woman, showing up to fundraisers for liberal politicians, talking loudly about the "rights" of workers—all of these are perfect substitutes for actually treating your employees with dignity and fairness.

Liberal political appointees are always "forgetting" to pay the Social Security taxes on their nannies and domestic help.

Arianna Huffington, the once conservative but now far-left pro-prietor of the Internet news site Huffington Post, built her business on the free labor of contributors. They did the work, they produced the content, but when she sold the company to AOL for more than $300 million, did she share the wealth? Did she redistribute the spoils of her corporate windfall?

Are you *kidding*? Of course not! She's a liberal. Liberals talk about fairness. They don't actually *act* fair.

This behavior is found in almost every realm. Liberals want to raise taxes on ordinary Americans, but they don't want to *pay* any taxes.

The Obama administration makes continual arguments about the need to raise taxes on the wealthy, about the inequities inherent in the American system. And yet, forty-one White House employees owe back taxes to the government, almost to the tune of nine hundred thousand dollars!

Billionaire investor Warren Buffett, another Obama partisan who loudly advocates raising taxes on the wealthy, is a tax-avoider of mas-sive proportion. His company, Berkshire Hathaway, owes nearly one *billion* dollars in unpaid taxes to the IRS.

Do as I say, not as I do.

In Hollywood, in Washington, D.C., in liberal enclaves all over the country, liberals operate under very different—and more lenient—standards of behavior than they'd allow the rest of us to operate under.

Consider, if you're not eating, documentary filmmaker Michael Moore.

Moore's first major film, *Roger & Me,* was a passionate indictment of Roger Smith, then CEO of General Motors, who Moore claimed was insensitive to the plight of GM's workforce and insufficiently sym-pathetic to the demands of the auto workers union.

Moore is a *very* liberal guy. Each one of his subsequent films—and his short-lived TV show, *TV Nation*—has advocated a very left-wing, very prolabor line. So you'd imagine that his movie crews and his television production used only union labor, right? His writers must have been members of the Writers' Guild, and his crewmembers were surely members of the filmmakers' craft guild, the International Alliance of Theatrical Stage Employees, right?

You're way ahead of me, aren't you?

Of course they weren't! He wasn't going to live up to his own rhetoric, was he? That would have cost him *money,* just as it would have cost Arianna Huffington to pay her writers, or Hollywood stars to offer health care to their employees.

These are liberals! They'd rather talk about fairness, and equity, and the dignity of the American worker than pay a fair wage, live up to their principles, and treat their employees with respect.

And while we're at it, let's talk about Detroit, Michigan. And all of those great union jobs that Moore celebrated in *Roger & Me.* Or more accurately, the end to all of those great union jobs that Moore celebrated in that documentary.

Because that's what Moore's film really did; it celebrated the layoffs of thousands of GM workers. Without those layoffs, Moore didn't have a movie. And he didn't have a movie because he would not have had a fake villain.

It turns out that Michael Moore's film was chasing around the wrong bad guy. Instead of stalking ex–GM CEO Roger Smith for days on end, he should have followed the president of the United Auto Workers' Union—and asked him some hard questions about why those plants were really closing. Presented the union boss with some hard facts.

- Did you know that Detroit was once the fourth-biggest city in America (1950), and once touted the highest per capita income in America, too (1960)?
- Did you know that since 1960, Detroit's population has gone from a high of 1.8 million to its current 714,000—the lowest it's been since 1910?

Then ask the union bosses why they continued to make more and more unreasonable demands on management until finally, finally, they managed to chase most of the jobs that used to be in Detroit to other states. Right-to-work states. States like Texas. Alabama. Tennessee. And Mississippi.

THAT would have been a good movie. A GREAT movie.

Liberals hate facts, but here are some more facts that will drive them crazy.

You may have seen the headline back in March 2011. Almost every major paper in America had one like this. This was from the *New York Times:* "Detroit Census Confirms a Desertion Like No Other."

And here was the opening of that story: "Laying bare the country's most startling example of modern urban collapse, census data on Tuesday showed that Detroit's population had plunged by 25 percent over the last decade. It was dramatic testimony to the crumbling industrial base of the Midwest."

The paper whose motto is "All the News That's Fit to Print" didn't bother to get into the real reasons for this collapse, especially the labor and industrial policies of a once-great state. But the writer, Katherine Seelye, did note that it was the largest loss of any American city in the past decade.

Bigger than New Orleans. Katrina drove 140,000 people out of town.

The union bosses drove 237,500 out of Detroit. No act of God necessary. It was acts of man—politicians and union bosses, primarily—that gave us modern, emptying, decaying Detroit.

That's the story Michael Moore should have told, but never will. It is the story of what happened to all of those jobs. And all of those people.

According to Michael Barone, and the Brookings Institution, there has been a remarkable internal migration happening in this country over the past few decades. Record numbers of Americans packed their belongings and headed South. Headed to states that are inhabited by folks who generally don't appreciate labor unions.

States that also just happen to love their Bibles. And their guns.

And we know how much liberals hate states like that. (See #37, The South.) According to the latest Census Bureau figures, the South was the fastest-growing region in America, up 14 percent over the past ten years. And black people are leading the charge.

The nation's African-American population grew by roughly 1.7 million over the last decade—and nearly 75 percent of that growth occurred in the South, according to William H. Frey, a demographer at the Brookings Institution.

What a story! That would make a heck of a documentary, tracking down some of those African Americans who've fled Detroit, fled the wretched schools, the crime, the chaos, the broken promises and corruption—and headed South.

Don't hold your breath waiting for PBS to make *that* documentary.

But how about just one more set of pesky, irritating facts for our liberal friends? In 1970, Texas had 11 million people. In 2010, it had 25 million. In 1970, Detroit was the nation's fifth-largest metro area. Today, metro Houston and the Dallas–Fort Worth metroplex are both pressing the San Francisco Bay area for the number-four spot, and Detroit is far behind. Far, far behind.

Why the boom in Texas, and the bust in Michigan? Some 37 percent of all net new American jobs have been created in Texas since 2007, according to a recent Dallas Federal Reserve report. The study is a lesson in what works in economic policy—and you'd think liberals would be crawling all over it, along with union bosses, to figure out why.

It turns out—and hold on to your cowboy hat, because this will shock you—businessmen actually like starting businesses in states where the politicians don't see them as the enemy. Where workers don't see them as the enemy.

In 1990, one of the world's biggest companies, Exxon Mobil, left New York City for Dallas. In a recent *Wall Street Journal* article, Exxon's former CEO, Lee Raymond, attributed his company's move in part to New York State's notoriously overbearing tax authority. But it was also about working amid a culture of competence. "It's just the attitude in Texas of getting things done and doing them well," he says.

Does anyone think of unions when they think of the words "culture of competence?"

Okay. That was big bad Exxon. But what about smaller businesses? The *Journal* tracked down Ed Trevis, a California-educated Brazilian immigrant and tech entrepreneur in Silicon Valley for twenty-five years. Mr. Trevis moved his company to Texas because, as he put it, "in California, you are always doing something wrong."

Then there was David Booth, who moved his financial firm from California to Texas. "It's just that they [the people in Texas] believe in the whole Horatio Alger myth down here," he told Dan Henninger. "It's hard to understand if you haven't lived here."

Does anyone think of unions when they think of Horatio Alger?

That's why people are moving. Because businesses are moving. Moving from heavily unionized states with serious public employee unions, and heading to less hostile grounds. They are following the work. They are following the jobs. They are chasing economic opportunity. As Americans have been doing for generations.

Americans actually like to work. We like to put in a good day's effort for a good day's pay. And we want to be held accountable for our work. And reap the rewards of our efforts.

Unions work quite differently. They want more for themselves without actually doing more. Indeed, it is in their interest to do less, so management is compelled to hire more workers. Which means more union members. And more union power.

Union bosses don't want people held accountable for their work. They want to shroud the workplace with rights of all kind. Protections of all kind. Rights for everyone but the guys who own the place. The guys who run it.

And once you join a union, once a plant has been unionized, good luck leaving that union. It's about as tough as leaving the Mafia. It turns out that fewer than 10 percent of currently unionized employees voted for the union in their workplace. The average union was established in 1976, according to data from the Department of Labor's Office of Labor-Management Standards.

Almost all of today's union workers didn't actually choose to be union members. The jobs they have came with a precondition; you either take the job—and union membership—or you don't have a job. And they make it almost impossible for workers to decertify their workplaces.

So much for caring about workers' rights!

And then there's that whole issue of how union bosses use member dues to advance their own political agenda. Exit polls from 2010 demonstrate that 42 percent of union households voted for Republican candidates, yet more than 93 percent of union political support went to Democratic candidates. To liberals.

So much for the whole notion of the benevolent unions.

Unions hate workers, or they wouldn't compel them to give money to politicians they deplore. Unions hate workers, or they would give them an option to decertify the places at which they work.

But if you really want to understand just how much union bosses hate workers, and care about nothing but their own power, look no further than the epicenter of unionism. The Ground Zero of unionism.

Talk to them about Detroit.

18 Teachers

Who's in charge here?

This is another one of those chapters that's really tricky. Because liberals spend a whole lot of time trying to convince us they love teachers. But dig even skin deep into the matter and it becomes evident that liberals hate teachers.

To understand just how much they hate teachers, consider the circumstances of their workplace. And compare it with yours and mine.

Think, for a minute, about what it might take for you to be fired from your job.

I know, I know. It's an unpleasant thought. With millions of Americans out of work, why bring it up?

Still: What would it take? Think about all of the things you could do at your place of work that would get you bounced out of there in a hurry—drunkenness, violence, acts of abuse, theft, or maybe just being really *really* bad at your job.

And that's a good thing, because that louse working alongside you is gumming up everything for everybody.

Now imagine, for a moment, that you're a public school teacher and a member of one of the powerful teachers' unions. Go through that list again. What would it take to get fired from *that* job?

Well, for starters, none of the above.

Public school teachers enjoy a huge amount of job security, thanks to their powerful unions and inflexible work rules. In New York City, for instance, bad teachers aren't fired—and *bad* here means not just bad at the job, but *bad* in other ways, too, like physical and sexual abuse. We're talking terrible. No, when school officials want to get a teacher out of the classroom, they have to go through an arduous multiyear process, involving hearings and appeals and lawyers and more hearings. All the while, the teacher draws full pay.

It's easier, in most cases, just to look the other way. In Southern California recently, a teacher who was literally *under arrest* for sexually abusing his students was *still* drawing his full salary.

All of these "protections" were put into place to provide public school teachers with the kind of job security and cushy work rules that United Auto Workers have enjoyed.

Which is why the American education system looks a lot like Chrysler and GM: out of touch and dependent on government bailouts.

Liberals don't care about that, of course. They're not interested in education. They're interested in the education *system*. And there's a big difference.

Education means teaching kids how to do stuff, and how to think about stuff. Education is a pretty simple concept with a very clear way to measure results: You give some kind of an exam—maybe it's one of those standardized tests all kids hate, maybe it's some kind of essay. But whatever it is, it'll measure the results and the kids will hate it. And then you look at what works and do more of that, notice the teachers who are getting great results and give them raises (and hire more just like them) and—pow!—education is achieved.

That's not how liberals think. Liberals want to figure out a system that will diminish the importance of real results—like, say, evidence that a kid is learning anything—and replace such evidence with a lot of stupid, liberal criteria, like a teacher's seniority (Who cares? Can they teach?) and a student's race (Who cares? Can he spell?) and a multicultural, child-empowering curriculum (Who cares? Can they do simple math?).

You can't improve what you can't measure, and liberals have resisted any kind of meaningful measurement of success in the classroom for decades. Instead of focusing on the three Rs, liberals have thrown up a barrage of silly things designed to distract us all from their awful stewardship of the schools.

School systems now routinely have more administrators than classroom teachers. They have armies of counselors and therapists and nutritionists and "multicultural learning facilitators." Schools insist that *everything* is under their purview—what your kids eat, what they believe, what they say on the playground. Because as long as the school system is doing *everything,* maybe you won't notice that little Johnny can't read. And that little Sally can't make change for a dollar.

But despite all of the noise about "honoring" teachers and "supporting" education and it being "all for the children," liberals—by their *actions*—reveal a very different truth.

A case in point: In August 2010, the *Los Angeles Times* got its hands on internal data the L.A. Unified School District had been assembling for seven years, tracking performance of their kids in math and English. The *Times* crunched those numbers to figure out which teachers were effective, and which weren't—something the Los Angeles School district *could* do, but didn't.

The *Times* focused on Broadous Elementary School, in one of the poorest neighborhoods in the San Fernando Valley, populated with hard-working Latino parents, most of whom never finished high school.

What did the study reveal? Well, for openers, that teachers matter. Highly effective teachers propelled student performance in less than a single year. The *Times* report noted that "there was a substantial gap at year's end between students whose teachers ranked in the top 10% in effectiveness and the bottom 10%."

It took a study to find that out?

Then the story went from the general to the very specific; we met two teachers from the same school, with the same kids, teaching the same subject, practically down the hall from each other.

One was Miguel Aguilar, a stocky thirty-three-year-old who grew up in the area. When the *Times* reporters showed up in his class—Room 26—they saw students on the edge of their seats and engaged in . . . a math problem!

It turns out Miguel doles out praise sparingly in his class—no gold stars for wrong answers—and he expects a lot from his kids. He expects results.

And the data revealed that Aguilar delivers. On average, students under his instruction *gained* thirty-four percentile points in math relative to their peers. Those gains, which he turned out each and every year, made him one of the most effective teachers in the school.

The *Times* then turned to Room 25—Joe Smith's classroom. He was teaching the same aged kids from the very same neighborhood the same subject.

Everything was the same but the talent and expectations of the teacher.

And the results.

On average, students under Smith's instruction lost—*lost*—fourteen percentile points in math during a school year relative to his peers in the district. Overall, he ranked as the least effective of the district's teachers.

Told of the *Times* findings, Smith, sixty-three at the time, expressed mild surprise.

"Obviously, what I need to do is to look at what I'm doing and take some steps to make sure something changes," he told a *Times* reporter.

Change? How about this for a change: *You're fired,* to quote The Donald.

What was the local union leadership's reaction to the *Times* exposé? The leader of the forty-thousand-plus-strong union called for a boycott of the paper.

Like I said, liberals *hate* teachers.

Why else would they pay Joe Smith and Miguel Aguilar the same? Why else would you pay the great teacher who drives student performance the same as the terrible teacher who couldn't care less about the kids and their performance? Why else would you set up a system where merit is not rewarded, and where mediocrity is not punished?

How on earth can that be seen as *respect for teachers,* setting up a system like that?

How in the world can that be called *support,* when bad teachers and good teachers are all lumped together, tainting the good ones by association, and sapping them of their zeal to teach?

I mean, think a minute about *your* job.

How hard would you work if you knew that almost nothing you could do could get you fired, and you knew that nothing anyone else did around you could get them fired?

How hard would you work if you had *tenure?*

And all of your coworkers had tenure, too?

The fact is, that isn't a world most Americans live in. Most of us actually fear the words "you're fired." Most of us actually want to impress our bosses, and are grateful to have bosses.

Most of us actually want to take care of our customers, and do a good job for our customers, because if we don't, our customers will soon become our competitor's customers.

And we won't have jobs.

All of which makes us much better employees. All of which would make teachers better teachers. Schools better schools. Students better students.

And all of which will *never* happen.

Because the teachers' unions will never let it.

Which is why liberals hate teachers.

And by proxy, of course, liberals hate students. (That itself could have been another chapter!)

Liberals hate teachers, and they don't much care for students, but they *love* the school system.

That's because to liberals and their vassals of power—the unions—teachers have two big functions: as a money source, with their union dues delivering cash and manpower to liberal candidates for office, and as foot soldiers in the liberal takeover of the mind of the American student.

17 Doctors and Patients

Who stole my health care?

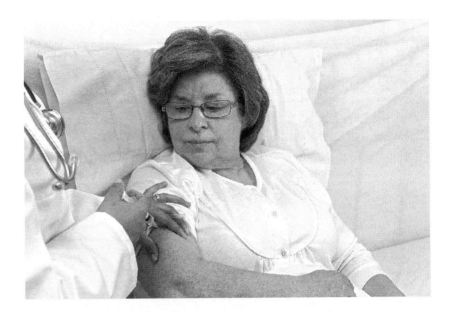

The best doctor's visit, I think we can all agree, is the shortest.

You don't really want to be hanging around a doctor's office, right? You want to be in and out—give some blood, fill up the small cup, undergo a minimum of jabs and probes, and you're on your way.

What you *don't* want to have happen is for the doctor to come into the examination room with a pile of test results, pull up that rolling chair, give you a sympathetic look, and say something like, "So, um, here's what we found . . ."

And then he might add, "But first, let me introduce you to the local deputy commissioner of the Health Care Expenditure Panel for this sector. He'll be able to answer any questions you may have about

214

the range of procedures I'm not allowed to perform and options that you don't have.

"And now if you'll excuse me, I'm due in court."

For most of us, that sounds like an absurd little scenario.

For liberals, that sounds *exactly* like the Patient Protection and Affordable Care Act of 2010—more popularly called "Obamacare"—and it's not absurd in the least. On the contrary, it's *coming soon* to a doctor's office near you. And liberals are positively giddy about it.

They should be. Obamacare is the culmination of decades of hard, relentless work by liberals to make sure that you and your doctor are never allowed an unsupervised moment.

Liberals hate doctors for many reasons, none of which make patients feel any better.

In the first place, doctors are know-it-alls. They've gone to medical school, passed exams, and demonstrated a mastery of the complicated insides of the average human.

Liberals hate that.

Liberals are always trying to figure out where the wiggle room is in any system. To a liberal, it's unfair that a person with demonstrable skills and a record of achievement should be given greater respect than someone without any of those things. And greater pay.

To a liberal, what matters is how much you (or your ancestors) have been oppressed. The qualifications that liberals really believe in, for any job, are: First, you must not be white, male, or Christian; second, it really helps if you've got two mommies. Or *are* two mommies.

So liberals are predisposed to hate doctors.

But it goes deeper.

Liberals think it's unfair that doctors are respected in society, thanks to their concrete skills. But they also think the whole idea of health and wellness is unfair, too. Liberals are obsessed with "fairness." When they notice unequal outcomes in *any* arena, look out. There's nothing so dangerous as a liberal out to make something more "fair."

That some people get sick and die, and some people get sick and are cured, is a fact of life that drives liberals into a rage.

To them, the only explanation for this bizarre set of outcomes is that someone must have made a mistake. The doctor must be responsible. When something bad happens to a liberal, his first question is, *Whom can I sue?*

That's why doctors are sandbagged under malpractice suits and hampered by terrified hospital administrators. Ask any doctor what his biggest challenge is, and he won't say "disease" or "cancer," he'll say "regulations" and "paperwork."

But that's the first thing liberals do when they want to get control of something. First, they bury it in regulations and forms. Then, they swarm it with something big and greasy and awful like the Patient Protection and Affordable Care Act of 2010.

The goal of every aspect of liberalism is to make everything the same. To even out the score. That's the idea behind their confiscatory tax code (*Hey! You've got more money than I do! Gimme!*) and their obsession with affirmative action (*Hey! You're the wrong race! Get to the back of the line!*) and now they're turning their sights on what happens between a doctor and his patient.

Hey! the liberals say. *Why are you getting cured faster? Why are you getting better care?*

So the liberal solution is to hobble us with a nationalized health-care system. Because the only way to make sure everyone gets exactly the same kind of treatment, with the same kind of odds, is to make *all* treatment and *all* health care mediocre.

The dirty not-so-secret behind Obamacare is, once it's fully implemented, there won't be any private insurers left. There won't be anyone else in the health-care business. It'll just be you, your doctor, and the National Health Care Administration representative, standing there with a rubber glove, ready to make sure you're not getting any health-ier, any faster, than anyone else.

Doctors, naturally, despise this. They hate the complicated Medi-care billing system, with its thousands of pages of price codes and pro-cedure allowances.

They hate the slow strangulation of what was once a noble—and, yes, lucrative—profession.

They know that it didn't used to be like this.

Doctors—before runaway malpractice lawsuits, before the liberals in government stepped in to "fix" the health-care system—managed to treat most folks pretty well. The ones who could afford it, paid up.

The ones who couldn't relied on the churches and charitable orga-nizations to set up hospitals, offer services, and take care of the needy. Which they did.

Liberals hate doctors because they know that the doctors are wise to this ruse, which is why a lot of doctors are opting out of Medicare altogether. It's too complicated. Too rule-bound.

And besides, the patients are complaining. But that doesn't bother liberals.

Because they hate patients, too.

The entire two-thousand-plus-page text of the behemoth called the Patient Protection and Affordable Care Act of 2010 can be summed up in three words:

Patients are screwed.

That's right: utterly, totally screwed.

Obamacare, despite the walloping lies told during its passage, is *designed* to remove your health-care choices. Liberals don't want you choosing your doctor—you might choose the wrong one!—or decid-ing which procedures you want and which you don't.

Liberals want to decide these things for you.

Actually, liberals *insist* on deciding these things for you, because if they don't, you might figure out how to get better health care than someone else.

Like, maybe, if *you* pay for it.

Liberals hate it when you pay for something, because then you act like a *customer* instead of the grateful recipient of liberal generosity.

And it offends their sensitivities to fairness and equality.

That's why all two-thousand-plus pages of the Patient Protection and Affordable Care Act of 2010 are vaguely worded outlines of what *future* regulations—written by liberals, enforced by liberals, informed by the liberal desire to make us all equally sick and poor—will be necessary to "implement" the law.

The Patient Protection and Affordable Care Act of 2010 isn't a law. It's a blank check, written against the earnings of every taxpayer, and every *future* taxpayer in America, toward the destruction of one of the most dynamic and advanced health-care systems in the world.

We'll all be lucky, when Obamacare is fully operational, if our system works about as well as the Canadian system, where patients wait for months for critical care, and procedures are routinely denied by local, unqualified, bureaucrats, all in the name of "fairness" and "equality."

In the not-too-distant future, American doctors and patients will barely be allowed to communicate, smothered and censored by a federal health-care bureaucracy. You'll have a closer and more meaningful relationship with the cranky lady at the post office.

Come to think of it, it'll be hard to tell the difference between the post office and the local hospital.

But liberals will march on.

If you don't feel sick now, wait until the government tries to cure you.

One of the big reasons liberals gave for passing Obamacare was that they were going to bend the cost curve.

Free market folks always find it amusing when the government shows up to save us from the rising costs of, say, anything.

Let's take education and health care, two areas where the federal government's Sasquatchlike footprint touches us most. The more they get involved, the higher prices skyrocket. Which prompts calls for more state intervention to help with those higher prices.

In the midst of one of our worst recessions, college tuition in America the past four years has risen almost 25 percent. With those kinds of increases, who needs help?

Then there is health insurance, which is what the Obamacare fight is really all about. Rather than learn from the way we insure cars, Obama instead applied the pedal to the metal on government intrusion.

When it comes to insuring our cars, insurance seems to work pretty efficiently, without much help from anyone. We get lots of choices, and pay for it out of our own pockets. We don't insure every small visit to the mechanic, or wear and tear on tires or transmissions—or our insurance prices would be through the roof.

So we instead insure against certain calamities, and pay for everything else out of pocket.

And because we pay for things out of our own pockets, we take much better care of our cars. We change our oil regularly, change the filters, the belts, the fluids and the brakes with diligence—lest we run the risk of even greater costs.

Costs we don't share with others via insurance. Costs we don't spread through third-party insurers like our employers. Or government-run car insurance.

Which is you and me!

Imagine if we ran our health-insurance choices like we handle our car insurance?

People would have incentives to eat healthier. To act healthier. To exercise more, and smoke less, and eat less. Imagine the savings to all of us if we just had more people pulling their own weight on the health-care front?

The markets simply can't exert their mighty magic the way we run health insurance. Which is crazy.

We get it right with cars, but can't seem to get it right with our bodies!

The private practice auto mechanics flourish.

While the private practice doctors flounder.

And the patients suffer.

The liberal answer to this paradox is more—much more—of the same old government medicine. And there aren't enough spoonfuls of sugar in the world to help this bad medicine go down.

16 Science

Who needs God? We have Al Gore!

Liberals say they love science, just as they say they love many things they actually hate. And in no single arena is the liberal hatred of science more evident than with the "environmental sciences."

You never hear liberals pining about quantum physics or astrophysics.

Or Einstein's theory of relativity. You know, the real kinds of science.

The only science you ever hear them extolling is the science that advances their agenda—the science tied to global warming.

And why? Because liberals love—love—the environment.

This gets a little tricky, but to understand all of this, one need look no further than your average liberal car bumper. You always know when you're driving behind liberals because their bumper stickers give them away: "Love Your Mother Earth" and "I HEART Gaia" are typical. But so are things like "Yoga Heals" and "Visualize World Peace."

Liberals believe all sorts of odd and superstitious things. They're into alternative medicine, homeopathic remedies, chanting cures, and group meditation to resolve world conflicts.

Many liberals think that the earth has a spirit and that ancient astronauts built the Great Pyramid. But for some reason, they think *conservatives* are the ones who are against science.

But it's liberals who hate science. And it's never more obvious than when they talk about the environment.

The earth is dying. Maybe you've heard. Thanks to plastic bottles and the internal combustion engine—in other words, thanks to *progress*—the earth is either warming up too fast or cooling down too slowly.

It's hard for liberals to pinpoint what, exactly, the earth is doing, but they're absolutely sure it's doing something bad, all because we keep choosing "plastic" instead of "paper" at the supermarket checkout.

Or maybe it's "paper" instead of "plastic." It's so hard to keep track.

Actually, it doesn't matter to liberals. They're not concerned with the facts, or the science, behind the study of the earth's climate. They're interested in manipulating data to achieve their political desires. Like everything else about the liberal cause of the day, it's never about what they say it's about—the environment, the children—it's always about power. Power over you and me.

Liberals hate science because eventually, the truth comes out. You can only say the sun revolves around the earth for so long until someone notices it doesn't. And you can only sound the alarm bells about man-made global warming until someone notices it's not happening.

And it's not, by the way. When a batch of emails sent among the "scientists" working on the Intergovernmental Panel on Climate Change was leaked to the media, what was revealed was a bunch of researchers who manipulated their own data, cherry-picked certain results, and squashed all dissenting views in order to "prove" their central thesis: that the earth is getting warmer with alarming speed.

Doesn't sound very scientific, does it?

And then again, in November 2011, *another* batch of emails was leaked, these between some of the scientists on the panel, trying to come up with ways to discredit climate change skeptics. Not with facts or scientific evidence, but muckraking attempts to tie skeptics to big oil, or big business.

So it's not science that concerns these scientists. It's political activism. How else could you explain the astonishing list of myths the eco-nuts have been peddling, especially when they're all so easily debunked by—you guessed it!—science.

Here's one example:

For as long as lefties have been wailing about global warming, they've been exercised over the melting of the Himalayan glaciers. IPCC "scientists" have made hysterical—hysterical as in hysterical-crazy, not hysterical-funny—claims about the melting of those glaciers. They predicted water shortages and droughts and dried-up river beds. They extrapolated from that millions of deaths, misery, and tragedy on a biblical scale.

Only one snag: The Himalayan glaciers *aren't* melting.

They're still frozen solid, up there in the Himalayas. Still blocks of slippery ice. If you go there to visit them, you'll still have to pack your mittens.

And what was the response from the IPCC "scientists" when it was incontrovertibly proven—using science, irritating and inconvenient science—to demonstrate?

They attacked the research, they attacked the findings, they attacked anyone and everyone who refused to believe the myth—that the Himalayan glaciers were melting quickly and would be gone in thirty years—and who instead believed the *scientific* evidence that the glaciers aren't melting, and are, in fact, *growing.*

There are dozens of examples of this kind of environmental freak-out.

When Al Gore famously predicted that the seas were rising, it only took another two years for him to be proven wrong. Did he then go back and correct the record?

You know the answer.

And yet liberals are always saying that conservatives don't trust science, when it's the liberals who will lie and distort and manipulate science to achieve their own ends.

It's liberals, especially in the media, who keep shoving this junked-up nonscience at us.

A few years ago, my producers called me early one morning. Usually, when I get a call like that, we have satellite issues, or the studio is down, or there is some other crisis to tackle before going on the air.

But they had good news. They were brimming with excitement over some sound bites they had unearthed from an interview Charlie Rose had with Michael Crichton.

Crichton, who recently died, just happened to know a thing or two about science and the culture at large. His science fiction, medical fiction, and thrillers—*Jurassic Park, The Andromeda Strain, Sphere, Disclosure, Timeline,* and countless others—sold over 200 million copies. In 1994, Crichton became the only writer ever to have works simultaneously charting at number one in television, film, and book sales (*ER, Jurassic Park,* and *Disclosure*).

But here's what most people don't know about Crichton. He was a Harvard Medical School graduate and a postdoctoral fellow at the Jonas Salk Institute for Biological Studies in La Jolla, California.

He did most of his own research for his books, and when he

started poking around the biggest scientific controversy of his day, global warming, he didn't like what he found.

After some analysis, Crichton was convinced the global warming crisis was overblown. He also believed that the politics of global warming was affecting the science. So he wrote a book called *State of Fear*.

It sent the global-warming crowd into a state of panic.

Crichton became their public enemy number one.

He might as well have announced plans to do hydraulic fracking in Central Park.

It was that bad.

All of which led to that interview around the big oak table in Charlie Rose's studios. And to that call from my producers. Here is a portion of that interview:

> CRICHTON: My conclusion is that we will have eight-tenths of a degree warming increase in the next hundred years, so I absolutely believe that warming is occurring, humans are involved, and it's going to continue for the next hundred years.
>
> ROSE: So what did you say that got everybody upset at you?
>
> CRICHTON: I'm not a catastrophist. And I said one other thing, too. I said I think it is not likely that carbon dioxide will prove to be the primary driver.
>
> ROSE: What do you think will be the primary driver?
>
> CRICHTON: The sun.

The sun! Oh, yeah, that faraway ball of flames that heats our planet.

Things got interesting when Crichton explained how politics can corrupt science.

> CRICHTON: You see these movements take over science. When I was young, every project, every grant proposal, had to be a cure for cancer,

because it was Lyndon Johnson's "War on Cancer," so there was no point. If you wanted to propose something, you had to find a way to say that this is going to cure cancer, true or not. . . .

ROSE: Rather than diabetes or . . .

CRICHTON: Right. You couldn't be doing just basic research.

Wow. That's the kind of nugget you'd think Rose would have run with. Politics corrupts science? But Rose moved back to global warming, and to the man behind the hysteria.

ROSE: Al Gore.

CRICHTON: I like him very much, but he's wrong on this issue.

ROSE: He's *wrong!*

It was as if Crichton had challenged some edict from the pope.

We isolated that clip on my show, and played it over and over and over again.

He's *wrong!*

Rose then calmed down and asked Crichton why Gore's arguments hold such currency. He gave a great answer.

CRICHTON: It's human beings. They line up for the catastrophe. They're ready for it. They're ready for overpopulation. They're ready for resource depletion. I know this. I've done this as a sort of test. Sit down at a dinner party and say, "The world is coming to an end, we have the most horrible things about to happen," and you get immediately the aroused attention of the table. Alternatively, you say, "You know what, basically, everything is good, the world is getting better . . ."

ROSE: Nobody cares.

CRICHTON: No. They get angry. Or they turn away. It's not what we want to hear. We want to hear disaster.

Which tells me Crichton went to dinner parties with lots of liberals. Then came the best soundbite of them all.

> ROSE: Did you have trepidation about doing this, because I think you're wrong, but I don't know, so therefore I can't prove it.
>
> CRICHTON: Yeah, I did.
>
> ROSE: Trepidation, like, "Why do I, Michael Crichton, need to go here? I mean, why not just keep my opinions to myself?"

He wanted to know why Crichton just didn't censor himself! Crichton's response was even more remarkable.

> CRICHTON: I had breakfast with a friend of mine and told him my dilemma, and he said, "No, no, you have to write it." And I said, "I'm going to get killed for this."
>
> And he said, "No, you have to write it." I'd like to say that as a result of that conversation, I decided to write it. I didn't. I went home and I thought, you know, I'm not writing this, it doesn't matter. As you said, keep my opinion to myself. I started working on something else, but I felt like a coward. And I thought, what are you going to do? You have looked at the data, and you really believe it is an effect, but that we as human beings should be worried about lots and lots of other things.

That's the power liberals possess to shut down scientific inquiry.

They throw their weight around with such mercilessness, they actually scared one of the richest writers in America to just, as Rose put it, "keep his thoughts to himself."

Forget the Godfather. It's those scientists you don't wanna cross!!

Indeed, the environmental Mafia have been doing whatever it takes to push a political agenda that has nothing to do with the environment, but everything to do with getting us to do as we're told.

And they're not about to give up.

Consider, for instance, the following headlines from national newspapers:

"GEOLOGISTS THINK THE WORLD MAY BE FROZEN UP AGAIN" –*New York Times*

"MOST GEOLOGISTS THINK THE WORLD IS GROWING WARMER, AND THAT IT WILL CONTINUE TO GET WARMER" –*Los Angeles Times*

"CLIMATOLOGICAL CASSANDRAS ARE BECOMING INCREASINGLY APPREHENSIVE, FOR THE WEATHER ABERRATIONS THEY ARE STUDYING MAY BE THE HARBINGER OF ANOTHER ICE AGE" –*Washington Post*

It's almost impossible to take them seriously.

By the way, the first headline above was from February 1895. The second one was from 1929. The last one was from 1974.

So we're getting colder and warmer and colder all the time.

The earth, according to liberals, is always on the precipice of environmental disaster. Our only hope is to use cheap toilet paper, ride our bike to work, take short, cold showers, and stop inventing new and cool stuff.

And yet, it's the new and cool stuff—better ways to extract oil from the ground, nuclear energy, more intelligent farming and lumber practices—that has made our environment safer and healthier than it's ever been. By every measure—every *scientific* measure—the air is less polluted, the water is cleaner, and the environment more sustainable that at any time in recent history.

Things are getting *better,* not worse, and we have science to thank for it.

Liberals hate that. They hate it when things get better. Things are supposed to get worse. That's the only way liberals will ever get control of things.

So when libs hear the good news about the Himalayan glaciers or the stabilizing sea levels or the improvements in air quality, they get absolutely bat crap crazy.

Science makes those things impossible to deny.

15 Algae

One of the greatest environmental tragedies of recent times was the BP oil spill in the Gulf of Mexico. Oil leaked into the pristine, crystal-clear waters of the Gulf at an incredible rate of over two million gallons *per day*, and the result was an environmental wasteland, a lifeless and desolate stretch of sludge and muck that extends the entire length of the coastline, from Louisiana to Florida.

The BP leak killed nearly all of the seabirds in the region, destroyed the delicate fisheries, rendered the beaches hazardous and unusable, and took a once-vibrant and bustling region of the South and turned it, almost overnight, into an empty ghost town.

Oh, wait a minute. That's not what happened at all.

That's what the environmental liberals *said* would happen, and what they imagined would occur, and thanks to the hysterical drama types in the media, that's what we all thought, as the oil cascaded into the Gulf.

That's what CNN's Anderson Cooper staked his entire show on. For week upon endless week, a breathless Cooper aired his nightly broadcast from New Orleans, and from the Gulf Coast.

And not because Cooper cares one bit about the people in that region. He only visits the region when there is something in it for Anderson Cooper, and only when the narrative comports with his vision of the world.

He loved the Katrina story, and parked his camera crew in New Orleans for what seemed like an eternity, all to excoriate the Bush administration, and support the Kanye West narrative: "George Bush doesn't care about black people."

Cooper decided to avoid taking his crew to the Mississippi coast, which actually caught the full force of Katrina, head-on. It was miles of destruction, as far as the eye could see. Casinos were wiped off their foundations, as were homes. It looked like the place had been bombed out.

But the state of Mississippi was ready for the disaster. Governor Haley Barbour was ready. Biloxi mayor A. J. Holloway was ready. And the people were ready. Almost immediately, Mississippi was taking care of business. Emergency crews were on the ground, private charities responded, and a competent government response offered a stark contrast to the goings-on in neighboring Louisiana.

What you didn't see in Mississippi were masses of people out on the street holding signs. Or blaming George Bush for their very bad luck.

Those people in Mississippi, many of whom were poor, too, were hit as hard as, if not harder than, the people in New Orleans, but they had family, church, local government, and state government taking care of business.

But *that* story didn't much interest Anderson Cooper.

Those people who make their living on the rigs in the Gulf of Mexico, those people who fish the waters, the people who run the restaurants and hotels from Biloxi to the Florida Panhandle are not Anderson Cooper's kind of people.

He wouldn't be caught dead vacationing in Panama City or Gulf Shores if his life depended on it; he's a Martha's Vineyard, Southampton, South Beach kind of guy.

Actually, he's so white that being on any beach is actually a health risk. He doesn't tan, he streaks.

Can you imagine Cooper in swim trunks, tossing around a football with people who bleed Alabama Crimson Red? Or wear Clemson Tigers T-shirts? I can't.

But for weeks on end, there he was every night on the Gulf Coast, excoriating BP, and rooting for the oil to wash up on the shores and ruin the place.

That's right. Anderson Cooper was rooting for the oil.

Indeed, Cooper was so invested in a bad outcome for BP, and a good outcome for himself (a Peabody Award or possibly an Emmy!) that he was actually rooting against the home team; he was rooting against the people he pretended to care about.

Indeed, he was hoping against hope that the BP spill would be the worst ecological disaster in world history.

He was yearning for those oil-soaked spots on the beaches to spread and multiply. For those oil-soaked birds and fish to start washing up on shore, along with the toxic sludge.

When that story didn't pan out, he had to be disappointed. When the carnage didn't come, he must have been depressed.

Two years later, here's what we know, and *not* because Anderson Cooper did some extensive follow-up reporting: The Gulf Coast is vibrant and bustling. The beaches are clean and the water is clear. Families still vacation there, especially on the beautiful Barrier Islands off the Mississippi coast. The fish are back. The shellfish, too.

So, um, what happened, Anderson? Where was this enviro-apocalypse we were promised?

As it turns out, crude oil leaks into the Gulf waters pretty much all the time. It's a natural result of having *so much* oil under the surface of the sea floor—it just seeps out. That's sort of the thing about oil and the Gulf—there's so much oil under the ground, it *wants* out, naturally, which is why BP and other oil companies are there in the first place.

The result of this entirely natural occurrence is, the Gulf has a natural mechanism to absorb and disperse huge quantities of crude oil: salt water and algae.

The salt water disperses the oil clouds, and the algae feast on them. Nifty handiwork by a power much higher than the EPA.

So two years later, the "worst environmental disaster ever" and the "oily wasteland" never really happened. Two years later, it's almost hard to find *any* signs of the oil leak in the region, unless you count the billions and billions of dollars poured into the area by a cowed and remorseful BP.

And what was the reason? Armies of environmentalists and college kids combing the beaches with paper towels and sponges? Skimmers and equipment battling the oil sludge?

It was salt water and algae.

Boy, do liberals hate that algae.

They hate it because it represents a powerful counterargument to their environmental panic.

You see, liberals love to tell us that the world is ending. That we're about to enter a dark time of strife and scarcity. They love to spin tales of a world covered with ice, and when that doesn't work, with a world too hot for human life. In the past forty years, liberals—and especially liberal scientists, which is an oxymoron—have told us that overpopulation will cause worldwide famines by 1985 (Remember those? Good times . . .), that the next ice age is upon us, that the globe is heating up irretrievably, that we're running out of oil, that we're running out of natural gas, that nuclear power will kill us, and that we'd all be better off if we went back to living in mud huts and growing our own food.

Okay, I added that last part. But I'm not too far off, am I?

Liberals aren't stupid. Well, some of them are, but most of them can read and think and do simple math. Most of them know that the earth is a massive engine of perpetual change, and that human beings are just a tiny part of a giant ecosystem. Most of them know that progress and prosperity are the key to solving our environmental challenges. Most of them—I think—have heard of salt water and algae.

So why the hyperdramatics?

Why the tears and wails and gnashing of teeth?

Why is it that every time some oil spills we're treated to a *telenovela* of overacting from the environmental left?

As the oil spilled into the Gulf, it was like one of those scenes from the Arab street, with the women in the burkas making that frantic ululating noise with their tongues and throat. You know the noise I mean? That's what the environmentalists sound like, every time somebody spills something.

Why?

Power, that's why. Because if you want to increase your power, the first thing you need is a really fat crisis. You need to scare everybody into thinking that this is really it. That the Gulf of Mexico is going to be a Dead Zone, that we've got only three years left to drive our cars, that the earth is turning into a sauna (or an ice cube; take your pick).

Only then can you pass more laws, issue more regulations, get more up into every American's life and business.

For liberals, there's only *one* solution to every problem. There's only *one* way to clean up an oil spill or solve an energy crisis: Give them more power.

Which is why they absolutely *hate* that algae.

Because the algae doesn't want power. It just wants to eat the oil.

14 V-8 Engines

Fast big cars

Here's what happens when you put the key in your car and turn on the ignition:

It *ignites*.

That's right: A bunch of sparks go off, and a series of tiny but powerful explosions burst in steady rhythm, and the car comes to life. As you drive down the street, your powerful, purring fire machine glides to the beat of hundreds of timed combustions.

We're so used to just turning the key and going that we often forget just what, exactly, is happening. It's just a car, we think to ourselves, and we don't really reflect on what an amazing technological marvel it is. Think about it: When you get behind the wheel, you become the master of a steel box on wheels that harnesses the awesome power of exploding fuel and turns it into something even more awesome: speed.

And if you hit the freeway at the right time of day and really open her up, you're suddenly connecting with a truly American kind of experience: the roar of an engine channeling fire into speed, the wind in your hair, and a sense of incredible freedom. Especially if you really crank up the tunes.

Boy, do liberals hate that.

To them, there's something just plain wrong about all of that power and freedom under the control of one person. They don't like it when we turn the engine over and tap the accelerator to hear that revving rumble of fire and pistons. They don't like it when we zip through the drive-through for a Big Gulp and a burger, and hit the freeway for a road trip. They don't like it when we move out to the suburbs—out to where the houses are larger and the lawns are spacious—just because we *can,* thanks to a car that eats up the road and peels out at the light.

The V-8 engine makes—or, I should say, *made*—all of that possible. Eight cylinders of gas-exploding potential. Eight pistons delivering freedom and speed to the driver.

Any driver. The classic American V-8 came with all kinds of cars—the muscle cars of the 1960s and 1970s as well as the family Caprice Classic wagon in two-toned Champagne Gold Firemist. Back then, it was almost a civil right to have that much power and thrust under your hood.

Boy, do liberals hate power and thrust.

What liberals want is for us to poke around town in silent electric cars with zero pick-up. They want us to creep out into the intersection when the light turns green, piloting our sad little mound of plastic car at moderate speeds. They want us to turn the music down, and switch it to boring NPR. They want us to stop hitting the accelerator—on our cars, on our ambitions, on our appetites, on *everything.*

Ever mash the pedal down on a Prius? Know what happens?

It *clicks*. It's a car that clicks. It doesn't roar or purr or rumble with power and fire and combustible potential.

It clicks. Like a golf cart.

And that's what liberals want: to cut us down to size.

And that's another thing liberals love to hate: big things. They hate Walmart because it is big. They hate the Texas Motor Speedway because it is big. They hate *American Idol* because it's big—it has a big audience, which proves it must be bad.

And what they really hate lately is big cars. Big cars with V-8s.

But size matters.

And size matters most in physics.

Take a simple test. Get into a nice big Chevy Tahoe, roll up the speed to about thirty-five miles an hour, and steer it straight into oncoming traffic at the first electric car you see. One of those silly-looking smart cars liberals are peddling to a not-so-receptive public.

Or one of those little four-cylinder cars that liberals think are so precious. The kind they are giving preferred parking spaces to all over this great country. And big subsidies.

See what happens.

News flash: The big car will crush the small car like a bug.

Indeed, the little car will fold like an accordion, while the big car will have some problems your local auto body shop can deal with in a week's time while you cruise around in your even bigger rental.

The driver in that little car will in all probability be severely injured, or worse, killed. You, the driver in the Tahoe, will walk away unharmed.

Why? Physics. Plain and simple. The force of something big and heavy crushing down on something small and light leaves that something small and light even smaller.

The same people who dictated seatbelts and booster seats and a list of federal regulations so long that our cars all pretty much have the same dull, drab look, and all in the name of protecting us from our own tastes and proclivities, have suddenly abandoned the notion of safety—the religion of safety—for a new religion: environmental safety. For an even newer and hipper science; the science of green.

Let the safety of the wife and kids be damned! That electric car they died in is saving the planet!

Ralph Nader wrote the book *Unsafe at Any Speed* some forty-five years ago to expose the intransigence of automakers on the safety front. It was all about how the now not so Big Three—GM and Ford and Chrysler—sacrificed safety for the sake of comfort and style. The Chevy Corvair got a full chapter, and was all but run out of production, and Ralph Nader became a rock star.

We're waiting for the *Unsafe at Any Speed* sequel.

We're waiting for the study that tells us how many more people have died because of this push for smaller, lighter, greener, smarter cars. And the science that supports it.

We're waiting for the study to tell us just how much money and precious natural resources we will gobble up scouring the earth to make those lithium batteries that will power us all around in our little green cars.

And we're waiting for that chapter on the Chevy Volt. And how it fares in crash tests with a Chevy Tahoe.

We're waiting for the studies on how those smart cars that look like Hunter Thompson's golf cart will fare in a head-on collision with a Ford F-150.

We won't hold our breath. Because that's the thing about liberals. They love science. But they love their religion more. And their religion du jour is green, green, green, green. And if that means making up some new science, or ignoring science altogether, so be it.

Let those V-8-driving, big-car-loving troglodytes eat cake (the low-fat and FDA-approved kind, of course)!

13 Bright Lights

Let there be light

It's right there in the Bible in the Book of Genesis, a passage most of us learn before we learn much of anything:

"In the beginning God created the heaven and the earth, and the earth was without form, and void; and darkness was upon the face of the deep. And the spirit of God moved upon the face of the waters. And God said, Let there be light: and there was light."

And so it was, until the 110th U.S. Congress said no. And the EPA agreed.

Last year, the last incandescent lightbulb factory in America, in Winchester, Virginia, closed up shop. When you remember that light is not just something that dates back to the Bible, that lightbulbs are the symbol of great ideas, sudden inspiration, and entrepreneurial aha! moments, the fact that the country of Thomas Edison would see the closure of the last incandescent lightbulb factory is a sad metaphor.

Maybe we no longer produce lightbulb moments, either.

A compact LED bulb flickering to life above the head of a cartoon character just doesn't feel quite the same.

By 2014, according to another stupid act of Congress (and this one passed in 2007, so it's not Obama's fault for once) the kind of lightbulbs that we all prefer—you know, the bright ones, the ones that actually illuminate rooms and objects—were essentially banned and replaced by those awful Dairy Queen–looking things, the compact fluorescent bulbs, that bathe the world in a gauzy dirty yellow haze.

It's sickroom lighting, state mental hospital illumination—the kind of lights they used in East Germany to keep everyone in the dark and under control.

It's the kind of light that funeral parlors put out. And government bureaucrats.

Our old lightbulbs were essentially banned until the cavalry rode in and stopped it in December 2011. At least for a while.

But know this. The liberals won't stop until they get their way.

Liberals who care about changing our toilets and air conditioners and plumbing will eventually get their hands on our light, too. It's just a matter of when, not if.

And when they do, it will cause big problems for the average American household. Your average three-thousand-square-foot house will need roughly a lightbulb for every square foot just to stop Americans from contracting squinting disorders. Shaving accidents will rise dramatically, and many men will give up the morning shave altogether for fear of lacerating a coronary artery.

Men, already impaired visually when it comes to color coordinating, will be rendered utterly helpless, especially single straight men.

But there will be problems beyond the aesthetic ones.

The compact fluorescents are harder to manufacture—something about all of those twisty tubes—and if something is hard to make, it ends up getting made in China, which is where all of our lightbulbs will come from eventually.

And that's how the Chinese will win, of course. We'll all be squinting into the sick gray light while they sneak in and take everything. Heck, they already own half of our debt. They might as well repossess our furniture, TVs, houses, and cars, too!

If it's dark enough, perhaps we won't notice.

To a liberal, the world looks better when it's dingier. Bright lights are too doggone festive. To maintain the proper downcast attitude, they want to make sure we're all a little less comfortable. A little less happy. A little less alert. A little less alive.

It's all about *less* with them. As far as the lefty environmental movement is concerned, we're running out of everything—polar icecaps, sea turtles, crude oil, food, water—and the trick is to cut our appetites down to size, to stop wanting to roll the windows down, hit the gas pedal hard, and sing along to seventies music.

It's not about speed or wattage. And it's not about natural resources, either, because we have plenty, and everyone knows it.

It's about optimism.

Either you think a more prosperous world is a good thing—that prosperity and ingenuity can solve most of our pressing problems—or you don't. Either you think that being able to buy a car that roars to life is a component of a complicated web of incentives designed to inspire the next Thomas Edison to invent something useful, or you think that we're done, we've invented everything already, and we need to divvy up a shrinking pie.

For the left, there are no lightbulb moments in the future. For the left, there's nothing bright on the horizon that we should race toward.

And that's why they hate fast cars and bright lights. Because both of those things remind us to keep pushing our potential.

Way back in the eighteenth century, there existed this same philosophical divide. It was between those who thought the future was one of unlimited improvement, men like William Godwin and even Jean-Jacques Rousseau, and those on the other side. On the side of pessimists, battling hard for the scarcity crowd, the doom-and-gloom crowd, was Thomas Malthus.

"The power of the population is indefinitely greater than the power in earth to produce subsistence for man," Malthus proclaimed.

Translation: We are all going to starve to death, because the people who grow food will not keep up with the people making babies.

Malthus was probably not a spectacular dinner guest. But his research and his theory were all the rage. And boy oh boy was Malthus ragingly, wildly, wrong! Thanks to the miracles of modern technology and science, we've managed to turn agricultural productivity into an art form Malthus could never have imagined.

There is now a surfeit of food in many places on the earth, we spend less on food as a percentage of our net income than ever before, and in the places in the world where people are actually starving to death, it has less to do with food than with governance. And really, really bad politics.

Indeed, in America, the wealthiest among us often look as if they need a meal. Badly. Young women all across this country strap themselves to treadmills and drink gallons of purified water in the hopes of looking like . . . a hungry person.

Meanwhile, take a look at the average girth of poor people in our country, and you'll think that the last problem they have is a food problem. Or at least a problem with food scarcity.

The affluent look as if they need an extra helping of ham and baked potatoes; the poor look as if they need to staple their stomachs and move more than just their bowels every day. That is not an exercise program.

What Malthus was to his time, so were the antinuke activists of the late 1970s to theirs; they were catastrophists. After the incident at Three Mile Island, we received a wave of "scientific" research predicting that the world would suffer multiple meltdowns, leading to mass casualties. And worse.

There were movies like *The China Syndrome* (it's always fun watching the late great Jack Lemmon have a meltdown on the screen) and *Silkwood,* and there were really bad concerts like the "No Nukes" show at Madison Square Garden—with ex-Woodstock wannabes and ex–Vietnam protesters looking for their next cause du jour, all decrying our nuclear-industrial complex and predicting the end of the world as we know it.

But to their chagrin, it just didn't happen.

Before them, there were the killer bee people, who kept trying to tell us that a swarm of bees was heading from Africa straight to America to terrorize our women and children.

It just didn't happen.

Then there were the Y-2K people telling us the end was near. Remember that one? Experts predicted that the world would shut down on January 1, 2000, due to computer glitches and programming and coding problems. Planes would fall out of the sky, security systems would be breached, power plants would shut down, and worse.

That didn't happen either.

And now we have global warming, and the Catastrophist in Chief, Al Gore, who predicted twenty-foot tidal waves hitting New York City, and polar meltdowns that would make the North Pole look like South Beach in twenty years.

That, too, will not happen.

That's the thing about being a liberal catastrophist, most of whom come from the world of academia, the arts, or lately, "the scientific community."

It means never having to say, "I'm sorry," or, "I was wrong."

And that's what is really behind the current push by the lightbulb police. They are scarcity people. They are pessimists. They are the glass is half-empty and emptying fast crowd. They all think the world is going to end because of global warming, and they are scurrying like crazy people to reduce our carbon footprints.

When all we want is to see our feet in the morning. And tie our shoes. Is that too much to ask?

12 The Berlin Wall

On a hilltop in Simi Valley, California, in the middle of a beautifully landscaped garden, sits one of the ugliest pieces of rock ever seen. It's a piece of the Berlin Wall, and it's covered with graffiti and it's a symbol of one of the most irritating and troublesome facts that liberals hate to face:

In the greatest struggle of the second part of the twentieth century—the titanic clash between the communist dictatorships and the forces of freedom—conservatives were right, and liberals were wrong.

Well, let's be a little more specific: *Ronald Reagan* was right. And pretty much everybody else in the liberal foreign policy establishment was wrong.

If you're reading this and you're over, say, forty-five years old, feel free to skip the next few paragraphs. But if you're under forty-five, you may need to pay special attention to this next part, because it's likely that no one ever taught you this in high school or college.

In 1945, at the end of the European part of World War II, American armed forces had marched all the way from the European Atlantic coast to the capital of Hitler's Third Reich, Berlin. And the armies of the communist Soviet Union, under the leadership of Stalin—who in many ways bested Adolf Hitler in the "Who is a Bigger Psychopath" competition—started marking their territory. They occupied Poland, Hungary, Czechoslovakia, Romania, and parts of Germany.

For a lot of reasons, some understandable and some not so understandable, the Allied armies accepted this. So Europe was divided into two. On the western side were the forces of democracy, freedom, and personal liberty. (If you're a liberal and you're reading this, just an FYI: Those are good things. Those were the good guys.)

On the eastern side, under the tyrannical rule of the Soviet dictator, were the forces of repression, fear, and enslavement. (If you're a liberal and you're reading this, just an FYI: Those are *bad* things. Those were the *bad* guys.)

Berlin, though, was an unusual situation. From 1945, Berlin was occupied by both sides. When Hitler's Third Reich was smashed, the Soviet army encircled the city, establishing what ultimately became one of the most sick and repressive regimes ever to exist on earth, East Germany—or what they called, without a trace of irony, the "German Democratic Republic," which was neither democratic, nor a republic, nor, since it owed its entire existence to its Soviet overlords, really German.

One way to gauge whether a place is good or bad is to count up the number of people who want to leave and subtract it from the number of people who want to move there. If the resulting number is positive—if more people want in than out—then you've got an indication that it's not such a bad place. If the number is negative, well, you've got some customer service issues to work out.

The problem for the communists was, *everyone* wanted to leave East Germany, and *no one* wanted to move there.

The solution?

Build a wall.

So in 1961, that's what they did. They divided the city, first with barbed wire, later with concrete blocks, and anyone who tried to jump over (lots did) or make a dash for it (lots did) or tunnel underneath (lots did) was shot.

Lots were shot.

So you'd think everyone would be thinking the same thing, right? "This is clearly wrong. Those people are evil. This wall needs to come down."

Okay, if you're over forty-five, you can start reading here. And if you're under forty-five, you've now had a lesson in history you probably didn't get in high school because you were too busy celebrating diversity or learning about the hippies in 1968 to learn about the single most important event in the second part of the last century. What followed, from 1961, was a lot of what liberals like to call *negotiation* and *dialogue* but what really is just another way of saying *appeasement* and *surrender*.

The correct, establishment-approved attitude toward the Berlin Wall was, *Well, it's an eyesore, of course, but what can you do? Who are we to lecture them?*

That was the liberal attitude toward everything Soviet, by the way, including the nuclear missiles they aimed at us, the despots they supported, the human rights violations they committed: *Hey, we can't criticize them! We're not so hot ourselves.*

For liberals, it was "tacky" to complain about the Soviet empire, to keep reminding everyone about the Berlin Wall. For liberals, the only way to appease and negotiate and placate the Soviet monster was, first, don't mention the Wall.

Don't mention the Wall! You could hear them all chattering, on the pages of the *New York Times* and in the halls of the State Department.

Which is sort of saying the same thing.

Don't mention the Wall! It's insulting to them! It's incendiary! It's rude!

And so in 1987, when a great American president named Ronald Reagan was planning his trip to Berlin, he was determined to remind everyone that there was a big, ugly wall dividing the city, and that on one side were the good guys (Spot Quiz #1: Liberals! Who was he talking about?) and on the other side were the bad guys (Spot Quiz #2: Liberals! Who was he thinking of?)

(Answers below.)

A young speechwriter for Ronald Reagan at the time, Peter Robinson, was dispatched to Berlin a few weeks before the trip to soak up the atmosphere and gather images for the speech. At a dinner party in Berlin, though, he made an embarrassing remark. He asked in a casual way if most people in Berlin had made their peace with the Wall. The reason he asked was that the official State Department policy at the time was, well, that most people in Berlin had made their peace with the Wall. They accepted it. They had learned to live with it. It didn't make them upset anymore.

A woman at the party heard the question and shook with anger.

Make our peace? she asked. Accept it? *Live* with it? Her sister, she said in a trembling voice, lived on the other side of the Wall. They hadn't seen each other in twenty-five years. How could that *not* upset them?

So what would you like the president to say when he comes here? Robinson asked.

He should tell them to tear down that wall! she answered.

Tear down this wall.

The origin of those four words—four words that shook the world, four words that tore down a wall—was a sister's clear-eyed outrage, a person's ability to see evil for what it was: something you don't appease or placate or negotiate with.

Tear down this wall.

The State Department hated those words. In the multiple drafts of the speech, they were excised, replaced, excised again. Foreign policy mandarins and appeasement bureaucrats argued all the way to Berlin—*These words are insulting! This language is incendiary! This is a mistake!*

But President Ronald Reagan wanted to say them. He insisted on saying them.

Because they were true.

Tear down this wall!

On a late spring day in 1987, in front of the Brandenburg Gate, President Ronald Reagan said these words, calling out to Mikhail Gorbachev, the then–Soviet dictator:

> We welcome change and openness; for we believe that freedom and security go together, that the advance of human liberty can only strengthen the cause of world peace. There is one sign the Soviets can make that would be unmistakable, that would advance dramatically the cause of freedom and peace. General Secretary Gorbachev, if you seek peace, if you seek prosperity for the Soviet Union and Eastern Europe, if you seek liberalization, come here to this gate. Mr. Gorbachev, open this gate. Mr. Gorbachev, Mr. Gorbachev, tear down this wall!

The biggest cheers, they say, came from the people no one could see. The ones on the other side of the Wall.

And in 1989, the Wall came down.

There are pieces of it all over the world, but the most moving piece is in the Reagan Library, in Simi Valley, California. Because it was President Reagan, a conservative, with a conservative's love of liberty and freedom, and a conservative's courage to speak the truth clearly and without apology, who struck the first blow against that terrible symbol of communism and totalitarian evil.

Whenever they see pieces of the Berlin Wall, liberals roll their eyes. Come on, the Soviet empire fell for *complicated* reasons. There were *larger forces* and *economic development issues* at work.

Yeah, right.

Liberals hate those pieces of the Wall. They hate that President Reagan was right. Right about liberty and freedom. Right about communism. Right about what people wanted and needed to hear.

ANSWER KEY

Spot Quiz #1: We were the good guys.

Spot Quiz #2: They were the bad guys.

If you got either of those questions incorrect, please stop reading here and go back to the beginning of this book and start over.

If you got both of these questions correct, feel free to continue.

11 Charity

The best thing about being a liberal is that, when tax time rolls around, filing your return is a breeze. After all, you don't have to hunt down all of those charitable donation receipts and add up all of those deductions.

That's because you don't have any.

Al Gore, the left-wing scold and environmental drama queen, famously deducted, in his 1997 tax return, a whopping $353 in charitable giving. Nice of him, don't you think?

On a more generous note, Vice President Joe Biden, in 2006, gave about $380.

Wow.

That's because liberals love to claim that they're charitable, but they're only charitable with Other People's Money. As in yours and mine. As in the U.S. taxpayer's money. But when it comes to actually giving themselves, well, that's a whole different story.

President Barack Obama, from 2000 to 2004, never gave more than 1 percent of his income to charity. Later, as he geared up to run for president, he bumped that up to about 5 percent. Perhaps he was visited by three ghosts one Christmas Eve.

The "Evil Dark Lord," Dick Cheney, on the other hand, routinely gives about 10 percent or more of his income to charity. And in one banner year, 2005, he and his wife donated almost 80 percent of their income to charity.

George and Laura Bush also tithe regularly. What's up with that? They're not even running for anything.

You'd think that this might cause liberals to think better of Cheney and Bush. People who routinely give away their money are what we call *generous,* which is a trait we often think of as a *good thing.* (To my liberal readers: If the italicized words are unfamiliar to you, please seek out your most conservative friend for an explanation.)

Liberals don't think of charitable giving as a good thing.

Liberals don't donate much to charity, but you can't blame them. The truth is, liberals hate the whole idea of charitable organizations doing good works. That's what the government's for.

So it's no wonder that Al Gore & Company were tightfisted when it came to giving their money away. To liberals, *taxes* are a charitable donation. They don't see why private charities even exist.

And remember this: The more government takes from those of us who would otherwise give to charity, the less there is for us to actually give to charity.

In the liberals' twisted view, the only way to make things better is by getting the government involved. The government *is* a charity to them, which is why liberal politicians always call their time in office "my time in public service."

"I want to *give back*," they say. "That's why I entered public service."

To them, working for the government is a charitable act. Despite the fact that they often leave office a lot richer than when they entered it. Despite the fact that it may have been the only real job they ever had in their adult lifetimes.

Funny how that works.

In fact, if you sat down to invent an institution more repellent to liberals, you'd have a hard time coming up with anything more awful than a private charity.

In the first place, there's that pesky word, *private*. When liberals hear the word *private*, they instantly recognize it for what it is: outside the control and direction of the government, which means that liberals can't tell it what to do.

And then there's another unpleasant truth: that a lot of these private charities—most of them, in fact—are *religious* in nature. That means that the people who work there are probably motivated by some kind of faith, by a sense that God wants us to help our neighbor. That's just wildly unacceptable to liberals.

You're not supposed to help people because you think that God wants you to. You're supposed to do it because the government requires it. After all, it's the *government's* job to teach children and help the sick and aid the poor. What does *God* have to do with it?

What liberals also hate about private charities is that each one has its own way of tackling a problem.

The Nature Conservancy, for instance, protects and preserves wilderness areas by collecting money from its donors and using those funds to buy up pristine lands on the open market, and by creating land banks that allow developers and other groups to donate land in exchange for permission to develop other, less valuable, areas.

Greenpeace, on the other hand, raises money from its donors to harass law-abiding companies and individuals, and to physically disrupt the building of power plants and other legitimate economic activity.

It's a free country, and if you want to throw your money down the sinkhole by giving it to Greenpeace, that's your right. As I am a deeply committed conservative, it's not my place to keep you from being stupid with your cash.

But the point is, these are two *private* charities, and you have a choice as to where to donate your money so that it can do the most good.

Liberals hate the idea of private charities because they hate the idea of allowing you to choose where to donate your money, and they *especially* hate the idea of your choosing to give it to someplace that's not sufficiently liberal.

Liberals hate the Boy Scouts, Catholic adoption agencies, evangelical day schools, free market–based environmental groups, the Salvation Army, and anything else that smacks of people doing good works for the wrong reasons. For liberals, the wrong reasons are anything to do with God, country, or a calling to serve.

Liberals hate private charities so much, in fact, that if given the chance, they'd starve them to death. In one of President Obama's budgets, he proposed limiting the amount of deductions for charitable donations allowed to taxpayers.

This might not mean much for folks like him and Joe Biden, but for people like Dick Cheney and George W. Bush, it's a clear attempt to diminish the amount they're able to donate. Liberals are hoping that the billions of dollars Americans donate to charities each year—not them, obviously, but the rest of us—will flow instead to the federal government.

Fewer donations mean fewer charities. And fewer charities means fewer pesky do-gooder organizations marching around trying to help people in accordance with their principles, which, let's face it, only serve to make people notice how inefficient and ineffective the government's attempts to tackle the same challenges are.

Private charities just make the government look bad, is how the liberals see it.

And they're absolutely right. They do.

Which is why liberals hate charity, and why they're trying to stamp it out.

There's an old saying that if you want to judge a man, look at his checkbook.

One of the best books of the past decade, *Who Really Cares* by Arthur C. Brooks, examined the actual behavior of liberals and conservatives when it comes to donating their own time, money, and even their own blood, for the good of their fellow man.

Conventional wisdom before the Brooks study would have favored liberals on the compassion and charity front. We're Scrooge, they're the Tooth Fairy, and it's always been that way because that's who we are, goes the old narrative. Conservatives care about money, not people. And liberals care about people, not money.

The Brooks study shattered that myth. Here are some of his findings.

Brooks discovered that four characteristics seem to drive the propensity for making people behave charitably: religion, doubt about the government's role in economic life, strong families, and personal entrepreneurship. Those Americans who have all four, or at least three, are much more likely to behave charitably.

Sounds like advantage conservatives to me.

Brooks discovered that conservative households gave an average of 30 percent more money to charity in 2000 than liberal ones. And that difference isn't explained by income differential. Brooks notes that liberals make 6 percent more per year than conservatives. And conservatives still manage to give more!

If you are a liberal, that's gotta hurt.

But there's more. Brooks learned that all classes of conservatives—rich, poor, and middle class alike—give more than their liberal counterparts. And while religion is a major factor, the figures don't just show tithing to churches. Religious donors give a whole lot more to nonreligious causes, too.

If you're a liberal, that's really gotta hurt.

Even those with incomes of less than fourteen thousand dollars annually, the "working poor," give three times as much as families on welfare. They're twice as likely to give, and twice as likely to volunteer.

The operative word is "working."

If you're a liberal and still reading, I urge you to stop now. This last part may just cause a seizure.

It turns out that in states in which George W. Bush got more than 60 percent of the 2004 vote, charitable giving averaged 3.5 percent of income. Compare that with states where John Kerry got more than 60 percent of the vote: charitable giving there averaged a mere 1.9 percent of income.

Red state folks give more than the blue state folks. We morons who supported that dope Bush actually gave more to charity than those smarty-pants liberals who loved Kerry.

That's gotta hurt liberals more than anything.

It also turns out that more conservatives than liberals donate blood. According to Brooks: "If liberals and moderates gave blood at the same rate as conservatives, the blood supply of the United States would jump 45 percent."

There's something fundamental about the urge to give. It's why so many of us don't understand the whole notion of helping more by paying more taxes.

We're already helping, and we'd help more if the government let us keep more.

Meanwhile, our government is trying to teach college kids how to give back by recruiting them to join certain organizations like Teach For America, where students are paid to volunteer, and even get their loans forgiven if they teach at an inner-city school for a few years.

That's right. *Paid* to volunteer.

They actually think volunteering should include pay.

Leave it to liberals to create a whole new mantra on the charity front:

"What's in it for me?"

10 Profit

Few things that liberals hate are as necessary to the liberal worldview as profit. And yet, as surely as there are carbs in Michael Moore's diet, liberals hate profit.

The "P" word is never mentioned by liberals without a qualifier. Profits are always of the "excessive" or "obscene" or "unfair" or "windfall" variety.

Liberals use the "P" word as if it were some kind of obscenity. Or virus.

The kind of profits liberals hate are normally made only by fat cats. To use these concepts in a perfectly constructed liberal sentence: *We must tax big oil's excess profits so we can lower gas prices and the sea levels at the same time while making sure those fat cats can't donate so much money to Republican Candidate XYZ.*

Hey, don't get mad at me! I said perfectly constructed, not perfectly logical.

Obviously, raising taxes on companies involved in the gasoline supply chain would only serve to raise gas prices, which speaks to liberals' uncomfortable relationship with logic and reality.

And for the record, I'm not sure I've ever encountered anything that would qualify as an "excess profit." What liberals might call an excess profit could lead to other horrible consequences known as excess hiring, excess 401(k) values, excess donations to charity, and so on.

Heck, unless you are GE, excess profits could even lead to excess taxes being paid.

In fact, excess profits from company A might lead to its placing excess orders with companies B, C, and D, which could lead to excess profits on their part also, which could lead to the problems of excess hiring, excess donations, excess stock values, excess taxes being paid, and so on.

Now to be fair, not all specific profits are hated by liberals. Just most of them, along with the general idea of them.

The profits made by Bruce Springsteen when he hauls the E Street Band on a world tour, the kind of profits that James Cameron makes on a movie like *Avatar,* the kind of profits Al Gore gets from all of his green energy holdings—those profits are always exempted from the wrath of the liberals.

Profits made by Apple Computers or Nancy Pelosi's vineyards are perfectly fine, too, even considering they are meticulously set up to remove one well-known barrier to profits: labor unions.

Of course, avoiding labor unions in an attempt to maximize profits is something that is considered evil and mean-spirited if the name of your company happens to be Walmart or Federal Express. Yes, that is the same Federal Express that Apple uses exclusively to ship its iProducts—which are made in very nonunion shops in China.

So if you're keeping score at home, it's perfectly fine for Apple to use Federal Express to ship as a way to maximize its profits, yet it is totally unacceptable for Federal Express to be a nonunion shop so they can maximize theirs.

Huh? Exactly.

Remember, we started off the chapter by warning you that profits and liberals have a very complicated relationship. Indeed, liberals hate profits while absolutely counting on them for much of what they advocate.

Oh, and speaking of China: "Outsourcing" is another way that some companies obtain profits, which of course is an unacceptable strategy unless you are one of the chosen few sufficiently liberal companies. Again, to demonstrate this concept in a sentence: *I just got a text on my iPhone from another Occupy group about how unfair it is that Walmart imports cheap goods from China. Let's discuss this over lo mein on the corner.*

Any adult discussion of profits necessarily leads to liberals' tying themselves in knots trying to reach some kind of logical conclusion. The overarching reason for the hatred is that profits all too often benefit the wrong people.

And moreover the wrong motivations.

You see, profits are quite often found to benefit folks who have—gasp—the profit motive. And any good Occupier knows that this is a mean-spirited Tea Party racist sexist homophobic motive and therefore evil.

Now this is clearly not the motive for the Pelosi vineyard, which exists only to fund Nancy's good works in Congress, right? And Steve Jobs was only motivated by making really cool products that really cool people could play with, not actually by money.

One of the most obscenely greedy industries, as we all know, is big oil. These folks are the worst of all worlds. In addition to making way too much money, they benefit from a product that pollutes and leads to political donations for Republicans. It's worse than big tobacco.

But an examination of big oil's profit on gasoline leads to some very curious outcomes. One is that big oil's margins are very thin. Something like 4 percent. When gas is at four dollars a gallon, that's sixteen cents a gallon.

When you consider that big oil actually discovered the oil, got it from the bottom of the ocean or from underground, got it to a refinery, refined it, got it to a distributor who then got it to your local neighborhood convenience store, that 4 percent is a real bargain.

It leaves you some money for a bag of Doritos and a large Coke.

Conversely, the government makes about fifty cents a gallon (depending on which state you count) on this gas, and it didn't do a doggoned thing but levy a tax on it. Which begs the question: If big oil's profit of four cents is obscene or excessive, what would you call government's fifty cents?

Theft, spreading the wealth around, and destructive are words that immediately come to mind.

But that misses the bigger picture on profit, and why liberals hate it so much. It is the profit motive itself that generated the competition at every step of the way that got the gas delivered at a 4 percent markup in the first place.

And it's not just the competition for profit that led to the gasoline either. It was present every step of the way, including the real estate transaction that led to the purchase of the corner lot and the building contractors who built the convenience store.

This same profit motive keeps the Doritos on the shelf and the Slurpee machine humming.

And unless you drive a Chevy Volt that I helped pay for, this process is also what delivered your car to the showroom. And your clothes, your home, your laptop, and so on.

Profit is what infuses efficiency into our economy. Milton Friedman has the powerful example of the five-cent pencil, which incorporates raw materials from numerous continents along with several levels of refining and manufacturing along the way, and what the world gets is a perfectly workable pencil for a nickel.

Yes, a full five-cent product that works exactly as advertised is the result of evil profit motivation at every step.

What would a profitless government pencil cost? Fifty bucks? At least.

And this is where the real hatred of profit is born for the liberal mind. From a basic misunderstanding of economics. Of life itself.

The socialist thinker George Bernard Shaw called profits "the overcharge." Karl Marx called it "surplus value." To the average liberal, profits are unnecessary charges added to the inherent costs of producing goods and services, driving up costs to the consumer. The socialist's dream was to get rid of all of those private businesses, and have the government run them, and those profits could be passed along to the consumers. Or the workers.

Why should owners and investors reap the rewards?

It all sounds perfectly reasonable if you happen to teach economics at Princeton like Paul Krugman does. The problem with socialists is that their ideas are always great. Until, that is, you try them.

According to Thomas Sowell, it was a Soviet premier—Leonid Brezhnev—who said that his country's enterprise managers shied away from innovation "as the devil shies away from incense."

Visit almost any DMV or U.S. post office, and Brezhnev's lesson lives.

What the liberal mind just can't bear—and can't stand—is that profit leads to opportunity and opportunity to success and success to freedom and freedom to a lack of control. And at the bottom of every liberal fantasy about how society should be organized is the liberal's desire to be the one controlling that organization.

It is the hope for profit, and the threat of losses, that actually forces owners in the free market economy to produce at the lowest possible cost. It is risks, rewards, and incentives that work in the real world. With real-life human beings.

Which brings us full circle to what I like to call the profit paradox. You see, liberals love tax revenue, and wouldn't you know it—taxes are based on profits!

Not a whole lot of revenue is generated from companies that go broke. Taxes go to fund all of the things that liberals love, like education, crony contracts to well-connected "nonprofits," and transgender programs for California inmates.

Liberals also love unions and union jobs are paid for out of what? Yes, profits.

All of this is just so complicated for liberals to wrap their minds around, which could explain why most of them are so unhappy so much of the time. Their worldview just doesn't comport with reality. The liberal hatred of profit simply misapprehends human nature.

9

Talk Radio

Fat loudmouthed bigots

Not too long ago, a reality television show had a call-in poll. The specific question escapes me, but it was essentially a referendum on the ouster of a certain contestant. Viewers were asked to send a text message to one number to answer "Yes," another number to answer "No," and a third number to say "Don't have an opinion." Each text message cost around $1.50, which meant that some dopes paid actual American money to broadcast to the world that they had no opinion.

It's funny, of course, but also kind of amazing. Americans like to express their opinions. So much, in fact, that they even like to express the fact that they *have* no opinions. (Although, as someone who has worked happily in talk radio for years, I've got to tell you: I haven't met many Americans who *don't* have strong opinions.)

Liberals hate talk radio. They hate it for all the reasons you'd expect: Talk radio hosts, and listeners, tend to be conservative. They also tend to be well informed, smart, and full of opinions.

Liberals hate that, too.

Liberals don't like all of that noisy dissent. Oh, sure, they talk a lot about the right to protest, and they love to use that phrase, "speak truth to power," but they don't like it so much when the people who are doing it disagree with them.

Talk radio, back before the Internet and Fox News Channel, was the only place you could find anyone in the media who dissented from the prevailing liberal lockstep attitude.

Talk radio truly spoke truth to power. The government's power. And the elite media's lock on power they'd had since the beginning of the modern media.

Back in the day, as the kids put it, we'd huddle up around the AM radio like refugees from a distant land, listening to voices from afar tell us that, no, we weren't crazy to think that government is too large and does too much; and that yes, there are folks out there who share our values and our principles.

Talk radio was a lifeline, a lighthouse in a time when liberals wanted us all to think that we were alone and isolated. Listening to talk radio in those early days gave a lot of us the courage to stand up for what we believe.

The liberals really hated it. They still do.

But compare the free-wheeling democratic conversation on talk radio to the canned and stilted talking-point-centered exchanges on CNN or MSNBC, where the liberal in charge keeps everyone on a tight ideological leash, and you can see why talk radio continues to remain popular and liberal cable news outfits are having trouble scaring up viewers.

Talk radio is still a crazy quilt of voices and opinions from all over the country. But the energy and passion that used to be contained in the airwaves has spilled out into Town Hall meetings and Tea Party rallies and dozens of new ways to make the conservative voice heard.

Liberals can hate talk radio all they like, but the horse has left the barn. The millions of Americans who listen to us every day know for a fact that they're not alone. They hear the callers on the line, they follow each other on Twitter and Facebook, and when they wanted to take to the streets and turn their talk radio–inspired dissent into talk radio–inspired action, they had the tools to do it.

Liberals fixate on the talk radio hosts—they talk trash about us, as if we have a blind and unquestioning audience of unthinking drones—but the truth is, they should be more concerned by the talk radio audience, which has moved past being informed about the issues and into being *active* about them.

My listeners are perfectly happy to push back against whatever it is I'm saying. My listeners are as passionate and as engaged as I am, and it makes me eager to come to work every day. But it scares the pants off the liberals.

That's why, if they had their way, they'd remove us from the air. And remove us for the good of the nation. And all in the name of fairness.

They have a plot to do just that, and it's called the Fairness Doctrine.

It's a misleading phrase, because it isn't a doctrine, and there's nothing fair about it. It all started in 2005, when Congresswoman Louise Slaughter (D-NY) and twenty-three cosponsors introduced the Fairness and Accountability in Broadcasting Act. It got nowhere.

But does that ever stop liberals?

In 2007, Senator Dick Durbin tried to stir that old hornets' nest up again. And I know why. My fellow radio talkers and I hit him hard for a speech he gave on the Senate floor back in November of 2005. It was one of those late-night speeches on C-SPAN 17 (or was it

C-SPAN 24, it's hard to keep track), when no one is listening but news junkies, and shut-ins at the local mental hospital.

It was a floor debate on an energy bill, when suddenly, Durbin took a bizarre detour and read a statement allegedly made by an FBI agent describing the treatment of a terrorist detainee by our soldiers at Guantanamo Bay.

This prisoner was, in the senator's opinion, "tortured" by having the air conditioner alternately turned up all the way and then turned off altogether. He was also chained in his cell and—humiliation of humiliations—forced to listen to rap music.

Sounds like any late-night stop at your local Taco Bell.

Durbin followed that description with the unintentionally comical claim that "if I read this to you and did not tell you that it was an FBI agent describing what Americans had done to prisoners in their control, you would most certainly believe this must have been done by the Nazis, the Soviets in their gulags, or some mad regime, Pol Pot or others, that had no concern for human beings."

It would have been hysterical if Durbin wasn't completely serious.

A sitting U.S. senator accused our men in uniform of behaving like Nazis, Soviets, and Pol Pot, and conservative talk radio was on the case.

In the good old days before talk radio, America would never have heard that absurd soundbite. It might have come to the attention of a producer on Dan Rather's staff or Peter Jennings', but both would have exercised their brilliant editorial judgment and quickly dismissed it as a slip of the tongue, and not worthy of news coverage.

Talk radio pounced on the soundbite, and played it again, and again, and again. Understandably, soldiers and their families were deeply offended, and they jammed my show with calls for weeks on end.

Durbin ultimately apologized. If not for talk radio, we would never have heard a peep about Durbin's Pol Pot speech.

Of course, if a Republican senator, say Trent Lott, had gone off on a riff at a private function honoring a dear friend, say the late Strom Thurmond, just as an example, and the comments were not nearly as bad, I'm sure that the mainstream media would have let it go, too!

Not so fast. It turns out if you have any kind words for a man like Strom Thurmond, it makes you a de facto racist in the eyes of the NAACP, and the left-leaning mainstream media. Lott went on a national apology tour, apologizing for what I don't quite know to this day. And he was ultimately compelled to resign as Senate majority leader.

That's what conservatives across this nation love about talk radio: it provides some balance in an otherwise imbalanced world.

That's why liberals hate it. And why they keep trying to block it.

On February 4, 2009, Senator Debbie Stabinow (D-MI) told radio host Bill Press, when asked whether it was time to bring back the Fairness Doctrine: "I think it's absolutely time to pass a standard. Now, whether it's called the Fairness Standard, whether it's called something else—I absolutely think it's time to be bringing accountability to the airwaves."

A week later, on February 11, 2009, Senator Tom Harkin (D-IA) told the same host, Bill Press, "We gotta get the Fairness Doctrine back in law again."

Later, in response to Press's assertion that "they are just shutting down progressive talk from one city after another," Senator Harkin responded, "Exactly, and that's why we need the fair—that's why we need the Fairness Doctrine back."

Former president Bill Clinton also weighed in on the Fairness Doctrine. He said: "Well, you either ought to have the Fairness Doctrine or we ought to have more balance on the other side, because essentially there's always been a lot of big money to support the right-wing talk shows."

What were they all talking about?

Well, it turns out that conservative talk radio is so effective, and entertains so many millions of people, and makes so much money, that it needs to be punished for its success. Meanwhile, despite the efforts of George Soros and many others, liberal talk radio never really captured an audience. It simply bled money, and millions a month in losses. Air America, the ill-fated attempt to counter talk radio, was so expensive, even their richest billionaires couldn't afford it.

So Air America was "shut down."

And thus the Fairness Doctrine.

In the name of fairness and balance, stations would be forced to shut down some of those profitable hit conservative talk shows, and put on those crummy, boring, unprofitable liberal shows—and all in the name of equal time!

The effect, of course, would be to destroy the bottom line of radio companies and syndicators, and thus destroy talk radio altogether.

That's how liberals deal with success of any kind, and any unequal or unfair outcomes. They simply do everything in their power to equalize the results, however low they have to set the bar to get their way.

Even if it means making everyone poor to get there.

Of course, many conservatives think that the liberal radio is alive and well. It's called NPR, and a good part of it is funded by the U.S. taxpayers. It leans decidedly left and has 33 million listeners. Somehow, that was exempted from the Fairness Doctrine calculus.

The fact is that talk radio is the great town square of the conservative movement, and liberals are probably right to hate it. And to fear it.

Because the kinds of conversations that happen on talk radio— the give-and-take of an argument, the personal connections between the host and the listeners—is more powerful than all of the MSNBC hosts, George Soros, Nancy Pelosi, and the entire Democratic media machine combined.

When Obamacare was being litigated in the summer of 2009, talk radio went into high gear, and my show did, too.

We talked to our audience about single payer, about the Canadian health-care system, and Britain's National Health Service (NHS). The more our audience learned, the more they wanted to know, and soon they wanted to know how they could effect change. We had them sign petitions, email their elected representatives, and we even urged them to show up at Town Halls during the summer to talk to their senators and congressmen in person.

The nerve of us!

And our audience showed up, and showed up in the tens of thousands. They showed up prepared. And educated. And with the means to capture what was happening at those Town Halls, and share it with friends. One of my proudest achievements as a talk show host was when I was able to present an anti-Obamacare petition with 1.9 million signatures to members of Congress through my on-air partnership with the National Center for Policy Analysis. It was cited at the time as the largest public policy petition ever delivered to Congress. We delivered the signatures in the back of an ambulance, just to underscore the point. To quote the positioning statement of the very first talk radio station I ever worked for, THAT'S "people power." That's talk radio in action.

On August 11, 2009, Pennsylvania senator Arlen Specter and HHS director Kathleen Sebelius were greeted by an angry audience in Philadelphia as they attempted to explain why the nearly three-thousand-page bill was good for Americans, and American health-care delivery.

When asked whether he had read the bill, Senator Specter admitted that he had not. He was rightly booed when he explained why: "We have to make judgments really fast." He went on to explain that the huge bill was broken down into sections to be read by different senatorial staff members. That explanation only made things worse.

HHS secretary Sebelius didn't fare any better when she came to Senator Specter's defense. "The Senate bill isn't written yet, so don't boo the senator for not reading a bill that isn't written," said Sebelius.

They booed her for trying to sell them a bill that hadn't been written yet, and would essentially control nearly 20 percent of the nation's GDP.

How dare they? Who do they think they are, anyway?

The exchange was captured by local TV stations, and also by talk radio fans who sent it to our attention via YouTube. And we played that clip to an angry audience. Needless to say, Senator Specter soon became ex-Senator Specter.

The good news for conservatives is this: The old days of the command and control media are gone. And the mainstream media don't like it. Neither do some on Capitol Hill who find the whole idea of an informed citizenry bothersome.

And messy.

And that's the great thing about talk radio. It isn't that it's talk radio. It's that it's talk *back* radio.

Liberals really hate it when we talk back.

8 American History

Have you heard the story of the high school football quarterback? After a nasty tackle, he lay on the field, dazed and half-conscious. The school doctor was called onto the field to be sure the player hadn't suffered a concussion.

"How do you feel, son?" the doctor asked the player as he checked his pupils.

"Okay, I guess," said the athlete, still groggy from the sack. The doctor was still concerned. The kid didn't seem to be entirely there, so the doc asked him a simple question to make sure his brain was functioning.

"Can you tell me who Ronald Reagan was?" the doctor asked. The high school quarterback thought for a moment, then answered.

"They haven't taught us that yet," he said.

Which was the moment the doctor knew he was all right, and sent him back into the game.

They don't teach American history in schools these days—at least not the way you and I think of it, as a collection of names and dates and great and small deeds, all arranged on a timeline that starts, roughly, with the settlement at Jamestown and ends, roughly, with the results of the most recent election.

Long ago, when the rest of us weren't paying attention, liberals decided to teach American history as a series of grievances.

To liberals, American history is an encyclopedia of crimes and outrages committed by guys who look like me—white and middle-aged—against, well, against *everybody else*.

For most high school students, the history of the great American experiment in democracy can be summed up by these key words: Indian genocide, slavery, white European hegemony, hypocrisy, civil war, racist imperialism, Jim Crow, religious insanity, the fall of capitalism, the New Deal, Japanese internment camps, Hiroshima, the civil rights movement, JFK, Vietnam, the peace movement, rock and roll, Watergate, and Gitmo.

The goal of the liberal American history educators is not to teach history; it is, first and foremost, to create the proper narrative.

Before liberals took over America's history education, kids in school learned a different kind of history of the great American experiment in democracy. The key words they learned were: Puritanism, religious liberty, individual property rights, the Founding Fathers, George Washington, the opening of the frontier, Civil War, Reconstruction, Manifest Destiny, the Gilded Age, World War I, the New Deal, World War II, the Cold War, and the civil rights movement.

Before liberals got their hands on it, American history was the story of challenges and triumphs, of brave leaders—Washington, Lincoln, even FDR—who guided the nation through wars and crises. American history used to be something that unified the nation.

But that's not a narrative that suits liberals. They have rewritten the American history textbook.

What liberals need, in order to improve us and correct us and to enact their progressive agenda, is to create a different kind of story, one that focuses on ethnic group grievances—the plight of the Native American; the hardships of slavery—not as an instructional tale of wrongs that were righted, but as examples of bad stuff that's *still happening*.

Author and talk radio show host Dennis Prager is a good friend of mine, and may be the smartest guy I know. Among his many passions is the Soviet Union, and he knows about as much about the place as anyone. He even knows a lot of dissident jokes.

It turns out that being locked up in a gulag was bad for your health, but the never-ending bleakness necessitated a good joke now and then to lift the otherwise dulled spirits. The target of the jokes was almost always the Soviet bureaucracy, and its unending fetish with re-writing—and even scrubbing—history.

One of Prager's favorite dissident jokes goes like this: "In Russia, the future is predictable. It's the past that keeps changing."

That's the world a lot of liberals would like us to live in.

A world in which our futures are predictable. A world in which we all live more modestly, more uniformly, and with less disruption from that big bad capitalist system. They'd prefer that we all be coddled by an ever-present nanny state.

And to make sure that we never find out that there was once a better way of living, that our past was different from our present, they have "historians" like Howard Zinn to do their bidding.

Who is Howard Zinn, and why should you care?

He is the most influential of all the anti-American historians of the

274

twentieth century. His cartoon caricature of American history has sold many millions of copies.

You should care because his writing is assigned reading for college and high school kids everywhere. You should care because this guy is trying to tell your kids and mine that they shouldn't believe all of their parents' mumbo jumbo about America's being a great country. It's all lies, lies, and more lies.

It doesn't help matters that celebrities like Bruce Springsteen, Eddie Vedder, and Matt Damon love Zinn, and never let a chance to plug his work go by.

In *Good Will Hunting*, Matt Damon's character tells his shrink, played by Robin Williams, that Zinn's work will "knock you on your ass."

It most certainly will, if it's the only book you've ever read. Which is probably the case for men like Springsteen, Vedder, and Matt Damon. Reading—and actually finishing—*any* book would knock them on their butts!

Zinn has never been bashful about his goals as a historian. "Objectivity is impossible," he once said, "and it is also undesirable. That is, if it were possible it would be undesirable, because if you have any kind of a social aim, if you think history should serve society in some way; should serve the progress of the human race; should serve justice in some way, then it requires that you make your selection on the basis of what you think will advance causes of humanity."

Wow! Most liberal historians are not quite as honest as Zinn, and most historians are very liberal.

We can tell what Zinn's "social aims" are from the title of his big bestseller, *A People's History of the United States*.

Author Daniel Flynn's superb deconstruction of Zinn's work is worth sharing. Flynn lets us know that if you've read your Marx (Karl, not Groucho), there's really no reason to read Howard Zinn. He goes on:

The first line of *The Communist Manifesto* provides the single-bullet theory of history that provides Zinn with his narrative thread—"The history of all hitherto existing societies is the history of class struggle." It is the all-purpose explanation of every subject that Zinn covers. On the other hand, why study history when theory has all the answers?

Flynn continues:

> Thumb through *A People's History of the United States* and you will find greed as the motivating factor behind every act of those who don't qualify as "the people" in Zinn's book. Zinn's Marxist explanation of the New World begins with Columbus who like every other settler in the New World was driven by the (evil) profit motive. "Behind the English invasion of North America, behind their massacre of Indians, their deception, their brutality, was that special powerful drive born in civilizations based on private profit."

Dare we ask what Zinn thinks of our Founders?

> They found that by creating a nation, a symbol, a legal unity called the United States, they could take over land, profits, and political power from the favorites of the British Empire. In the process, they could hold back a number of potential rebellions and create a consensus of popular support for the rule of a new, privileged leadership.

Zinn's book is 776 pages of this garbage. It's a relentless, old-fashioned lynching of capitalism. A scalping of the whole idea of American greatness.

Zinn's success has spawned imitators, and history departments at colleges across America are filled with professors hoping to advance their "social aims" at the expense of objective scholarship. Discover a new grievance, or advance an old one, and you're on a fast track to tenure. Follow that American exceptionalism trail, and you'll be consigned to part-time janitorial work while you slave away on that Ph.D. to nowhere.

The results of all of this are certainly depressing, but grimly hilarious. Native-American groups compete with African-American groups in the who-had-it-worse sweepstakes. The winner gets bragging rights and the loser, presumably, gets to open a casino.

Jewish Americans chime in with their specific grievance—that the American government was aware of the deadly anti-Semitism in Europe and still turned Jewish immigrants away. Irish Americans remind us that they were discriminated against in Boston—so is everybody, that's what makes it *Boston,* but try convincing them of that—and Italian Americans want us all to stop assuming that they're all connected to the Mafia.

Only 80 percent of them are.

I'm kidding! See how bad this gets? We can't even joke anymore.

The great story of American history—how Americans of all stripes and types blended together to create a new nation, a new way of self-governance—gets lost in the cacophony of ethnic complaints and demands for redress.

You can't blame the high school quarterback for not knowing the name of the fortieth president of the United States, because that's just a name, a fact, an item on the timeline.

The American history that he's been taught is about all of the bad stuff that white Anglo-Saxon guys did to everyone else, and since everyone insists on jumping in with their sob story, you end up with a lot of material to cover.

There isn't room to talk about *Marbury* v. *Madison* or the Great Awakening or the Marshall Plan. And besides, what's the point of teaching a kid that stuff anyway? That stuff isn't going to make him feel guilty.

American history in general, with its great stories of courage, its amazing debates and philosophical clashes, the sheer scale of the continent that contained the imagination and dreams of generations of pioneers, inventors, presidents, villains, and heroes doesn't fit neatly into the preferred liberal narrative, which is basically: factories in the nineteenth century were pretty awful places, and then we got OSHA.

Vote for the liberal.

That's why liberals hate real American history. Because it might get in the way of their real agenda: advancing America's inexorable movement toward socialism.

7 The Military

"Our monsters in uniform"

Picture this scene: You're a happy autocrat, ruling your people with the benevolence and wisdom that only the anointed possess. You've ordered your subjects' lives in the manner that is best for them. They are not always happy, but they don't always know what's good for them, or they would be.

It's not easy being an autocrat. Sometimes you have to crack the whip. Sometimes it's necessary to throw some of your people in camps, break up their families, or eradicate the occasional village. This is the price of order.

Whether you are progressing toward socialism, communism, fascism, Islamism, or that special Latin American dictatorship you can call your own, it is the power of your state that makes everything possible.

Then one day your entire world is turned upside down.

You've done something to anger the United States of America and to your surprise, there are suddenly American soldiers everywhere. They're destroying your statues; they're liberating your people. And ungrateful as they are, your people are joining the Americans in hunting you down and bringing you to justice.

As you, the formerly great despot of Durkadurkastan, are dragged out of your spider hole, you realize that your destiny has been sealed by young men and women wearing the uniform of the United States.

That's why liberals hate the American military.

Their liberal vision—one of centralized control, state domination, and the suppression of individual liberty in the name of progress—is often the same as that of many of the autocrats our military has crushed.

C. S. Lewis once remarked that the most oppressive of tyrannies is a tyranny that is exercised for the good of its victims. And this describes the project of liberalism to a tee. Liberalism, at its core, is the contention that all governance and policy ought to be judged, not by its outcomes, or its means, but by its *intentions*.

You can't make an omelet without breaking a few eggs, say the liberals.

And boy, have they proven themselves the master chefs of the not-so-delicious omelet of failed governance around the world.

This is the core ethic of the liberal.

And it gives us the key to the three reasons that the liberal hates our military.

The first is the U.S. military's long-standing record of smashing the liberal project on every continent, in every era. When Americans destroyed German militarism in World War I, liberals understood that we crushed a particular model of centralized, aggressive state control that they themselves aspired to.

When the Americans again crushed the Axis in World War II, liberals knew that with those powers died a vision of centralist, corporatist, hierarchical governance that they not-so-secretly revered.

And when the American military, under the hated Ronald Reagan, laid to rest once and for all the hope of communism, liberals were once again deprived of a model of totalitarian control for which they had much sympathy.

Today, in this age, we see the American military engaging in combat and conflict from Central Asia, to the Middle East, to the vast interior spaces of Africa. And in doing so, our soldiers, sailors, airmen, and Marines embark upon what the liberal has been trained to think of as imperialistic, colonialist, and yes, racist work.

From the tribal wastelands of Afghanistan and Pakistan to the pirate havens of East Africa, the military of the United States is on a classic civil mission, daring to impose Western values upon indigenous cultures. And keep Americans safe at the same time.

The liberal trained at Berkeley or Brown or Williams no doubt has a meltdown at the thought of confident, aggressive, and victorious Americans failing to respect the multiculturalist ideas that provide the basis for their entire worldview.

Where the liberal espouses the false equality of cultures, the American soldier demonstrates with the rifle and the MRE the intrinsic superiority of ours.

Where the liberal pays lip service to the validity of all mores and beliefs, the American soldier embarks upon missions every day to forcibly eliminate tyranny.

And where the liberal subscribes to a creed of American impotence and our inability to change the world, the American soldier demonstrates that American power changes the world for the better every day.

"Peace through superior firepower" is a credo the American soldier lives by.

"Give peace a chance" is, well, a really bad song by a guy who also imagined no heaven, and no countries.

The American soldier could never imagine living in that world.

And that's another thing about liberals. They don't even like American soldiers. They don't like who they are and where they come from.

How can I say this?

Just listen to liberals talk about soldiers.

During the Iraq War, liberals were constantly saying things like, "We are for the soldier, we're just against his mission."

That's like being for McDonalds, and against the beef.

That's like being for the football players, but against the coaches and team.

That's like being for freedom, but against democracy.

Or being for the people who work at corporations, but against corporations themselves.

Oops. I forgot. That's what liberals really think about those things, too.

Telling a soldier you are for him, but against his mission, may make the liberal feel better, but not the soldier—who is risking his life for the mission!

But liberals also don't like our soldiers for other reasons. For one, a disproportionate number of our troops come from the South, believe in God, love guns and football and NASCAR—and love their country so much that they decided to fight for her. And possibly die for her.

Liberals see it differently. They see soldiers as being victims of economic circumstances that compel them to join. They see the military as an outpost for uneducated bumpkins and inner-city kids who join the military because they have no other options.

I'd love to see a liberal actually say any of this to a soldier's face. Don't hold your breath.

They keep their condescension to themselves, because they know that the concerned, smug look on their faces might be wiped off with one punch.

When the liberal's favorite soldier, John Kerry, returned from his four-month summer vacation in Vietnam (cameras in tow), he flew straight to Washington, D.C., threw the medals he didn't earn into the Potomac, and testified before a bunch of senators that the guys he was fighting with were a bunch of animals.

Liberals ate it up. And the liberal media, especially.

This ambitious Yale man—Kerry was chairman of the Liberal Party of the Yale Political Union—was trotted before the Senate Foreign Relations Committee (a committee he would later chair) to tell his story about his service in Vietnam.

And what stories he told.

Not his stories, but stories by a group called the Winter Soldier's Project. Stories Kerry didn't bother to fact-check. Why bother, when they fit your agenda perfectly?

That the stories were largely proven to be pure fabrications didn't stop Kerry. Or prompt an apology.

"They told the stories of times that they had personally raped, cut off ears, cut off heads, taped wires from portable telephones to human genitals and turned up the power, cut off limbs, blown up bodies, randomly shot at civilians, razed villages in the fashion reminiscent of Genghis Khan, shot cattle and dogs for fun, poisoned the food stocks," Kerry told a somber Senate panel, in his weird, affected Masterpiece Theater accent.

Sounds like an average week for Saddam and his sons when they ruled Iraq.

But Kerry was describing the U.S. soldier. He was happy to smear all GIs—and do so with that dour, haughty pomposity we have come to know Kerry for, and all to advance his own standing. And his own political career.

Here is how he described his fellow soldiers.

"The country doesn't know it yet, but it's created a monster, a monster in the form of millions of men who have been taught to deal and to trade in violence, and who were given the chance to die for the biggest nothing in history."

The liberals *really* ate that up.

And Kerry, a warrior for the liberal cause, kept on feeding them more.

When asked about why he thought our soldiers—the so-called monsters he described—did what they did in Vietnam, Kerry went straight for the cultural jugular.

"I think clearly the responsibility for what has happened there lies elsewhere. I think it lies in large part with this country, which allows a young child before he reaches the age of fourteen to see twelve thousand violent deaths on television, which glorifies the John Wayne Syndrome, which puts out Fighting Men comic books on the stands."

John Wayne syndrome? I didn't know liking John Wayne was a disease, Senator Blue Blood.

Kerry didn't blame the soldiers for being monsters. They couldn't help themselves. It's the country they grew up in—those John Wayne movies and those comic books—that turned those poor bastards into monsters.

That's what liberals really think about our soldiers. And the country they serve.

But there's a second reason why liberals hate the military, a deeper one. It is their belief that moral judgment is primarily rendered on intentions.

Nothing can be further from the ethos of the American military.

In the United States military, as anyone who has served in it would tell you, judgment is rendered not on the basis of good intentions, but on the basis of competence, excellence, and achievement of the mission.

Outcomes matter. Results matter.

The liberal project, having spawned nothing but failure throughout its existence, is the antithesis of the culture of the U.S. military.

Merit matters to soldiers. Merit rules in military units. Imagine a sniper getting the job, and not being a good sniper. Imagine a pilot getting the job, and not meeting the high standards set by his commanders.

It's unthinkable.

Can you imagine what a politically correct military would look like if liberals were in charge?

Think the staff of Starbucks, without weapons.

Ironically, in the place where merit rules the day—our armed forces—minorities fare quite well. It turns out that African Americans can perform without having the bar lowered on them. In the military and in the world of sports, African Americans manage to excel without any "help" from liberals.

That's because the soft bigotry of low expectations may have a home in the liberal mind, but not on the battlefield. Or the ball field.

And then there is the third reason liberals hate the military. His name is George S. Patton, and all that he epitomized. Just running through some of his most famous quotations would give any liberal a migraine.

"A good plan violently executed now is better than a perfect plan executed next week." Liberals hate that one, because they are always in search of perfection.

"If everyone is thinking alike, then somebody isn't thinking." Liberals hate that Patton gem because what they seek is conformity.

And then there is this Patton classic: "Battle is the most magnificent competition in which a human being can indulge. It brings out all that is best; it removes all that is base. All men are afraid in battle. The coward is the one who lets his fear overcome his sense of duty. Duty is the essence of manhood."

Battle? Competition? Winners and losers? Duty to country? Manhood?

That's why liberals really hate the U.S. military.

Because our soldiers believe in all of that stuff crazy old Patton believed in.

And they're willing to pay the ultimate price for those beliefs.

6 The Founding Fathers

Old white guys with wigs

Imagine, for a moment, that you're one of those high-powered market-ing guys. You know the type I'm talking about: the guy who's dressed in one of those zillion-dollar suits, pointy shoes, edgy ties, and really complicated eyeglasses.

And then imagine it's your job to find a really diverse and balanced group of people to come up with the next Constitution of the United States.

Okay, so you're going to need some women. About half, actually. And then some African Americans, some Native Americans, and don't forget the fastest-rising group in America, Hispanic Americans. Asians are important, too. And let's not forget a healthy dose of our Arabic friends.

You might want to get out a pad of paper. It's going to be a very long list.

Don't worry about forgetting any group or ethnicity. The minute word of the project gets out, you'll be swamped with emails, Twitter campaigns, shout-outs on MSNBC, and your office will doubtless be surrounded by protesters and petitioners, all demanding that this or that group be represented, this or that race, creed, or religion be given a "seat at the table," this or that specific class of person get special attention, special mention, special notice.

As Willy Loman's wife said, attention must be paid.

And just imagine, for a moment, that you somehow manage to do all of that. That you somehow manage—I know, I know, impossible, but we're doing a thought experiment here—to satisfy the race-hustlers and the ethno-politicians and the professionally aggrieved, and you actually get a "diverse" and "inclusive" and "rainbow coalition" of folks together to sit down and redraw the United States Constitution.

What do you think the resulting document would look like?

Maybe a better question is, What do you think the resulting document would *smell* like?

Because you know exactly what it's going to *be*. Which is: nothing you'd want to carry around in your pocket.

The United States Constitution—heck, *all* of our founding documents: the Declaration, the Constitution, the Bill of Rights, you name it—was written by a bunch of white guys in tights and powdery wigs. I know, I know—terrible, right? But somehow this exclusive and non-diverse group of men managed to condense the most powerful and lasting declaration of human liberty into a slim set of principles, so elegantly, so thoughtfully, that when the whole thing is printed, it's small enough for every citizen to carry around in his back pocket.

As every citizen should.

And they managed to do it in language that—despite its age and the passage of time—is crystal-clear and easy to understand, as long as you're not serving on the Supreme Court of the United States or the Ninth Circuit Court of Appeals, where apparently some of the language is baffling.

Or just a general nuisance, because it makes it harder for these so-called judges to act like legislators.

Or better still, philosopher kings, which was the job they prepared for during their stints at Harvard Law, Yale, and Berkeley.

The Founding Fathers managed to do this for all of the usual reasons—they were smart, they had a lot of free time, they were educated in the tradition of Anglo-Saxon philosophy and religion, they didn't refuse a glass of wine or two in the middle of the day to relax a bit and take a break—but also for reasons that can't be so easily quantified.

They did this because they knew it was right.

Not perfect. Not infallible. But right.

Right in the sense that they knew in their hearts that personal freedom and liberty and human dignity are gifts from God, not from a governor or president or king.

So when they sat down to debate and politick and frame the document that has led us here, to 2012, the longest democratic experiment in the history of man, they started from a simple premise: The constitution they were writing wasn't going to be a list of the rights that the people *retained*. It was going to be a document that restricts the *government*.

The Constitution doesn't tell the people what they're allowed to do. It tells the government what *it* cannot do.

It draws a line in the sand: this far, and no further.

The Constitution also creates a complex series of checks and balances between the branches of government, and even within each branch. And all to block too much power from consolidating in any one place.

When politicians complain that they can't get things done, when pundits complain that there is gridlock in Washington, D.C., that is precisely what the Founding Fathers were shooting for when they wrote the Constitution.

Gridlock was the point, not the problem.

Not bad work for a bunch of old, crusty, eighteenth-century rich white guys who dressed like women, sucked down more Skoal than a major league baseball relief pitcher, and smelled worse than your average Occupy Wall Street protester on his best day.

And you can carry the whole document around on your iPhone.

Really. There's an app for that.

Boy, do liberals hate this.

They hate the idea behind the whole enterprise. The whole idea of a document that restricts government—government! What could be more loving and nurturing than government?!

It all just drives them nutso, like a rat in a coffee can.

Why do we need to restrict it? Especially when there are so many things that government needs to do, like choose your doctor and teach your children and correct your diet and save your money and organize your business and a host of other things that the Founding Fathers would shake their heads at if they were alive today.

Seriously. If we could somehow transport the Founders to the present day, giant clouds of wig powder would erupt in cumulus plumes, as they shook their heads in unison at all of the things we the citizens ask of our government, and all of the things that the government shoves down our throats.

They'd be disappointed. But I'm not sure they'd be surprised.

And that's why liberals really hate the Founding Fathers. Not just because they were all white and all guys and all loved tobacco. (Although, boy, does that stick in their craw!)

They hate them because the Founders knew, *knew* in their hearts, that without constant vigilance and strict attention, government would creep over everything, like crabgrass. They knew, *knew* in their hearts, that men were not angels, that man is by his very nature fallen, that men with too much power are dangerous, and that there is only one path to perfectibility—and it is not through the social engineering of politicians and government.

It is through Him. It is with Him.

Those crusty old white men, most of whom were Christians, even got that part right. They didn't impose some kind of old-man theocracy on the masses. One nation under Baptists, one nation under Episcopalians, one nation under Catholics was not good for America. Or religion.

It didn't hurt that the document they revered even more than their portable Shakespeare and Montesquieu—the Bible—itself calls for separation of church and state ("Render unto Caesar the things which are Caesar's, and unto God the things that are God's"). But the First Amendment, with the establishment and free exercise clauses, manages to protect the church from the state, and the state from the church.

That kind of depth and foresight would be too much for any liberal brain to fathom. So, too, would that kind of dynamic tension. That sheer political genius.

So let's go back to our politically correct, perfectly balanced, ethnically sensitive constitutional convention.

What do you imagine the "rights" will be that they come up with? The right to pursue liberty and prosperity? The right to be free from government intervention?

Done laughing now?

You know what it would look like. Not an enumeration of the restricted powers of the government, but a list of things the government—that is, me and you, the taxpayers—*owes* to the people. Free this and free that. Free health care. Free education. Free lunches. Free breakfasts. Come to think of it, all of that is free for half of America right now.

If this politically correct, culturally diverse crowd had their way, it would be guaranteed goodies as far as the paycheck can stretch.

It wouldn't be a constitution. It would be a Christmas list.

Actually, somewhere down along Article XXIX, paragraph 21, section ii, there'd be a new rule that you can't even use the phrase "Christmas list."

It would be a Winter Solstice Celebration Gifting Guideline.

It would be housed in a big impersonal government building, with lots of government employees carefully monitoring the gifting, and would ultimately become a part of the executive branch.

Think about it: We already have the Treasury Department, the Department of State, the Department of Defense, the Department of Justice, the Department of the Interior, the Department of Agriculture, the Department of Commerce, the Department of Labor, the Department of Health and Human Services, the Department of Housing and Urban Development, the Department of Transportation, the Department of Energy, the Department of Education, the Department of Veterans Affairs, and the Department of Homeland Security.

And you think it is a stretch to think that one day there could be a Department of Gifts and Giving?

That's why the Founders would really be spinning in their graves if they came back to visit America. The modern administrative state, and the unelected bureaucrats who run and regulate our lives, would have been unimaginable to them.

And that's why I would hate to see that new Constitution written by that politically correct and culturally diverse crowd, because I couldn't carry it around in my pocket. It would be way, way too big. And way, way, way too complicated and long.

Which is why the Founders wrote the document the way they wrote it. To keep that kind of thing from happening. (Or, maybe, in light of what's occurring right now in Washington, D.C., to at least *slow it down a bit.*)

And that's what drives the liberals crazy about the Founding Fathers. Liberals hate the Founders because the Founders had their number, all those years ago.

They had them pegged.

5 The States

I was traveling once on a flight from New York to Dallas when I heard a question I'll never forget. *"Who the heck lives in Oklahoma?"*

It wasn't just the question. It was how it was delivered. With sheer contempt. Like someone would have to be crazy, or worse, to choose a state like Oklahoma in which to live.

It was two buddies who were talking, and one of them mentioned that after some business in Dallas, he was going to rent a car and drive to Oklahoma City to visit friends. And that's when the other guy said it: *"Who the heck lives in Oklahoma?"*

What he was really saying was, *"Who the heck chooses to live in Oklahoma?"* And I knew right away he was a liberal. I didn't even have to ask.

294

Some years ago, I remember Bryant Gumbel was talking to someone on some morning TV show somewhere when an anchor mentioned he'd be in Indianapolis over the weekend. Gumbel quickly shot back, "India—no—place?"

Everyone on the set laughed. I didn't get the joke.

Now I've always known Gumbel was a liberal. And I've never liked him, not because he's a liberal—I'm not quite that shallow—but because he is an arrogant, aloof, self important ex–sports reporter turned ex-newsreader who thinks just a little too highly of himself.

But the reaction on the set was what stunned me. Everyone laughed. Everyone in front of the camera. And behind it.

And I thought to myself as I watched this crass regional bigotry on display: *"Who do you think watches the dumb morning show you put on every day so you can sell soap and toothpaste and pay the bills? Your sophisticated friends in Manhattan?"*

And I might add, most of the folks on that set—all of the sophisticated media types—all came from someplace else anyway.

Places like Oklahoma City.

And India-no-place!

We all know how little regard liberals have for flyover country.

But the contempt goes deeper than mere culture. Liberals don't quite understand why we give those rubes in the states so much power. So much control over their own lives and money.

And there's one simple answer.

The Tenth Amendment.

That damned Tenth Amendment.

When you tell a liberal that you actually believe the Tenth Amendment is as important as, if not more important than, any other amendment, he looks at you as if you'd just sprung a new head.

"The Tenth Amendment?" they'll squeal. "You still believe in that states' rights nonsense?"

Of course, they'd be referring to the dark chapters of southern segregation, when racists used the Tenth Amendment as a pretext to deprive African Americans of their Fourteenth Amendment right to equal treatment under the law.

Those folks weren't states' rights advocates. They were racists, using a very bad legal argument to advance a very bad social policy.

Sort of like liberals do just about every time they make any legal argument.

When I tell a liberal that I think the states should be allowed to run their own health care and other internal affairs, I get an incredulous smirk. *"Have you ever met a state legislator? Those yahoos can't run anything!"*

To which I immediately reply, *"Have you ever met a federal legislator? Or a federal bureaucrat?"*

And that's the rub. At least I can actually meet my state legislator. I can drive to my state capitol and show up, and if I'm with just a dozen or so people, I'll get his attention. And if he doesn't listen to me, I can email him, call him, drop by his house, or his aunt's house, or call the local paper and radio station and even drop by his favorite restaurant or watering hole in town, and just make a general nuisance of myself.

Somehow, the state is something I can wrap my taxpayer's head around.

But the federal legislators and their staffs? And the phalanx of suitors and lobbyists seeking favors? I haven't a clue. Or a chance.

It's pointless to point out to liberals that the federal government's foray into regulating every single aspect of our lives hasn't exactly been an impressive display of governmental competence. They don't deny the federal government's shortcomings—but their explanation is that the federal government doesn't have *enough* power.

Or *enough* money.

So it's better not to bring these matters up with liberals. Because the states' rights argument is one that actually challenges their entire worldview.

Are there better arguments to bring up as for why the states should run their own internal affairs? You bet! But actually it's better not to bring those up, either. The federal government is to liberals what Jesus Christ is to the Christians. They worship no other gods before the federal government, especially not the states.

In fact, the states are a competing set of gods—fifty of them, to be precise.

And liberals hate that.

You might be tempted to point out that the Constitution itself says the states should be running their internal affairs. Under Article I, Congress doesn't have the power to regulate commerce generally, only interstate commerce. And unless a power is given to Congress specifically in the Constitution, the states are in charge.

Alas, deploying the Constitution against liberals is also a pointless exercise. You ask liberals whether they're worried that their latest scheme might be unconstitutional, and you'll get Speaker Pelosi's famous response on the constitutionality of Obamacare: "Are you serious?"

You might also be tempted to point out that letting the states run their own internal affairs increases democracy. Surely having majority rule in each of the fifty states is more responsive to what people want than pure majority rule in the country as a whole.

Democracy should divide self-determination into the smallest units possible—the individual first of all. That's the meaning of liberty! Alas, pointing that out is also a useless exercise. Liberals don't trust people to govern their own affairs. That's why they hate the states but love the nanny-state federal government.

Those yahoos can't run anything! With that expression of cultural elitism, liberals reveal what they really think of the Constitution, democracy, and liberty itself.

In the famous old case of *Hammer* v. *Dagenhart* (1918), the Supreme Court struck down a law of Congress that outlawed the interstate transport of goods made in factories that had employed child labor (below the federal standard of fourteen years old). This ruling caused much anxiety among liberals. How could the Supreme Court protect the exploitation of children?

The liberal reaction was nonsense. The issue in the case was not whether child labor was wrong. Everyone agreed that it was wrong. All of the states had child labor laws on the books. In fact many states imposed stricter standards than the federal one, and the trend was clearly in favor of tightening the standards further in all the states.

The real issue was why the *federal government* should be involved in regulating child labor. The Constitution gave Congress no power to regulate the purely internal commerce of a state. In fact, at the time, not even liberals would have argued otherwise.

You've come a long way, liberals.

Now, a majority of Congress was at the time against child labor for the simple reason that a majority of the people in each of the states was against it. And sure, state legislators would want to compete for industry to locate in their states. But you know what? They liked their jobs even more, and the people who elected them were against child labor. That's why the states, on their own, had moved forcefully to limit and eventually abolish child labor.

Heck, maybe those yahoos could run their own affairs after all!

Then came Franklin Roosevelt, whose New Deal arrived to smash one constitutional principle after another. Liberals steamrolled everyone, and the casualty was the Tenth Amendment. And the rest of the Constitution.

The Supreme Court Roosevelt inherited didn't immediately cave to his demands. Indeed, they let him know that they were not going to allow the federal government to regulate everything under the sun, and concentrate all power in Washington. That they actually took their job to guard the Constitution seriously.

And he said, *"Oh yeah? Well what if I appoint five extra judges to the Supreme Court?"*

At that point, the Court realized that its goose was cooked. It abdicated its role as protector of the Constitution, and let the new majority have its way. Congress could now regulate whatever it wanted.

The New Deal should really be called the New Constitution. Because the Constitution no longer imposed any limit on federal power. The limits of the Constitution were replaced with the principle of national majority rule—unrestrained by any constitutional principle. Tyranny of the majority, you say? Liberals call that social justice.

But here's the thing. If the federal government, armed with the power of taxing and spending, can regulate everything under the sun, then what's to stop a transient liberal majority from confiscating everyone's property and spending it on themselves and their voters?

Nothing, that's what.

The federal government has become an instrument for rent-seeking on a massive scale, controlled chiefly by liberals who think they know exactly how we should all run our affairs.

The liberals' approach to government is totalitarianism, armed with the power of confiscation. Your money doesn't belong to you—you're lucky they let you keep any of it.

Liberals think that everything they give away is free. But deficit spending is just taxation deferred for another day and another generation. They say they're about generosity, but what they're really about is confiscation.

Confiscation as social justice. Confiscation as the instrument of their benevolent rule.

The reason liberals hate the states is that their very existence is a thorn in the liberal side. The idea that people should run their own affairs, which is the basic justification for the continued existence of states in our Constitution, totally contradicts the liberals' most basic tenet—which is that *they* should control every aspect of our lives.

It's a familiar argument: democracy versus totalitarianism. Conservatives hate the latter. Liberals hate the former.

4 The Constitution

We the people . . .

"We the people."

Those are the first three words of the U.S. Constitution. Not "We the bureaucrats." Not "We the politicians." Not "We the judges."

Just "We the people."

And the Founders spent the rest of their time writing a Constitution that gave life to those three words.

Which is why liberals hate The Constitution.

Oh, boy, do they hate the Constitution! I mean, they have even termed the Tea Party's adherence to the Constitution a "fetish," which is downright scary considering the folks making the fetish claim live in places where you can actually make a living being a dominatrix.

They nearly broke out in hives when someone in Congress came up with the idea to read the entire Constitution on the House floor.

What a waste of time!

Now there are many reasons why liberals hate the Constitution—and many ways they demonstrate that antipathy—but what really steams them is that this old, outdated document starts with those pesky three words I started this chapter with: "We the people."

Those words disrupt all of the great liberal plans.

As State Senator Barack Obama complained to National Public Radio a number of years ago, our Constitution was a document of "negative liberties" in that it stated what the government cannot do. At the time, he was talking about something called "redistributive rights."

Because that's what the Constitution is to him. A bunch of weirdly worded and oddly subdivided collections of paragraphs and sentences that are designed to protect "We the people" from their own government.

And that just messes up everything for him.

There's that pesky Bill of Rights, which is just an endless series of "thou shalt nots" for government.

And we know how much liberals love "thou shalt nots."

Which is, not at all.

President Obama doesn't like all of those "thou shalt nots"—negative rights—because they get in the way of his plans to create a whole series of "positive rights."

Like a right to an education. A right to health care. And so on and so on.

Then there's that crazy idea called separation of powers, which liberals hate because it creates gridlock. And liberals hate gridlock because it means that they can't get to spend all of that money they don't have.

I can't count the number of times President Obama blamed his inability to "get things done" on the legislative branch—Congress—holding him back.

That pesky Article I.

Back when Obamacare was being debated on Capitol Hill, President Obama convened a bipartisan get-together where everyone could talk through their points, and reach some sort of compromise.

Obama called on Senator McCain, and called him "John."

I know this might seem like an obscure point, but it is actually what poker players call a "tell."

It reveals Obama's true feelings about McCain's status, and his.

Oh, how I wish, "John" had replied, "Now, Barack, I am a U.S. senator, and being that I serve in the first branch of government—the people's branch—I hope you would do me the honor of calling me Senator, and I'll call you Mr. President."

Okay. Maybe I'm asking a lot. I mean, McCain graduated from the U.S. Naval Academy, and understands these kinds of things.

That rules matter. That protocol matters. That respect matters.

Obama went to Harvard Law, where he was taught that he was special, that the rules were dumb and didn't apply to him, and that the Constitution was just a bit archaic.

How do I know they think that way at Harvard and Columbia Law?

Listen to their graduates talk about the Constitution!

Heck, listen to Judge Ruth Bader Ginsburg, herself a Columbia Law graduate, who, on a trip to Egypt, was asked what Constitution she thought Egypt should model their new Constitution after: "I would not look to the U.S. Constitution if I were drafting a constitution in the year 2012. I might look at the Constitution of South Africa. That was a deliberate attempt to have a fundamental instrument of government that embraced basic human rights, had an independent judiciary . . . . It really is, I think, a great piece of work that was done, and much more recent than the U.S. Constitution."

There you have it! They teach this kind of stuff at Columbia Law.

A sitting Supreme Court justice recommending South Africa's

Constitution as a model for other countries is like having the Ford CEO drive around in a Volkswagen.

Okay. You think I'm being picky. Let's take Justice Stephen Breyer, a Harvard Law graduate who also taught at Harvard Law. He believes in what he likes to call a "living Constitution" so deeply that he actually wrote a book about it.

Which basically means that the old one is not very useful in a whole lot of cases, so why not just make up some laws as we go, and keep up with the changing times?

He also thinks international law should play a role in a judge's decision-making process. Who needs the U.S. Constitution when we can read Denmark's?

There you have it. They teach that at Harvard Law School, too.

In fact, they teach everything but the actual Constitution at our nation's finest law schools. Because that would be sooooooooooooooooooooo . . . boring.

It's much more fun playing that Harvard Law School game, "Let's Make Up the Law."

I mean, who wants to do all of that dour, tiring research into the Founders' original intentions? The kind of dreary work that old workhorses like Justices Scalia, Thomas, Alito, and Roberts do?

Now that Justice Anthony Kennedy, he has the right idea. You never know how he'll sway, or how he'll vote. Because sometimes, he thinks the Constitution actually governs our nation. And sometimes it doesn't. He goes right. He goes left.

He's the key swing vote in almost every single close case we have at the Supreme Court these days. Ah, the joys of being a one-man constitutional convention.

All of that would bug the Founders, but what I suspect would astonish them is the size and scale of Washington, D.C. And those government agencies, places like the EPA, HHS, DHS, FDA, DEA, FBI, CIA, DOE, DOD, HUD, and SPUD.

Okay. I made up SPUD. But give it a few years, and I'm sure we'll have one.

I think the Founders would be stunned to see the power many of these agencies have over every aspect of our lives.

And what would bug them the most is that these people don't answer to "We the people."

They don't run for office, and we can't fire them.

The Founders worked hard to create a limited government with a whole bunch of enumerated powers reserved to the states. And the people.

That is what the United States was all about—that is, before all of this hope and change and fundamental transformation buried us under a mountain of debt and an army of nameless, faceless bureaucrats.

The biggest threat to our republic may well be that army of bureaucrats. Even when Obama leaves office, he will leave behind a society so infested with government hacks that there is no telling how long it will take us to recover.

If we can recover.

You see, with so many bureaucrats at the federal, state, county, and city levels, almost everyone's "special cousin"—the one who can't get a real job—is now employed as a bureaucrat. Yep. Someone pulled some strings somewhere and he "got on" with the "guvmint"—doing God knows what.

Bless his heart.

But the problem is, all of these bureaucrats now have some kind of crippling authority over someone's private business—you know, the business that hired the smart cousins who are able to do that real job.

This is a huge army of folks, all of these "special cousins."

Think millions and millions of Barney Fifes blowing their whistle and pulling out their ticket pad every time someone wants to do something productive.

The notion of limited government is just not possible with so many government employees gumming up everything we do and touch.

How can you have limited government when there's a department of something to screw up on every corner? This is why you have straight-faced government employees shutting down lemonade stands run by kids—and acting all self-important to the media when doing so.

Yes, Google "lemonade stand busted" and you get forty thousand hits.

One example is from Midway, Georgia, in the summer of 2011. Police Chief Kelly Morningstar was on patrol and drove by a stand set up by three ten-year-old girls. Our intrepid law enforcement hero shut 'em down. When their parents complained, Morningstar bravely stated she told the pretty young perps: "We understand you guys are young, but still, you're breaking the law, and we can't let you do it anymore. The law is the law, and we have to be consistent with how we enforce the laws."

Yes, this was said with a straight face—and the town's mayor backed up the head cop. Aren't you picturing Mayberry's buffoonish mayor right now?

Now I know what you're thinking. You're thinking, "wait, this is a cop and I thought we were talking about bureaucrats." We are. This is illustrative of how we are being taken over by bureaucrats and don't even know it. The cop, who is obviously insufferably left-brained to begin with, was carrying out a bureaucratic fiat.

What "law" was this police officer upholding?

Midway city law requires business and food permits (fifty dollars a day), even though the stand was at the home of one of the girls. So this local government expects these girls to plunk down fifty bucks to some bureaucrat and then fill out some paperwork, all so they can maybe make twenty-five dollars.

And learn a little about how to run a business.

According to Morningstar, who was apparently gunning for the Barney Fife lifetime achievement award, "We were not aware of how the lemonade was made, who made the lemonade, of what the lemonade was made with, so we acted accordingly by city ordinance."

Gee, I dunno. Maybe lemon juice, sugar, water? Just a wild guess.

Keep in mind, however, that this is not really about lemonade stands. This is the bureaucratic maze that our entire free enterprise system is now engulfed in. And it's proportional.

Yes, several days lead time, paperwork, and fifty bucks is what the city extracts from an enterprise that may last two hours and gross twenty-five dollars. Imagine the cost and bureaucratic maneuvering any real entrepreneur faces.

My point is, bureaucrats are swallowing us whole and many of us don't know it.

But it gets worse. Not only are these bureaucrats ruining our businesses and our lives, "we the people" are paying for it. And paying them, on average, twice what we make in the private sector when you factor in health and retirement benefits.

This is not the experiment in self-governance that our Founders contemplated with the Constitution.

This is not what "we the people" want, but it is what too many of the politicians want. As luck would have it, many of these cubicle dwellers belong to government unions. Government unions, as we now know, exist to stand behind liberal politicians at political rallies, all wearing the same T-shirt and holding up the mass-produced union signs.

Oh, and they vote and pay union dues—dues that are then funneled into the campaign coffers of those same liberal politicians, who have promised to pay them more money if they are elected, which will lead to more union members and even more union dues . . . and . . .

You see where this is going?

Remember, it is always *our money* they are throwing around ultimately, too. Our tax money.

Liberal judges make rulings that support this bureaucratic entitlement culture by using the rule of law to force us to pay for more bureaucrats. They will then spend more of our money to fill out more paperwork to justify their existence, and it all leads to even more government employees who vote for even more liberal politicians who appoint even more liberal judges.

All of which flies in the face of the limited government laid out in our Constitution. The plain truth is, "we the people" don't need all of these faceless bureaucrats. But they need us. Who else is going to pay them and pay for their health care and their pensions?

Liberals must ignore the Constitution—and "we the people"—in order to live with themselves.

That's why they love talking about their "Living Constitution."

Because the old one is dead to them.

3

E Pluribus Unum

"From the one . . . many?"

If you asked a team of expert psychologists and sociological researchers to come up with a design that was sure to infuriate and offend liberals in America, they'd probably come up with what we call the Great Seal.

The Great Seal has got it all—everything liberals despise is there, front and center.

In the first place, you've got your eagle, holding arrows. What good could those arrows possibly serve, aside from celebrating the violent blood lust that liberals see in Americans? It doesn't matter to them that in the eagle's right talon he's clutching the olive branch of peace—making the visual point that Teddy Roosevelt made 150 years later with the words "Speak softly and carry a big stick."

Liberals don't think we *need* those sharpened arrows.

Liberals would prefer it if the bald eagle on the Great Seal was holding olive branches in both talons, or, better, an olive branch in one, and maybe a soft cushion in the other, to entice our enemies to lie down and snooze.

Or, perhaps, the olive branch and a bottle of lavender massage oil. Or maybe one of those loofah sponges they use in spas.

Anything, actually, from the Brookstone catalogue would work.

The key, for liberals, would be to get rid of those awful arrows. We don't need arrows, or a big stick. We just need a couple of Nerf toys and a pleasant, hopeful expression.

And that's another thing that's wrong with the Seal: that eagle looks too *angry*. Too hurtful and judgmental.

Liberals, given the choice, would replace the scary eagle with something more like the popular children's television figure, Barney, the purple dinosaur. *I love you!* the Great Seal would project to all who gaze at it, a big purple dinosaur holding up a juice box and a gender nonspecific plush toy.

Liberals hate the eagle and hate the arrows. But they also hate the banner—a design that echoes the American flag—and the medallion of stars above the eagle's head.

Both of those elements seem so aggressive and militaristic. And worse, both of them seem so *proud*. Banners and medallions are the kinds of things that fly during battles, and both are the kinds of things that seem to ignore the awful, shameful things that liberals associate with America.

It would be better, for liberals, if we replaced those symbols of pride with what they might call little "snippets of shame."

Maybe replace the medallion with a photograph of some victim of American Evil. Thanks to Photoshop technology, maybe it could even be a *rotating* photograph, cycling through the great Victims of American Aggression.

The American Indian, a slave, a couple of lesbians, a vegan or two, Rosa Parks, and pretty much anyone from a country south of the United States border—there would be no need to *choose.* Rotate 'em all in.

So now we've "fixed" the Great Seal of the United States. It's no longer something liberals hate. It's a happy, loving purple dinosaur, holding up a healthy snack and a soft cushion, and above his head is an ever-changing scrapbook of the Great American Victim.

But what about the most troublesome part of the Great Seal?

What about that awful motto?

E pluribus unum, Latin for "Out of many, one," flutters on a banner around the eagles'—excuse me: around the *purple dinosaur's*—head.

"Out of many, one" is the national motto, and what the Founders imagined it meant is that out of the great and celebrated differences between us, comes one nation and one larger purpose.

E pluribus unum is perhaps the most obnoxious motto the Founders could have come up with, as far as liberals are concerned. They don't mind the *e pluribus* part—they love to note the things that divide and separate us. But they positively despise the *unum* part.

The truth is, the Founders anticipated this. When they gathered to form a nation, almost three centuries ago, they were a collection of very different men. The Puritans from the North had complicated and not totally friendly relations with the Quakers from Pennsylvania, who in turn pretty much hated the Virginia Cavaliers, who, for their part, viewed the Scotch-Irish Georgians and Carolinians with contempt.

They were different, in other words—*pluribus* kinds of guys—but they knew that if America was to succeed, it would have to find some way to get an *unum* out of all of that *pluribus.*

Liberals hate this. They hate any attempt to find common ground among Americans, because their political principles, and their political *agenda,* is all about dividing us, drawing distinctions, making lists of in groups and out groups, turning us all into victims or victimizers.

Which one do you think *you* are?

Because that's the message that liberals send to Americans: Pick a side. You're either owed something, or you owe. They don't believe in an *unum,* because that would mean that all Americans would be governed by a single set of principles.

It would mean that all of us, no matter what part of the cacophonous *pluribus* we come from, would be, essentially, locking arms together to build the future.

Liberals hate that idea, because it robs them of their ability to pit sides against each other. That's the hot molten center of every liberal crackpot scheme—identify a victim group, apply political pressure, create a "program" to address the "wrong," and confiscate money from the "victimizer" group to pay for it.

That's why liberals love to identify new racial and ethnic groups. That's why they like to append a qualifier to the word "American." It's not enough to be just "American." You've got to be an African- or Muslim- or Gay- or Asian- or Pacific Islander—or, really, any qualifier you like kind of American. You can't be part of the *unum,* to a liberal. You always have to be a *pluribus.*

In fact, liberals look at the federal government, and the federal budget, as one vast lawsuit settlement. It's not a budget for the future. It's a series of payoffs for what liberals see as the crimes and misdemeanors of the American past. For them, the American taxpayer is just a poor, evil sap who owes reparations.

That's why they hate our motto, *e pluribus unum.* They hate it because it's all about building a future. Not about litigating the past.

There was a story in the *New York Times* that showcased the absurdity of the *pluribus* crowd (aka the diversity nuts).

It was about a girl named Natasha Scott, who was described as a high school senior of mixed racial heritage from Beltsville, Maryland.

She was venting about a personal dilemma on College Confidential, the go-to electronic bulletin board for anonymous conversation about admissions.

"I just realized that my race is something I have to think about," she wrote, describing herself as having an Asian mother and a black father. "It pains me to say this, but putting down black might help my admissions chances and putting down Asian might hurt it."

There you have it, from the mouth of a teenager, no less.

Look at what the *pluribus* crowd has done to this poor girl. She is acutely aware that the college admissions system favors one part of her ethnic heritage over another.

Oddly enough, Asians are a much smaller "minority" than African Americans in this country. But because Asians are so successful, college admission officers don't feel sorry for them, so they are not a preferred "minority."

What the *pluribus* crowd managed to accomplish with all of this ethnic engineering is not just to pit Natasha against other students in the quest for diversity.

They managed to pit Natasha against *herself*.

But the story got worse.

"My mother urges me to put down black, to use AA—Africa American—to get into the colleges I'm applying to," Natasha confessed. "I sort of want to do this, but I'm wondering if this is morally right."

Fantastic job, *pluribus* people! The only person with any common sense in the room is the child. She knows what she's doing is wrong. It's the adults who don't.

That Natasha's mom—herself an Asian—told her own daughter to check the African-American box is not just bad leadership; it is something much worse: It is cynicism incarnate.

Her mom is teaching her daughter to game the system and lie about her own ethnic heritage. Or at the very least, erase half of it to advance herself.

This flies in the face of everything our Founders tried to accomplish when they wrote the Constitution. Did they recognize that we've all got differences? Of course. But they also knew that the only way to move forward in freedom and prosperity was to dedicate the nation—the *pluribus*—to the *unum*.

The only way America works is if we act like *America,* instead of a squabbling group of distinct ethnic and racial subsets, which we are.

In 1994, Al Gore gave a speech at Institute of World Affairs in Milwaukee about—you guessed it—world affairs. This was during some down time in his remarkable career, somewhere between the time he invented the Internet and the time he discovered global warming. In that speech, the subject turned to "*E pluribus unum.*"

"We can build a collective civic space large enough for all our separate identities, that we can be *e pluribus unum*—out of one, many," he said.

Out of one, many. That's what he said, I swear.

Gore was quickly mocked for what some thought was an error. But it wasn't an error; it was a Freudian slip. Because it's what liberals really want the Latin phrase to mean.

Out of one, many.

Contrast Gore's talk with a speech in 2005 by Dr. Larry Arnn, president of Hillsdale College, a wonderful place where students are actually required to study the Constitution. Arnn was addressing the ways in which our Bill of Rights actually breeds harmony among Americans:

One may pray all he pleases, and others are left free to pray or not, and with all their property intact. Short of slander, libel, or treason, one may say what he pleases and do no harm to another. One can see how the right to property, properly conceived, has this same attribute. If my property is the fruit of my labor, and not of yours, then we have no conflict. My having my good deprives you of none of yours, and your having your good leaves me secure in mine. The interesting thing about this understanding of rights is the harmony it breeds in society. This harmony—or to use the political term, this justice—is the reason why our Constitution has lasted so long and our nation has prospered so well.

Brilliant point, Dr. Arnn. Liberals love to talk the harmony talk, but our Founders walked the harmony walk. And "we the people" have been the beneficiaries.

So let's go back to where we started this chapter, shall we? We fixed the Seal—the eagle is now a purple dinosaur, the banners are now the Pantheon of the Downtrodden, the arrows are incense and a loofah sponge.

But the motto remains tricky.

E pluribus angry?

E pluribus oppressed?

E pluribus omnipotent (government, not God)?

Something like that, right?

2 Apple Pie

Hold the sugar and ice cream

Naturally, liberals hate apple pie. I mean, there's that saying "as American as apple pie," which all but certifies the great American dessert's status. It's almost a requirement that apple pie falls on the liberal hate list.

You know, along with everything else in the old advertising jingle "baseball . . . hot dogs . . . apple pie and Chevrolet . . ." And then there's "Mom and apple pie" and so on.

Liberals cannot abide any of those things.

Take hot dogs, for instance. Do you have any idea what's in those things? They're stuffed with so many bad things that liberals think Americans would be better off grilling turkey dogs. Or tofu dogs.

Fat chance.

The assault on hot dogs reached its apotheosis last August when *USA Today* published a story that warned readers that hot dogs were dangerous for your health.

It turns out that the nonprofit Physicians Committee for Responsible Medicine said the processed meat in hot dogs carries a cancer risk on a par with cigarettes.

Hmmmm. Smoking Camel cigarettes is as dangerous as downing a couple of Nathan's Coney Island specials every now and then? Who knew?

Well, there's something you should know about the PCRM, the group that commissioned and promoted this so-called study.

It turns out that PCRM isn't just any group of doctors. They're vegans, with a very vegan agenda. There's nothing particularly wrong with that. But they've also been repeatedly accused by the American Medical Association of distorting the facts as a means of promoting their agenda. There is something particularly wrong with that.

Although hot dogs are not the gourmet snack of the health-conscious liberal vanguard—they do pack a heck of a lot of sodium, which all doctors agree is dangerous—most docs still think hot dogs eaten in moderation are okay. Just like most other things that are bad for you.

Like gambling. Or drinking. Or gunning the car to a hundred miles per hour on the open road. Or eating a gallon of Breyers Vanilla Bean—which I knock out by the end of the first quarter of a Dallas Cowboys game when they are losing.

Okay, so we've dispensed with hot dogs. Let's take Chevrolet. No, I mean literally. The liberals did take Chevrolet. They took Chevrolet—and the rest of General Motors—from its rightful owners, and gave it to the same unions that had, in effect, put it out of business.

So it's okay for liberals to not hate Chevrolet. Of course, these same liberals wouldn't be caught dead driving one unless it was the

Chevy Volt, but now that the labor unions own the company, it's off the hate list. For now.

And then there's that old American standby—the apple pie. Liberals don't hate it because it's bad for you. Oh, sure, apple pie conjures up thoughts of butter and flour and all kinds of other non–Michelle Obama approved substances.

Let's not forget the à la mode requisite. I am not sure why God made warm apple desserts and vanilla ice cream for each other, but He surely did.

We all know apple pie is not as healthy as a pile of steamed arugula, and yet we still love it. Which is a problem with liberals, loving something that's not good for you.

Unless you're talking about unprotected sex or marijuana.

Then it's okay, because liberals are all in favor of those things, and in favor of taxpayers' picking up the tab for the results, too.

But what really irks liberals about apple pie is what apple pie represents.

As demonstrated by the "American as apple pie" cliché, it represents America itself. And in a good, wholesome way.

There is nothing wholesome about America to your average liberal, who would prefer to associate our country with something bad like racism, sexism, or imperialism.

You know, like "America is a racist nation" and "America's chickens are coming home to ROOST."

Let's not forget that pie-eating patriot Michael Moore, who once said, "I like America to some extent," and once asked, "Should such an ignorant people lead the world?"

Gives you goose bumps, doesn't it? Then again, I'm thinking that, like me, Moore loves pie more than just "to some extent."

Of course, apple pie is also associated with some of America's great traditions. You know, like, Thanksgiving. Now there's a holiday that liberals really hate for a bunch of reasons. First, it represents part of the founding history of this nation, and for crying out loud, if we have learned anything from liberals, it's that the planet would be much better off without America.

Thus anything that has anything to do with a celebration of its founding is simply evil. Period. Not only that, but Thanksgiving is all about white people and eating birds and religion and God and all that stuff. YUK.

Of course, some folks associate apple pie with Christmas, too. The horror!

Christmas? As in CHRISTmas? Oh, we can't be having that.

Now to be fair and inclusive—and to make sure we get our facts straight, there is one holiday celebration that does not associate itself with apple pie: Kwanzaa.

You know Kwanzaa, the "ancient" and "sacred" tribal tradition that was started way back in, well, 1966 by Dr. Maulana Karenga. Dr. Karenga was chairman of the Black Studies Department at Long Beach State, and created this ancient and sacred tribal tradition as a way "to bring African Americans together as a community" after the Watts riots.

You'll see no apple pie at Kwanzaa, which was promoted by Karenga himself as a "black alternative" to the "white religion" of Christianity. After all, ancient Kwanzaan tradition holds that Jesus was psychotic. All the way back to 1966, which makes the sacred holiday about the same age as a VW van at a Grateful Dead concert.

Of course, if it wasn't bad enough that apple pie is associated with Thanksgiving and Christmas, the fact that this dessert is a staple at July Fourth celebrations just puts liberals into seizures.

Studies have come out in the past year that indicate that kids who go to patriotic parades or who wave the flag or who celebrate the Fourth of July are more likely to become—gasp—Republicans! Oh, no! Yes indeed, and the study comes from Harvard.

This is so rich I'll have another slice of pie, please!

And I am not exaggerating the findings. Check out the Huffington Post headlines about the story: *"July 4 Celebrations Make Children More Likely To Become Republican: Harvard Study."*

Well gosh. And then Google July Fourth and apple pie and *whammo!* 1.75 million results.

Of course, the academics who did the study tried to assign this outcome to evil plots by folks like Karl Rove and Dick Cheney and the like with the idea that *"the political right has been more successful in appropriating American patriotism and its symbols during the twentieth century"* and so on.

They just can't face it. Conservatives love America more than liberals do, and that's just the way it is.

In fact, it is one of the traits that determines whether one is a liberal or a conservative. To paraphrase what the liberal academics who performed the study said: *The political left has been more successful in appropriating anti-American sentiment and its symbols during the twentieth century.*

There. I am right, and so are they.

Where liberals so often go wrong is in correlation analysis. Or, as I like to call it, the Homer Simpson Factor. The D'oh! Factor.

Of course the political right appropriates patriotism and its symbols better than the left, because conservatives like patriotism and patriotic symbols and liberals do not.

Of course the political left has been more successful at appropriating anti-American symbols, because liberals like to hate America and conservatives do not.

This is much like when liberals figured out that folks who own a home are much more likely to be responsible with their money and successful than those who do not.

The conservative answer would be to help more people be responsible and successful—but the liberal answer was to give more people homes.

Now how did that work out?

Which just points out how dangerous liberals are when they get power.

They hate America and all it stands for.

And nothing stands for America better than apple pie.

1 America

The last not so great ex-hope.

(See Chapters 2–50.)

Acknowledgments

Thanks to my ever-patient and supportive boss, Greg Anderson at the Salem Radio Network; to Tom Tradup, the Salem radio executive who always has my back; to Ed Atsinger, the CEO of Salem Communications and broadcasting visionary, who has been so supportive over the years that I have worked for his company; to Roger Ailes and the Fox News Channel for inviting me to appear there for more than a decade; thanks to my loyal and hardworking crew: Producer Lance Anderson, Operations Director Eric Hansen, and Creative Services Director Peter Rief; to my business manager, Joey Hudson (who is like the brother I never had); to Mitchell Ivers, one of the best editors in the business; to David Vigliano, an extraordinary literary agent; and to my collaborator and writing partner, Lee Habeeb, whose constant optimism always inspires me. I'm blessed to be surrounded by many professionals who are so good at what they do. Most of all, thanks to you for allowing me into your home, car, or office through my radio show and my work on Fox News Channel. I'm a very lucky guy. God bless America.

Author's note: After the publication of 50 Things Liberals Love to Hate *in hardcover, I invited listeners to submit their own written chapter on the perfect "51st Thing." Here is that winning entry:*

Two-Parent Families
By Ron Wood

The loss of two-parent families is a disaster for America but a great opportunity for the liberal elite. They can step in and help! The dilemma of impoverished single mothers especially gives liberals the motivation to tax more, to spend more, and to use other people's money so the government can become the provider of choice for *all* their needs!

A story to make my point: I saw a handsome young man walking in my direction down the city street one day. He was probably in high school. Maybe an athlete. Moving fast. He tugged on his pants, pulled them way down, and uncovered all of his boxer shorts. He held on to his belt with one hand and kept on walking, although now with a waddle in his gait. He didn't notice me but I sure noticed him. "Hey! You! Pull your pants up!" I yelled.

"Who, me?" he tossed over his shoulder as he kept walking. "You don't even know me." He tugged upwards on his belt until his pants were now halfway up over his underwear, a little less in danger of exposing himself.

I thought to myself, yeah, son, I do know you. You're a wayward son. You're a momma's boy who's gotten too big for her to manage. Your daddy abandoned you and now you've grown up but you don't know how a man ought to behave. I know you because here you are, strutting down the street, a young rebel with no self-respect.

Tough love speaks up. It may sound like a father's voice. It may be a mother's insistence. But tough love will confront a wayward son. Why? So he will be spared from hell, kept from jail, and learn how to be a mature man for the sake of the next generation.

The absentee father problem in America may be the biggest problem we face. It's actually an epidemic. More than 72 percent of African Americans are born to single moms, and the number for all American babies is 40 percent. That is a catastrophe of epic proportions.

Indeed, there is no greater economic crisis or social issue. *Listen up:* America's power is not in its military might but in its culture. Our culture was once anchored in two-parent, multi-generational families based on the Bible. But sadly, America has changed.

Liberalism and liberal ideas changed it.

Now, too many homes have an empty chair at the head of the table. Sons feel it. Fatherless boys are more likely to see women as sex objects. They haven't seen an example of a faithful man loving a woman as a husband should. Boys raised with no man in the house are more likely to seek out gangs. Why? They find acceptance, authority figures, and feel authenticated by acting brave and getting noticed.

Boys have it tough in public schools too. Girls grow up faster and excel in a female-oriented school environment. Boys check out, go passive, and lose motivation to learn. Many studies have shown that simply putting a man in the classroom, just to be there, not even to teach, causes boys to suddenly do much better.

Mothers abandoned by their baby-daddy are more likely to go on welfare and have a lower standard of living while the renegade man's standard of living goes up after he bails on his family. Not fair is it? But it happens all the time.

Underage sex has very serious consequences. While the baby-daddy walks away with another notch on his belt, the baby-momma is left with stretch marks; she quits school, does stints at low-wage jobs, has a markedly diminished chance of being happily married, and a hard life beckons.

There is also the moral dilemma of abortion, the higher taxes we pay to pick up the bill to replace a two-parent family's income, the health-care and child-support costs, and the lost talent and training a skilled young woman could have contributed to our nation's benefit except she dropped out of school to raise a baby.

Leave it to liberals; they hate two-parent families so much they're willing to create a state option that produces outcomes that destine people who use it to a lifetime of bleakness and poverty.

It is hard enough in today's world to keep kids safe from drugs, violence, hatred, and the pervasive effect of TV's moral neutrality. But try doing it with no man in the house! Who is going to answer the door? Who will demonstrate hard work? Who will train life's values? Who will hug their son or their daughter and provide the reassurance every young person needs?

It is no wonder that girls may look for affection in the wrong place if a father is absent. They may give sex in order to get affection from some male. And young males will happily oblige, right? The truth is that all young men desperately need a grown man as a role model. A dad can teach a son to respect women, to keep his word, to grow into responsible manhood. It takes a man to teach a man how to be a man.

There is no greater crisis in America today than the epidemic of absentee dads, the increase of babies born out of wedlock, the break-down of the historic American culture that gave us strong families as economic units. Where have all the fathers gone? What happened to getting married *before* having a baby?

It's been said that if you do the following three things, the odds are in your favor that you will never be on welfare: 1) Stay in high school until you graduate; 2) Don't quit one job until you have another; and 3) Don't make a baby until you marry.

It's that simple. And we all know it's true. The fact is, no nanny-state can ever supply what America's children need. All the money in Washington can never replace the power of a two-parent family. A father is irreplaceable. So is a mother.

And that's why liberals hate the two-parent family. Because the best social program ever invented to prevent child poverty is a mom and dad.

Ron Wood is a writer and pastor and has worked in broadcast news. He graduated from Southeastern University in Lakeland, FL.

Made in the USA
Lexington, KY
02 July 2015